B

monroe

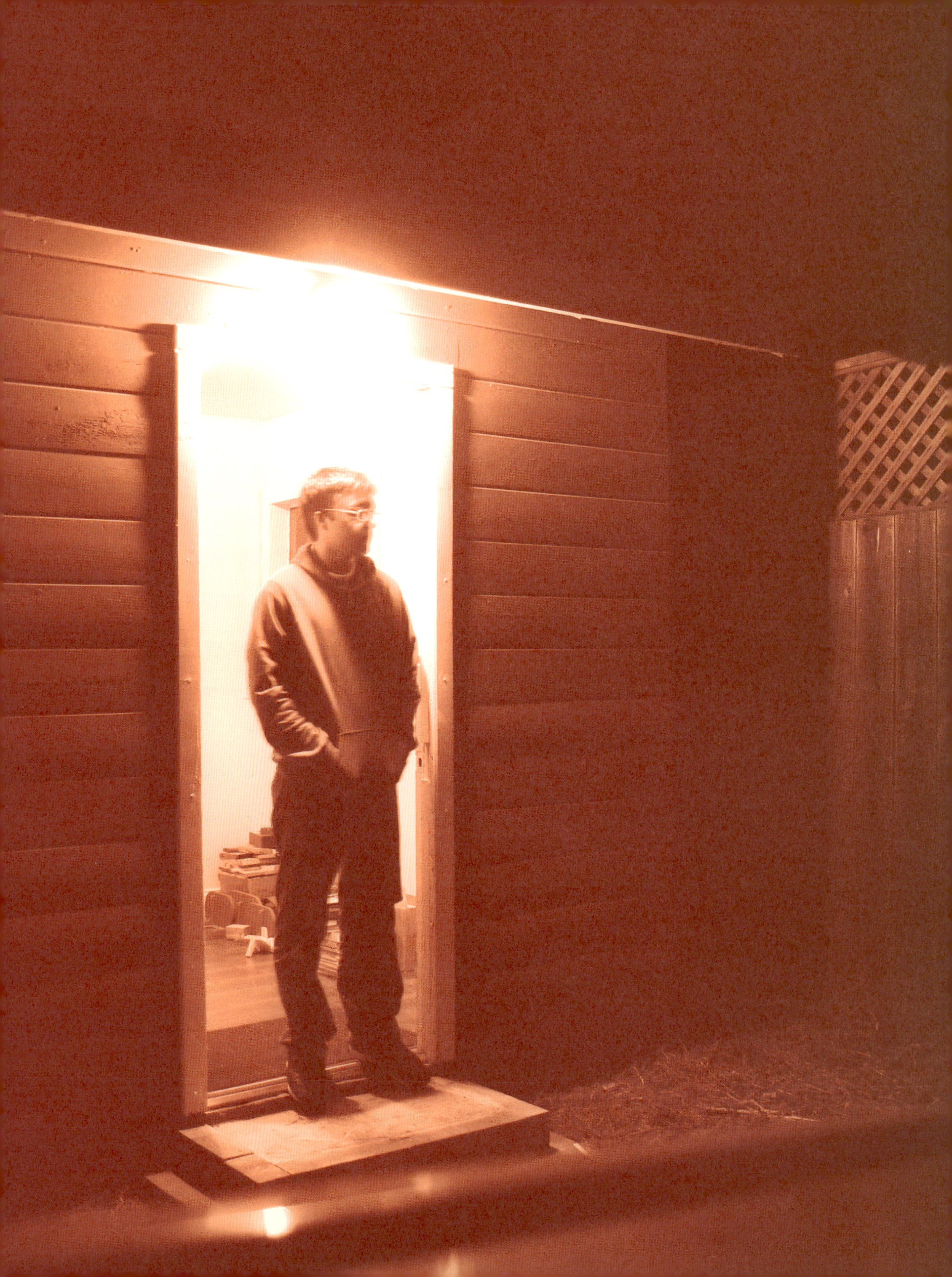

brendan monroe

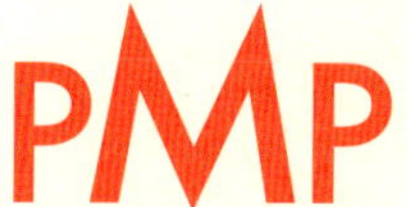

Inquiries should be addressed to:
Paper Museum Press
220 Clement St.
San Francisco, California 94118
www.paper-museum.net
p. 415.386.7275
f. 415.386.7272

•

Distributed by Gingko Press
5768 Paradise Drive, Suite J
Corte Madera, CA 94925
www.gingkopress.com
books@gingkopress.com

•

Printed in China
ISBN 978-0-9788739-1-2

All images and photos © 2008 Brendan Monroe unless otherwise noted

•

° Design / Jordan Stark
www.productetc.com
° Editor / Jordan Stark
° Assistant Editor / Brendan Monroe
www.brendanmonroe.com
° Copy Editor / Kevin B. Chen

•

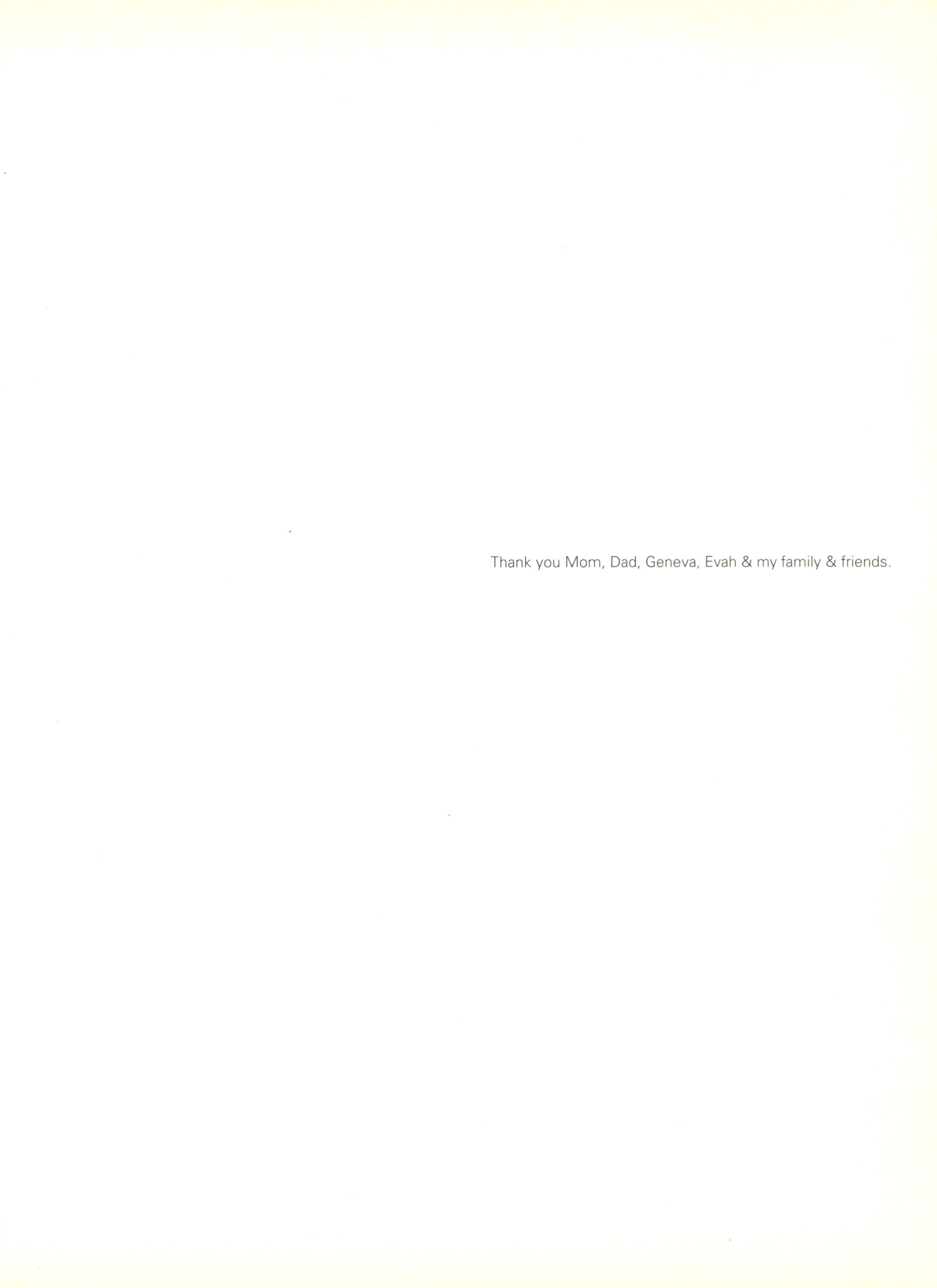

Thank you Mom, Dad, Geneva, Evah & my family & friends.

Table of Contents

Contributors

Mike Kelley is the Director and Owner of Junc Gallery in Los Angeles, California. Since 2003, Junc has established itself nationally as a leader exhibiting the best emerging and established artists within its genre. The gallery's website is juncgallery.com. He also curates outside the gallery and is a founding member of the Silverlake Gallery Alliance.

Shana Nys Dambrot is an Art Critic, Curator and Author based in Venice, California. Her art and design reviews, features, and interviews have appeared in scores of regional, national, international, and online publications. She is currently the Los Angeles Managing Editor at Flavorpill.com and a Contributing Editor at its affiliate publication Artkrush.com.

Dr. Simon F. Park is an internationally recognized microbiologist, from the Faculty of Health and Medical Sciences at University of Surrey, United Kingdom. He has published numerous research papers in international refereed journals, books, and other periodicals. His conviction is that collaborations with artists can lead to powerful concepts through which the true and sublime nature of the microbial world can be communicated in a way that transcends the usual forums offered by newspapers and popular science magazines.

Introduction
Mike Kelley

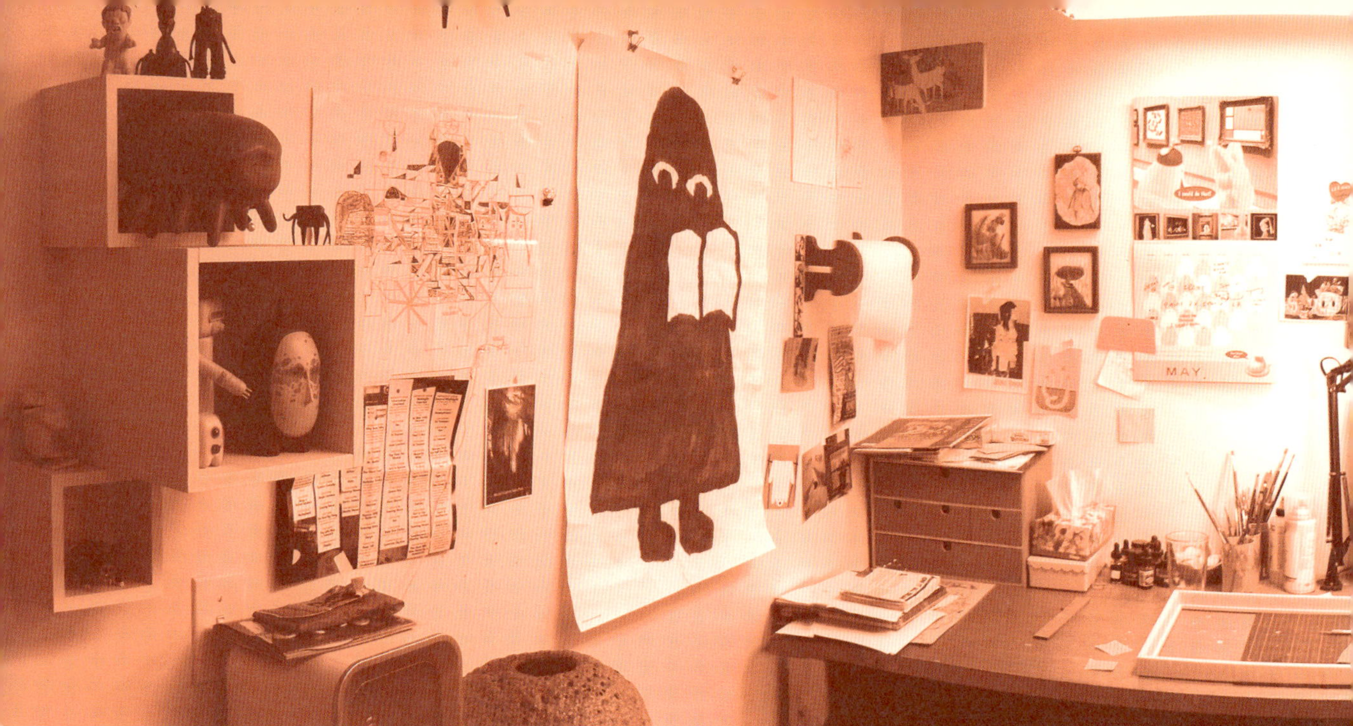

Brendan's a perfectionist; I had the chance to observe this fact first hand when he had his first solo show at my gallery. His was the first show in the newly renovated space when we moved up from a tiny to a small space. Despite the modest jump in scale it was an exhausting three-month process that made me physically sick. The night before the reception I gave Brendan the keys so he could do his install, then went home and curled up in the fetal position.

The next morning I walked in to an amazing installation. The entire space had been considered to create an expanded experience. A subtle silhouette of trees was painted as a backdrop to the larger paintings and drawing installation that hung against the back wall in a cluster reminiscent of leaves on a tree. Small mounds of dirt were strategically placed around pedestals and in corners of the room complete with live plants. From the ceiling, hung at varying lengths, were small sculptures that moved into the gallery, creating the verticality of trees in a forest and adding yet another dimension of spatial drama. It looked awesome and in my fragile state it was a big relief!

That night drew a big crowd, people were blown away, and the whole thing went off without a hitch. It was fun. You could say it was a coming out party for Brendan and Junc. In that sense we sort of started out together.

It was also the beginning of my respect for Brendan's completeness as a "professional" artist. The view of the "the big picture" that he demonstrated in his installation is also his advantage in the art business (sorry, yes this is a business). He has an uncanny understanding of how each show, zine, print, project, etc. is not just an ends but also a means of progressing to the next level, artistically and professionally. Of course it all starts with the work and it's essential to his success that he paints phenomenal pictures all the while continuing to evolve as an artist. So it's almost a miracle that with all these qualities he also happens to be a really nice and gracious person.

Biology as Destiny

Brendan Monroe reminds me of an archaeologist for a couple of reasons, for one, like an archaeologist, he maps out a specific terrain, then painstakingly uncovers it inch by inch, over years if necessary, obsessing over each potential clue for what it might reveal about our humanity. The other reason is that they both deal with a lot of mud. In Monroe's case, it's images of mud beautifully rendered through a range of earthy tones that swirl together like calligraphic ribbons perpetually reassembling themselves in the requisite forms.

In our video age it's tempting to think of him as a contemporary shaman opening a portal to our hazily remembered primal motivations; or to view the work as a testament to art's mystical power pitted against the combined forces of electronic media and mass consumption. Monroe's work investigates the primal, it suggests an innate need for ritual and associates biological processes and the resulting physical and

Evah Fan & Brendan Monroe's Studio
Jordan Stark, 2007

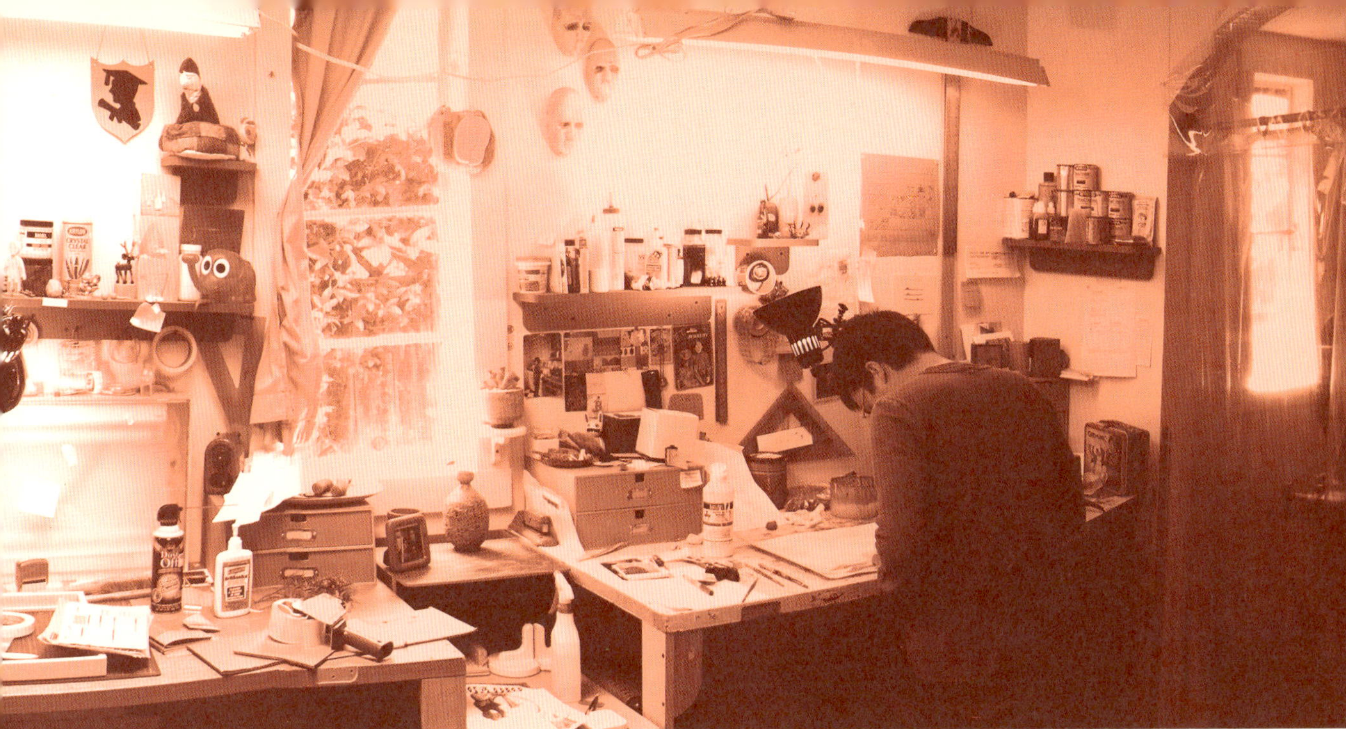

psychological trauma as a defining characteristic of man. Biology as destiny, it's a message that at times feels at odds with esoteric investigations of social identity in art that often perplex the uninitiated and are praised by critics.

Monroe's work is more populist. Without pandering, he combines familiar lessons from illustration and abstraction with reflections on the body and our duality creating a place for humanist content in contemporary art. Through these paintings we are reminded that we are bound by the terrestrial forces of nature so fundamentally that to reinforce the point the paintings have evolved to the point where they often look like they were painted entirely with the earth itself. The anthropomorphic creatures are our stand-ins, tending the brood, performing rituals and other primal activities. By relieving them of cultural features that could reveal political and philosophical affiliations, we're left to focus on fundamental human drives, the body's vulnerability, and our own mortality.

Actual humans in the paintings are used to illustrate the drifting divide between our modern and primal selves, the call of the wild vs. the indomitable tow of progress. In "You're So Blobby" [pg 10] a human dirt clod clings to a teenage boy who's trying to exit the composition while glancing back with pronounced disinterest. The relationship of co-dependency has long since grown cold and the embrace has the appeal of a suffocating ex who refuses to accept it's over. What they represent is clear; the creature (our primal self) is looked on as burden to the young man determined to move on. What's not so clear is their collective future or if one could actually exist without the other.

Another example of this paradoxical relationship is "Personal Ninja" [pg 61] in which a man peers out from behind a suit of organic compost (made from paint scrapings). Extraneous clues to the suit's exact function are omitted, leaving us to ponder instead their true relationship. Is the covering providing protection in a symbiotic relationship or a force threatening to smother and consume him?

As the titles suggest, both paintings are tinged with offbeat humor, which is characteristic of the work rescuing them from less optimistic conclusions and creating an appealing balance between the artist's insight and his picture making skill. His ability is not limited to painting though. From the beginning, Monroe has also made sculpture created with equal accomplishment as the paintings which he integrates into gallery installations giving each exhibition the added bonus of a theatrical materiality.

That's what good art is: a considered point of view engagingly illustrated in some fashion. In Monroe's work it's his unrelenting point of view that ultimately fuels the art, makes it relevant, and there is no sign of the well going dry any time soon.

Paintings

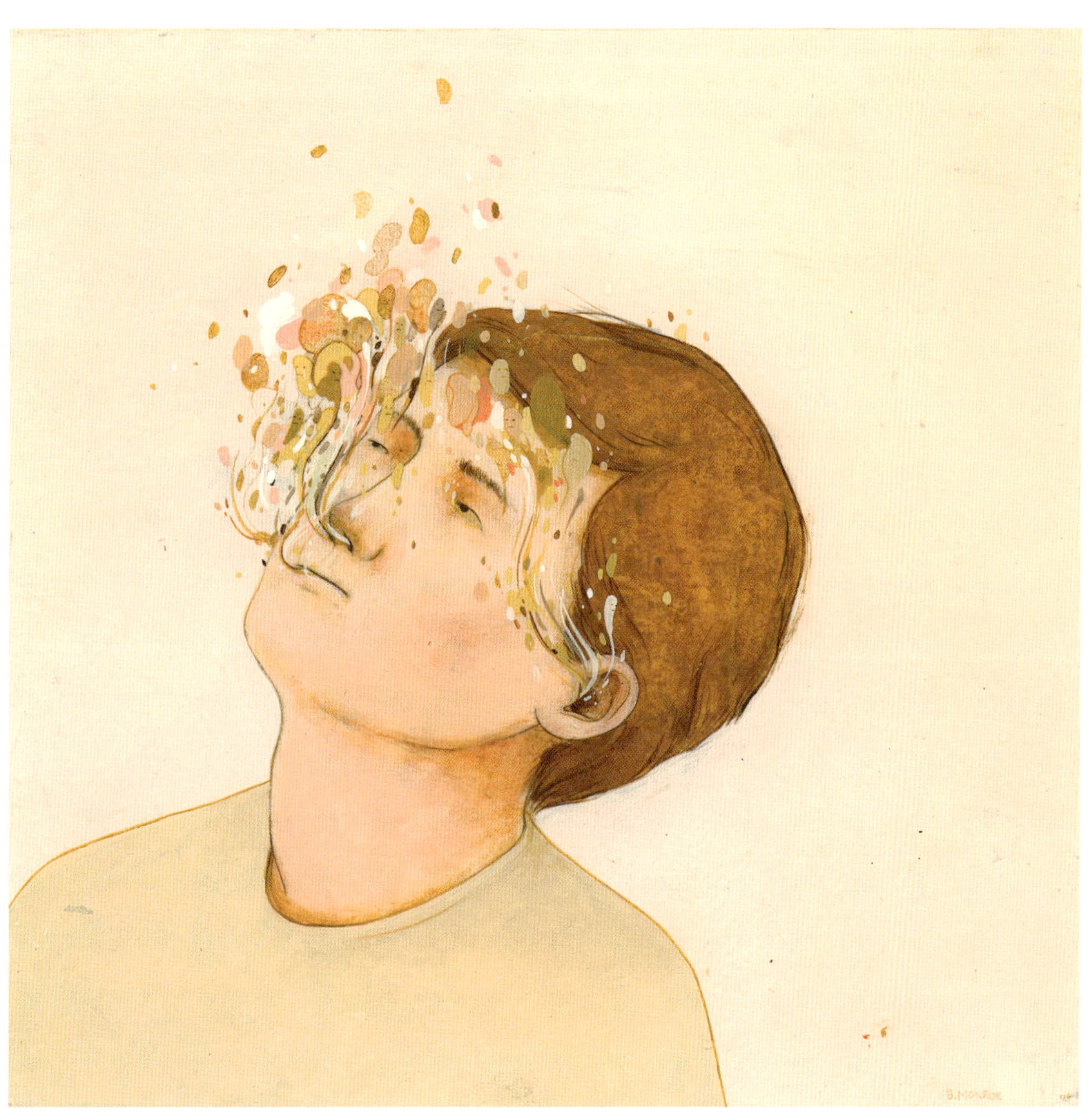

It Began Inside
2006 — acrylic, collage on paper
6 x 6 in / 15.2 x 15.2 cm

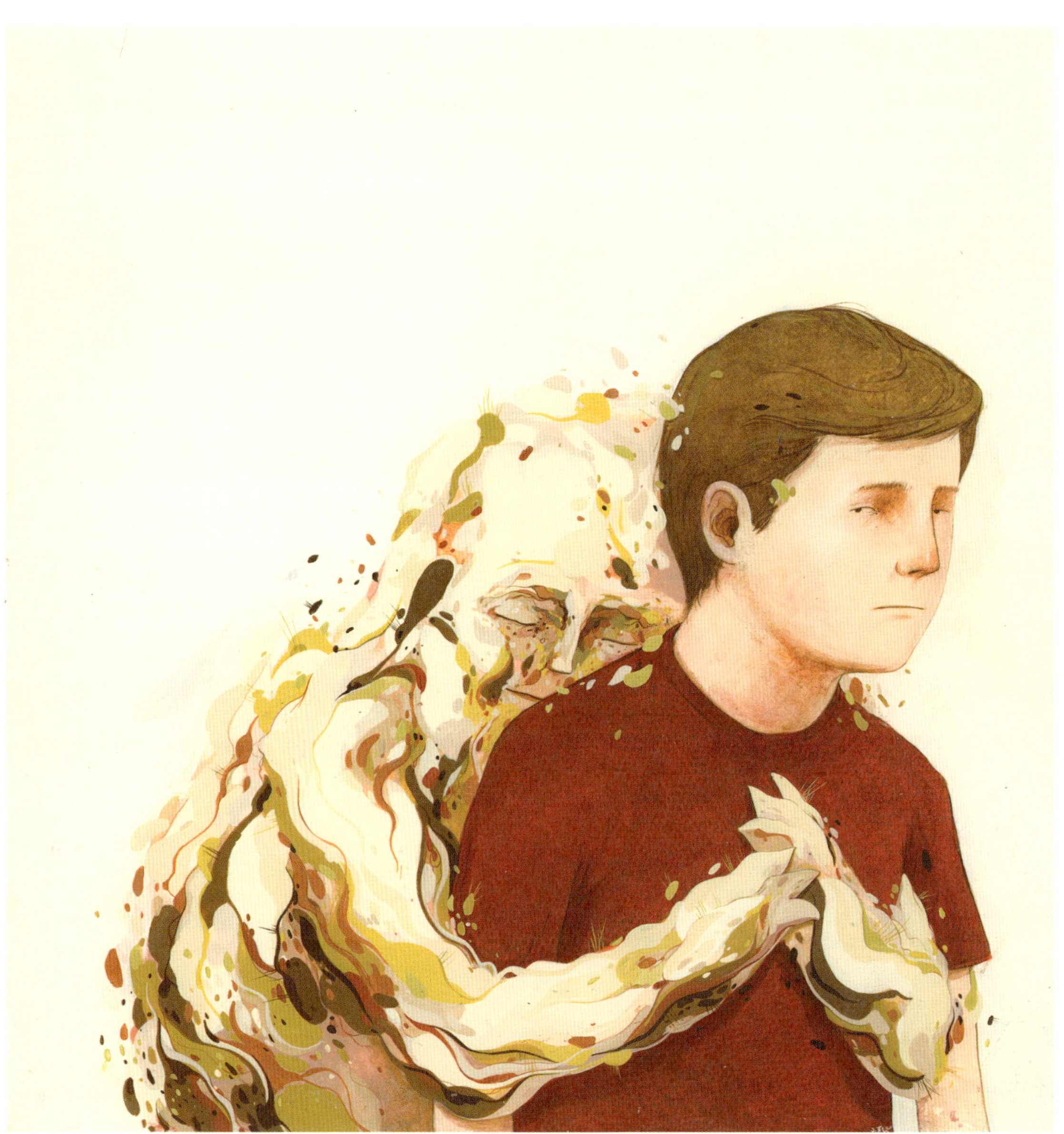

You're So Blobby   2006 — acrylic on paper
10.5 x 10 in / 26.7 x 25.4 cm

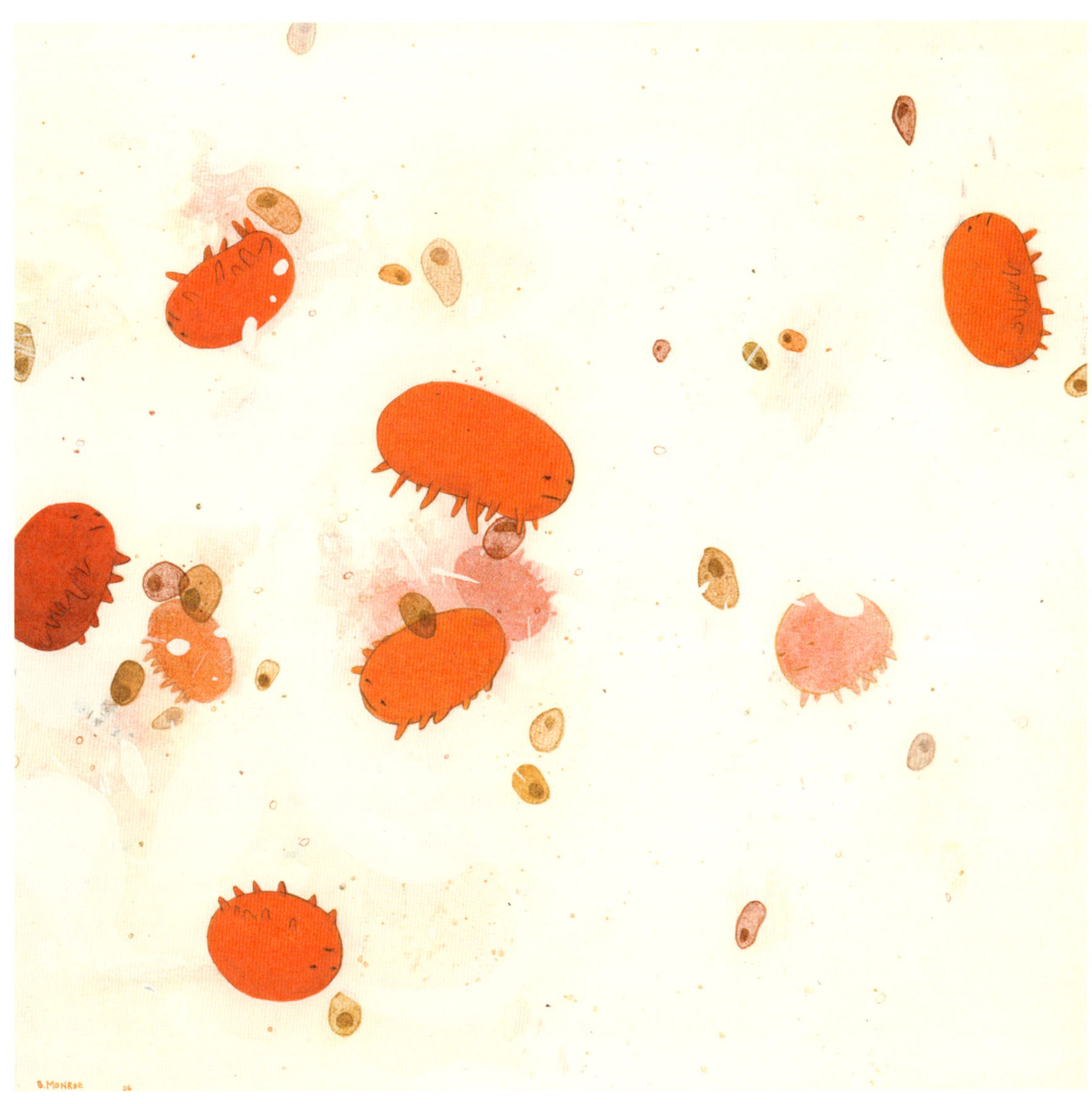

<table>
<tr><td>Contaminated</td><td>2006 — acrylic, collage on paper
7 x 7 in / 17.8 x 17.8 cm</td><td>(overleaf)
Stowing Away</td><td>2006 — acrylic, collage on paper
23 x 33 in / 58.4 x 83.8 cm</td></tr>
</table>

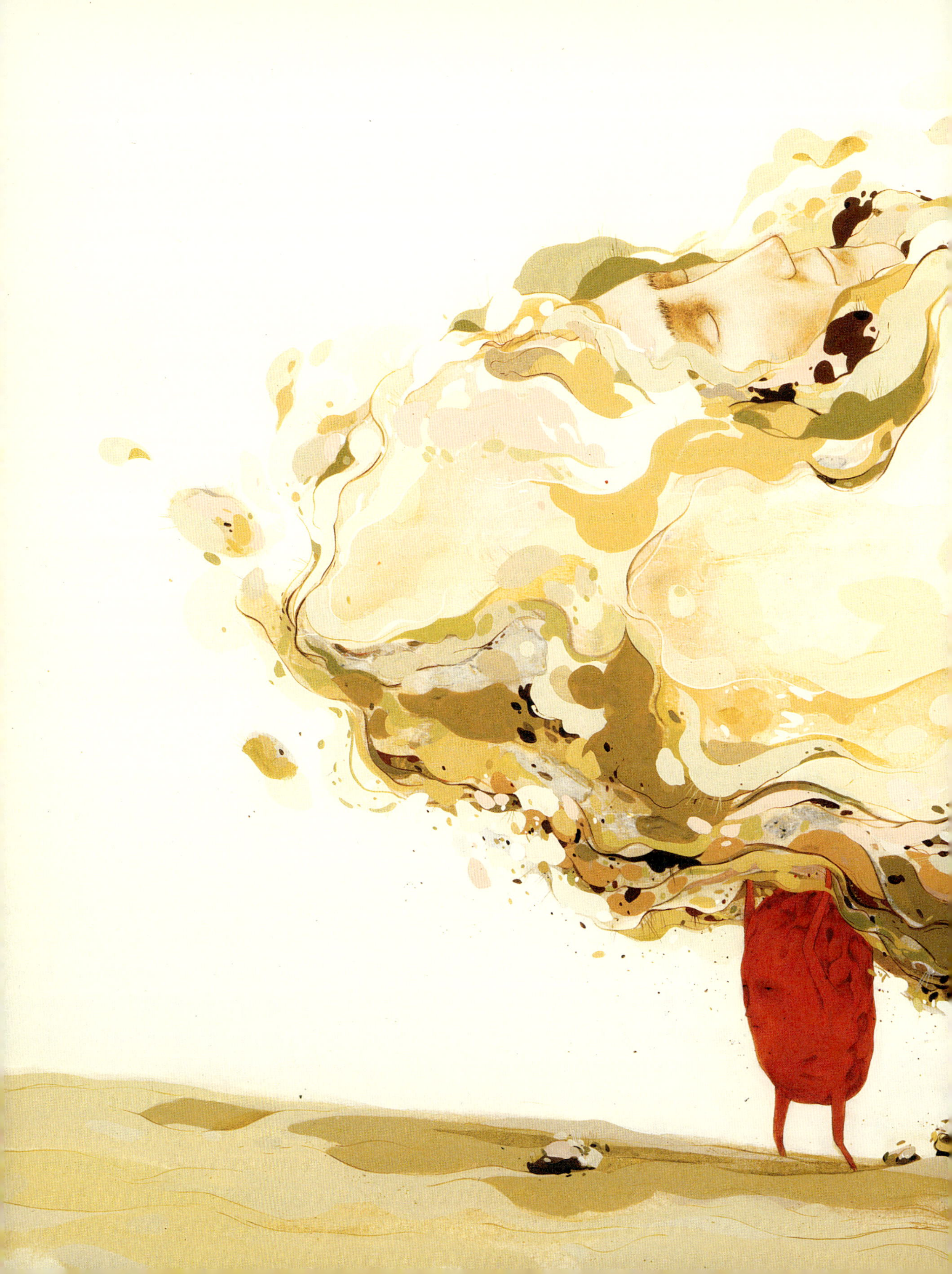

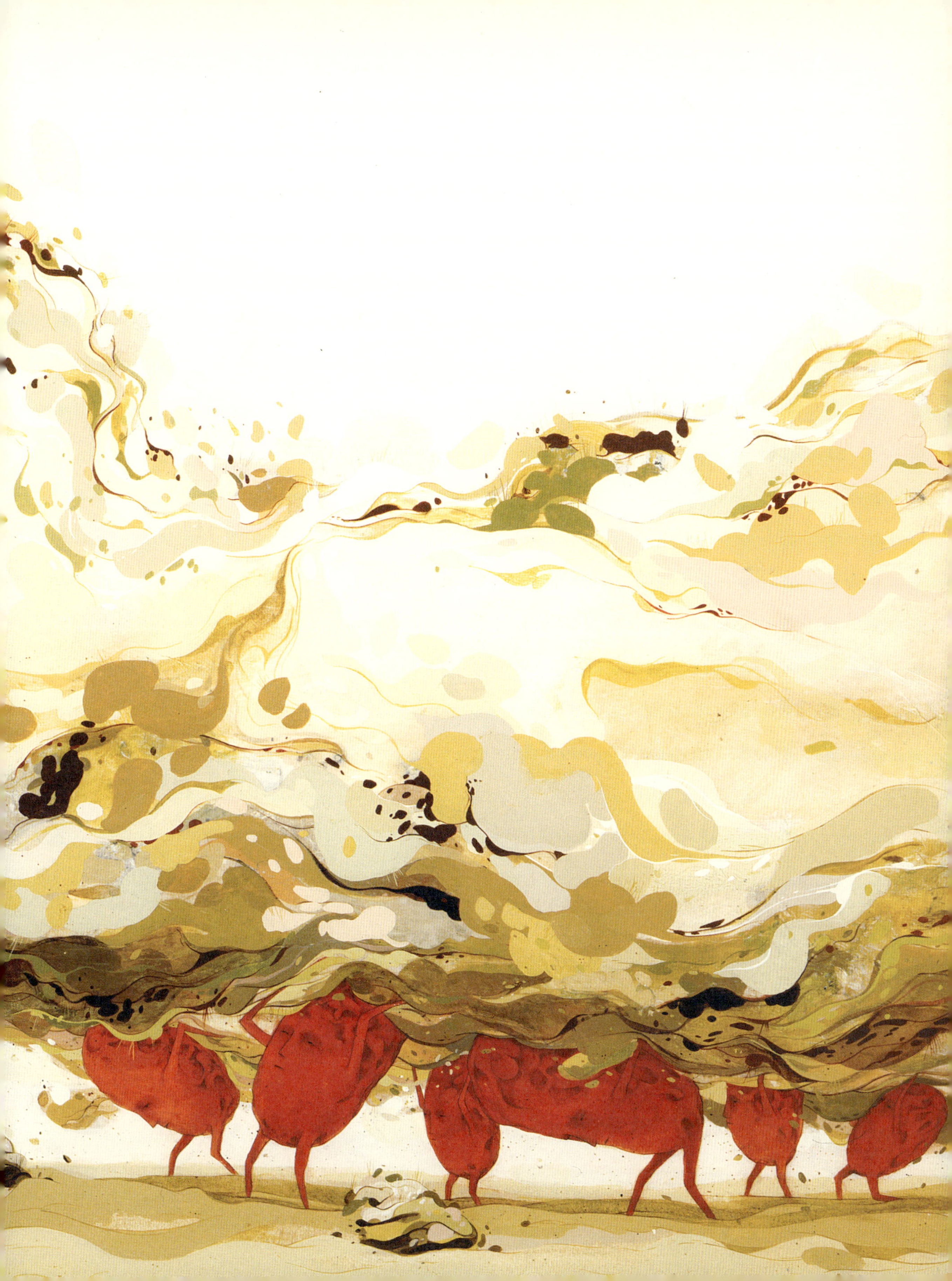

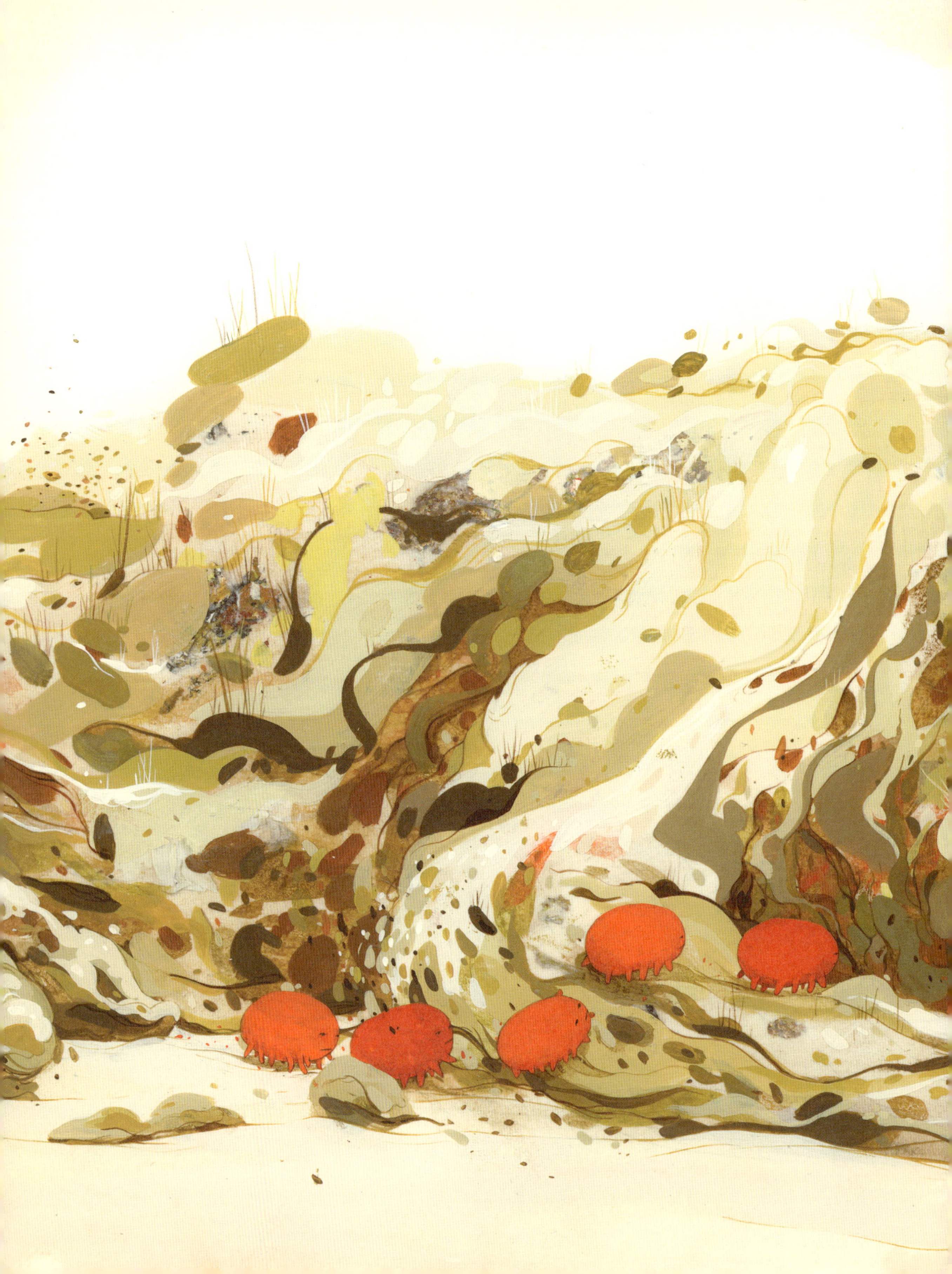

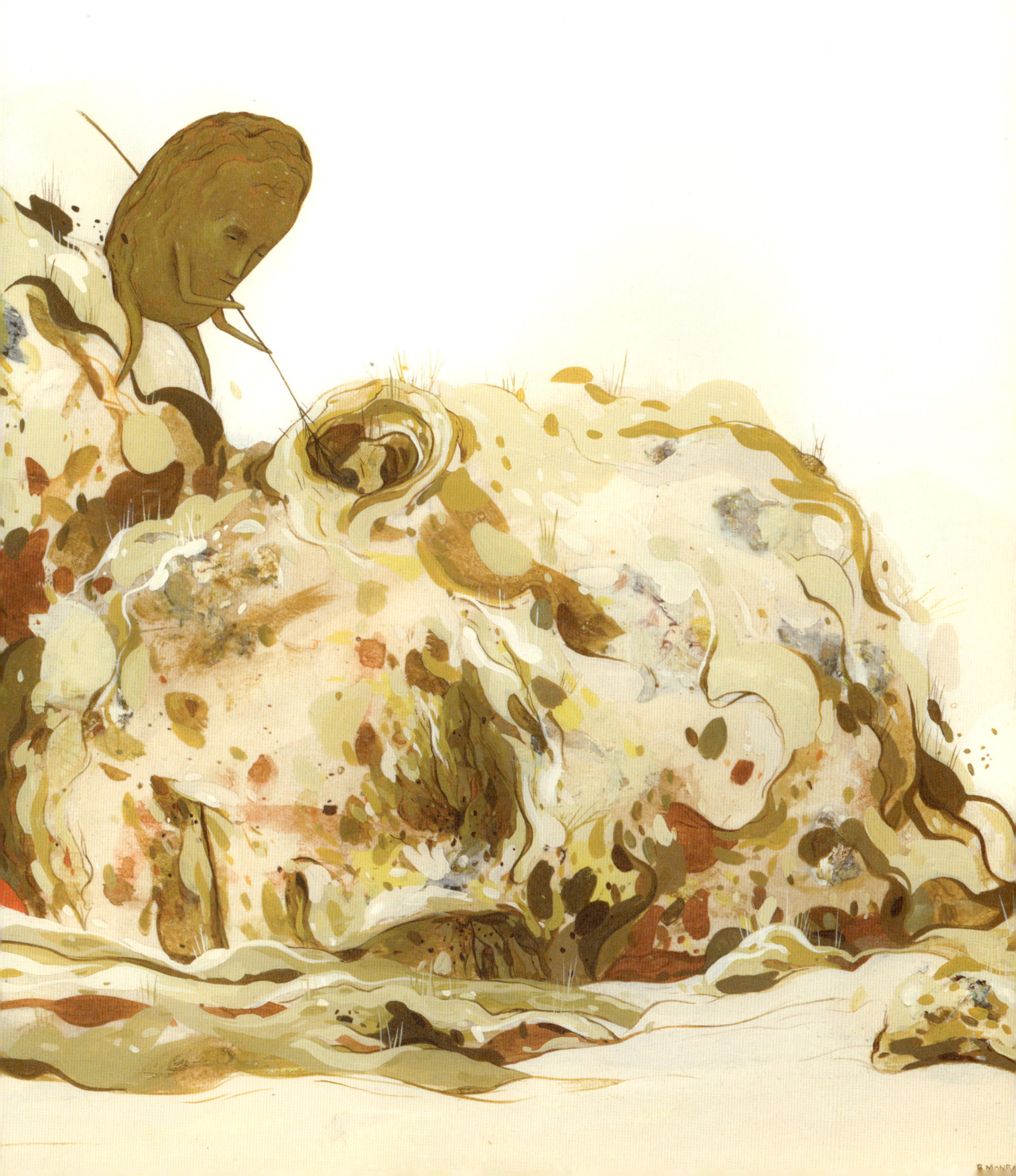

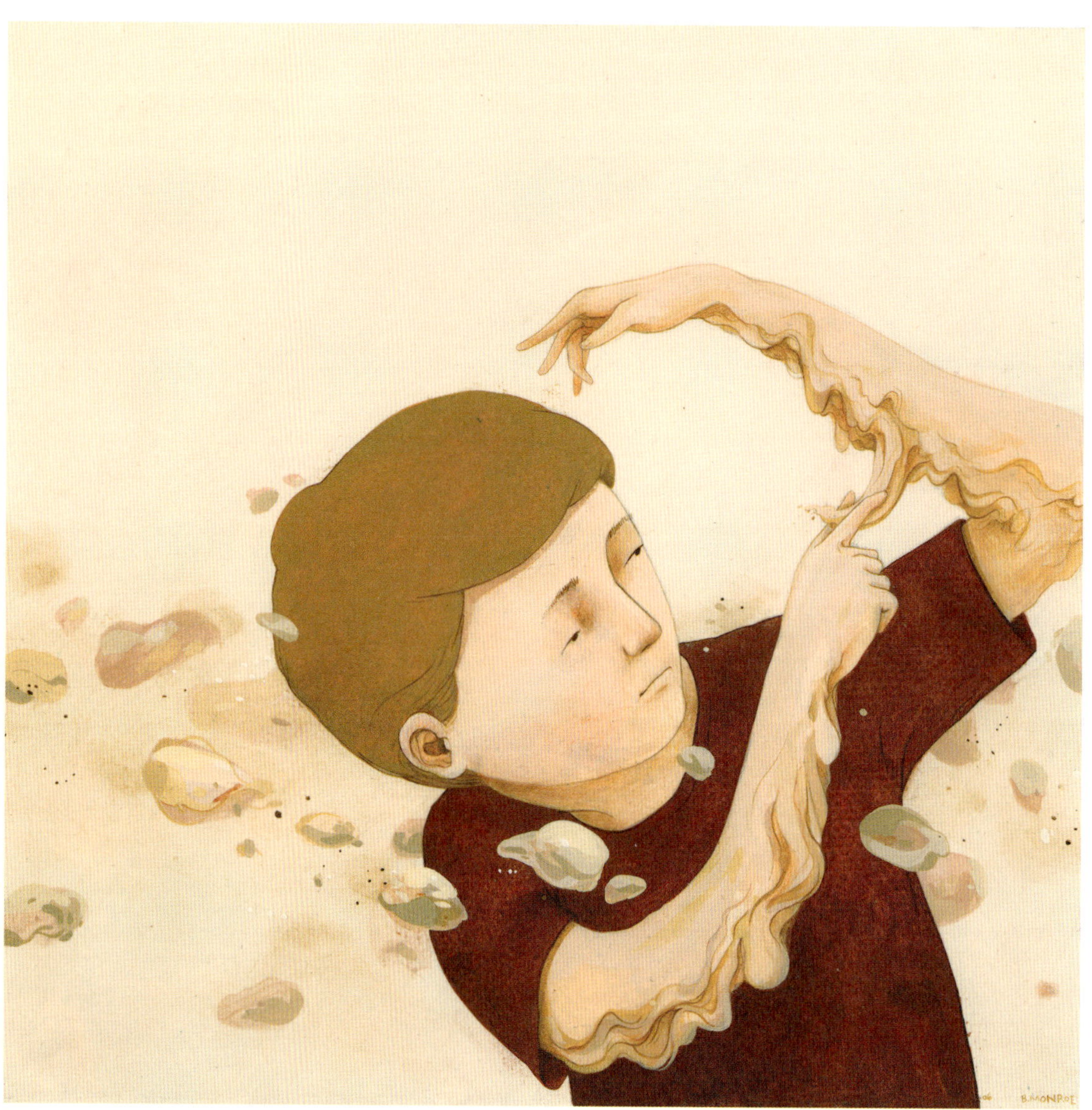

(overleaf)

Sleep Deep   2006 — acrylic, collage on paper
                        11 x 21 in / 27.9 x 53.3 cm

Allergens   2006 — acrylic on paper
                       8 x 8 in / 20.3 x 20.3 cm

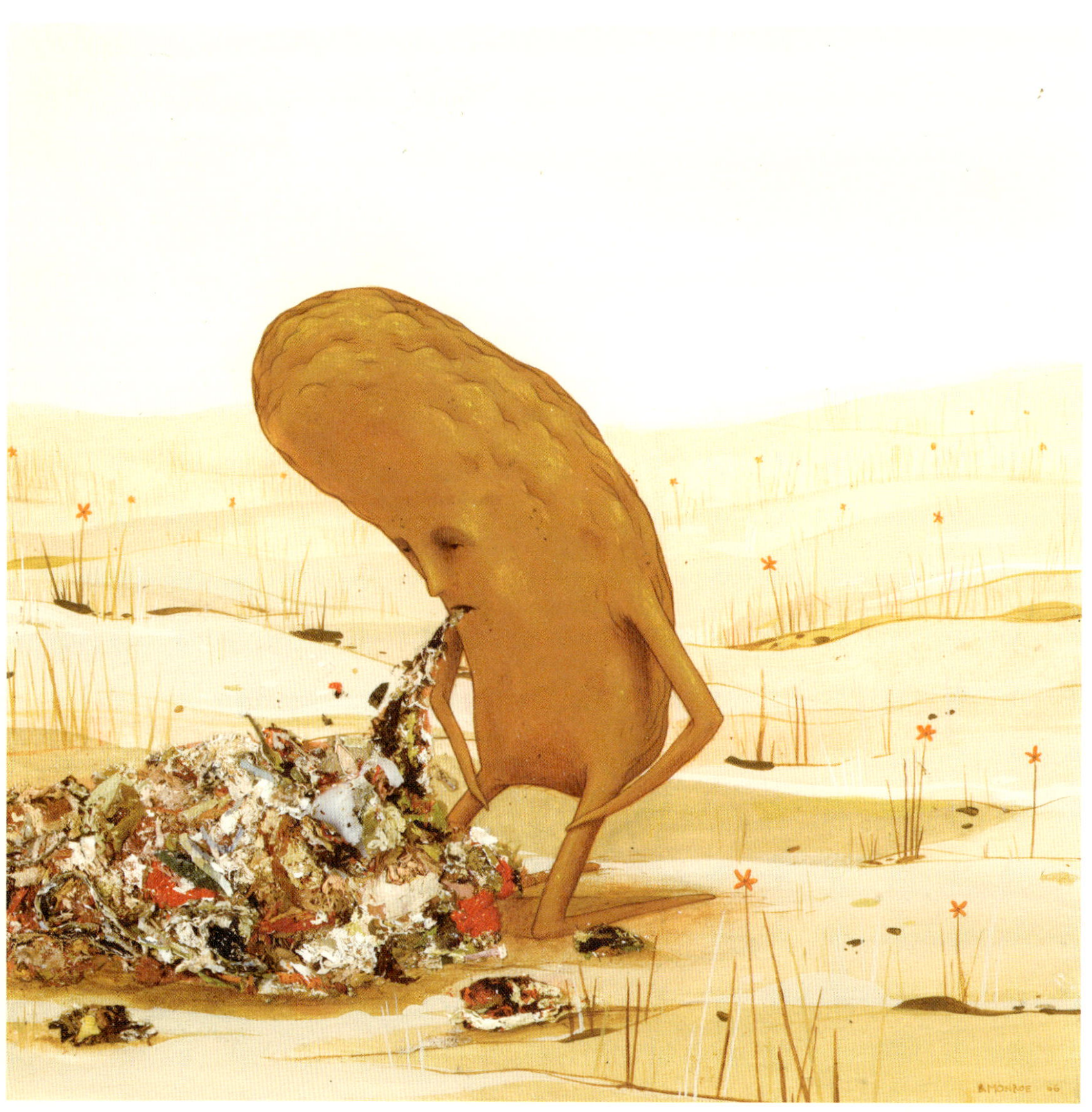

Can't Keep it Down 2006 — acrylic, collage [ps] on paper
7 x 7 in / 17.8 x 17.8 cm

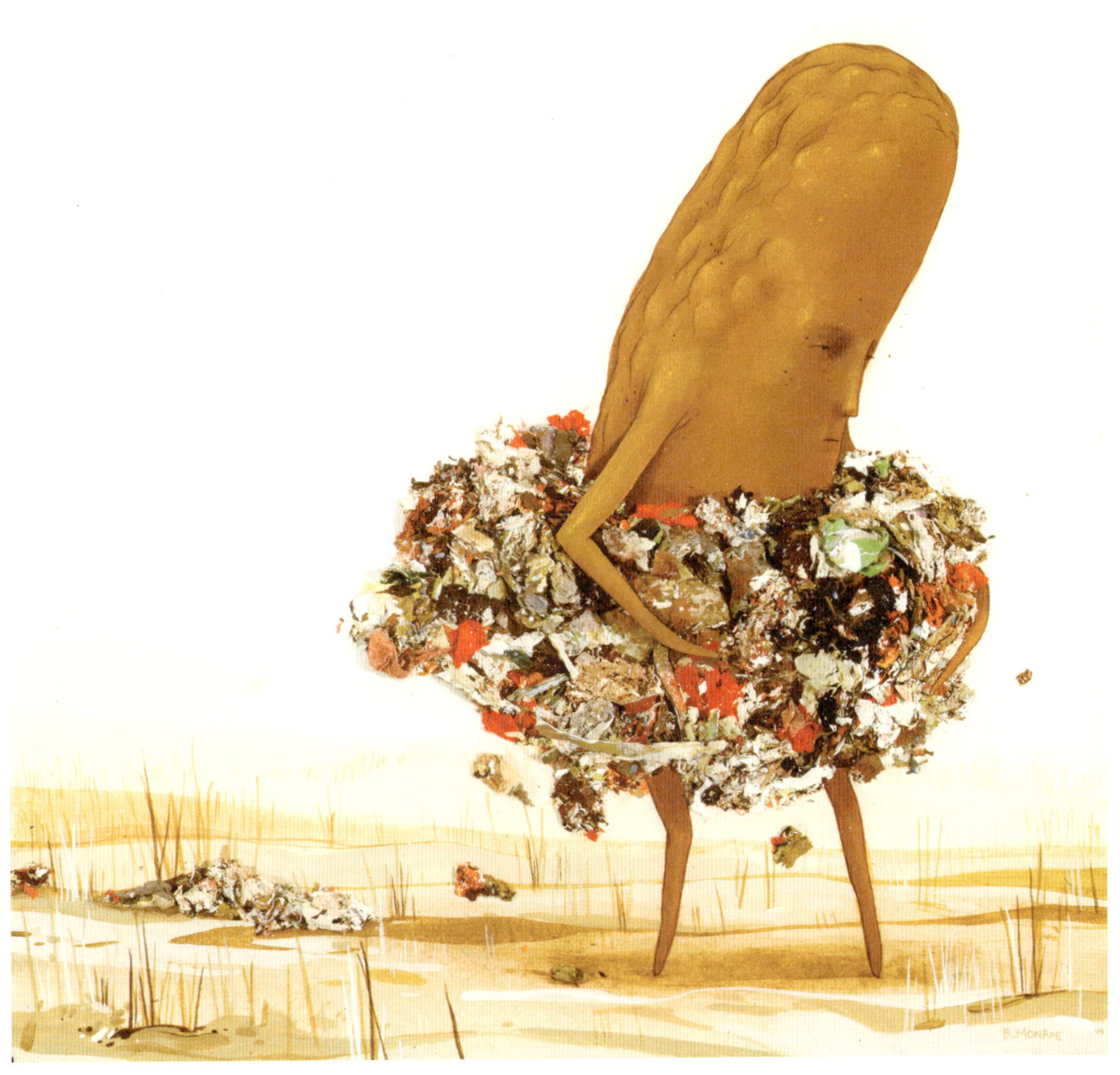

Can't Hold it Up   2006 — acrylic, collage [ps] on paper
7 x 7 in / 17.8 x 17.8 cm

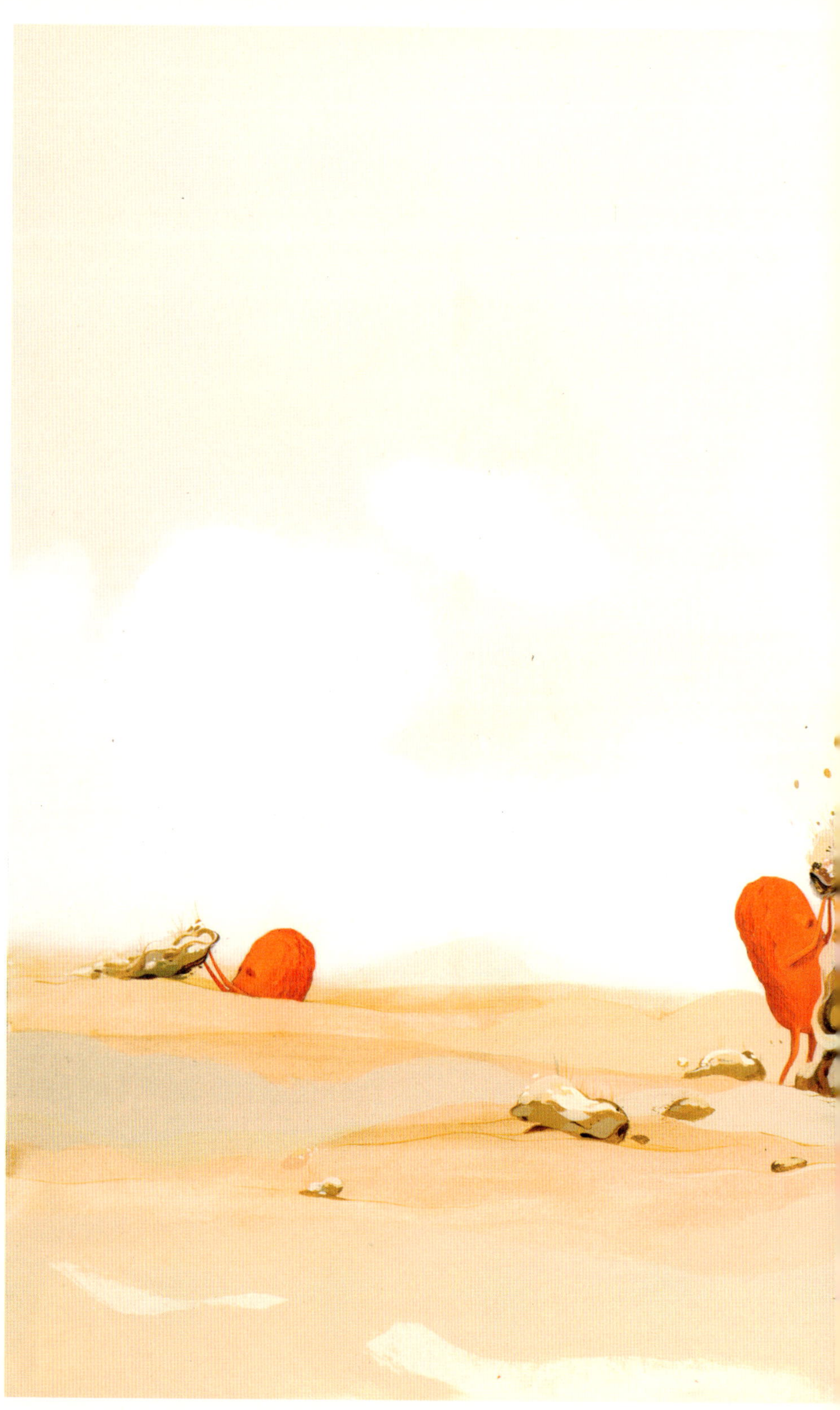

Holding Seams   2006 — acrylic, collage on paper
26 x 40 in / 66 x 101.6 cm

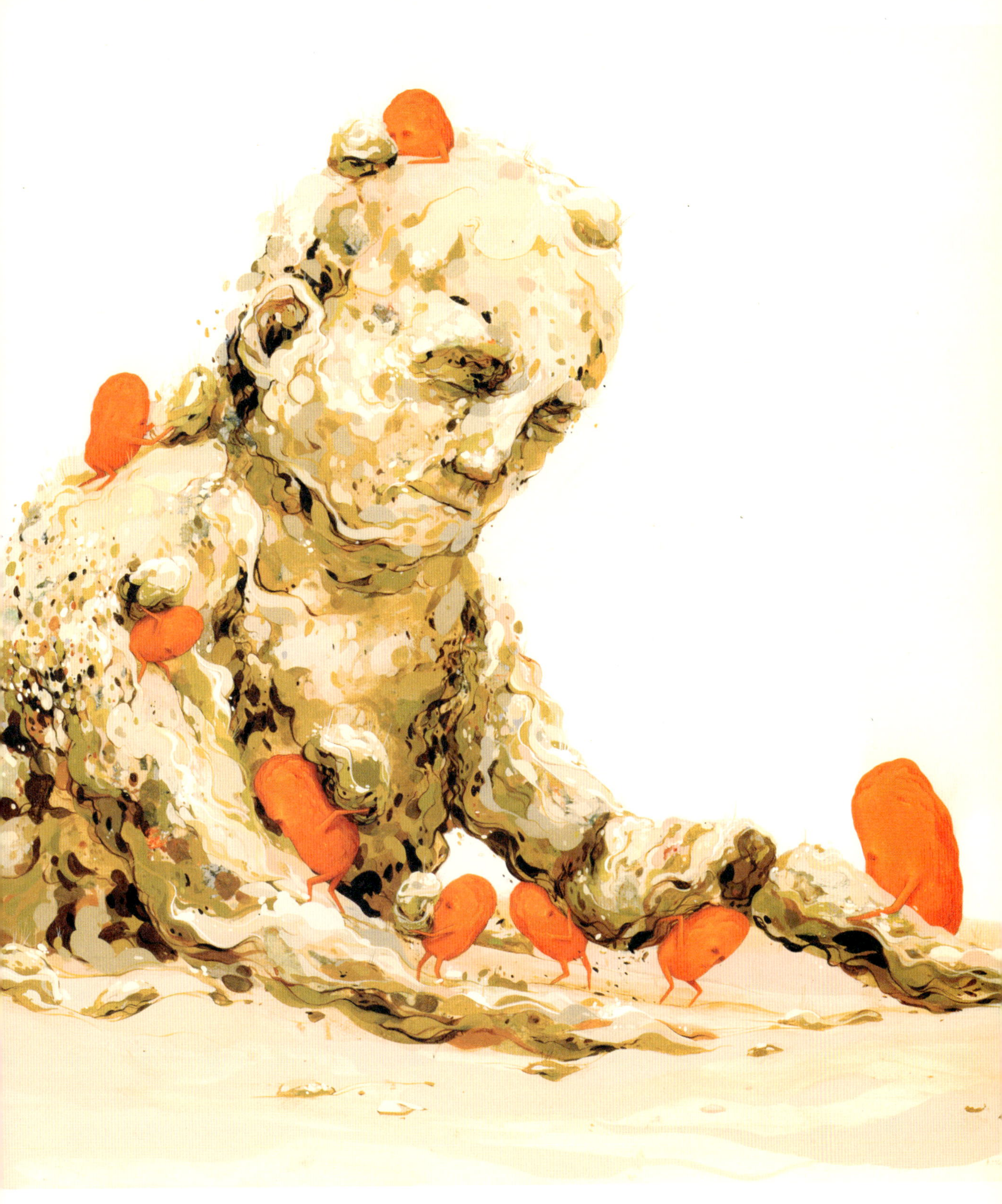

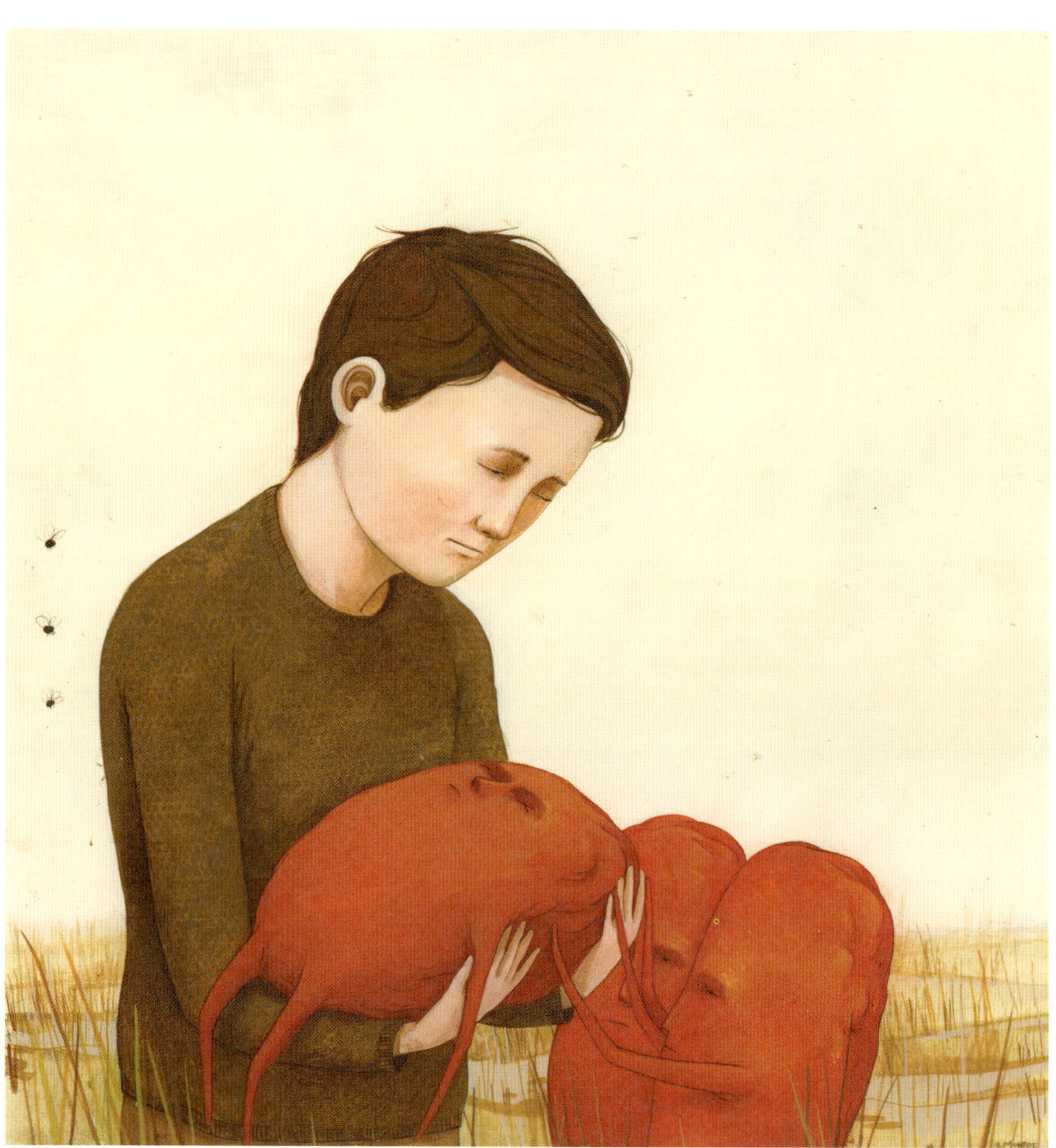

Having No Other Choice   2006 — acrylic, collage on paper
9 x 8.5 in / 22.9 x 21.6 cm

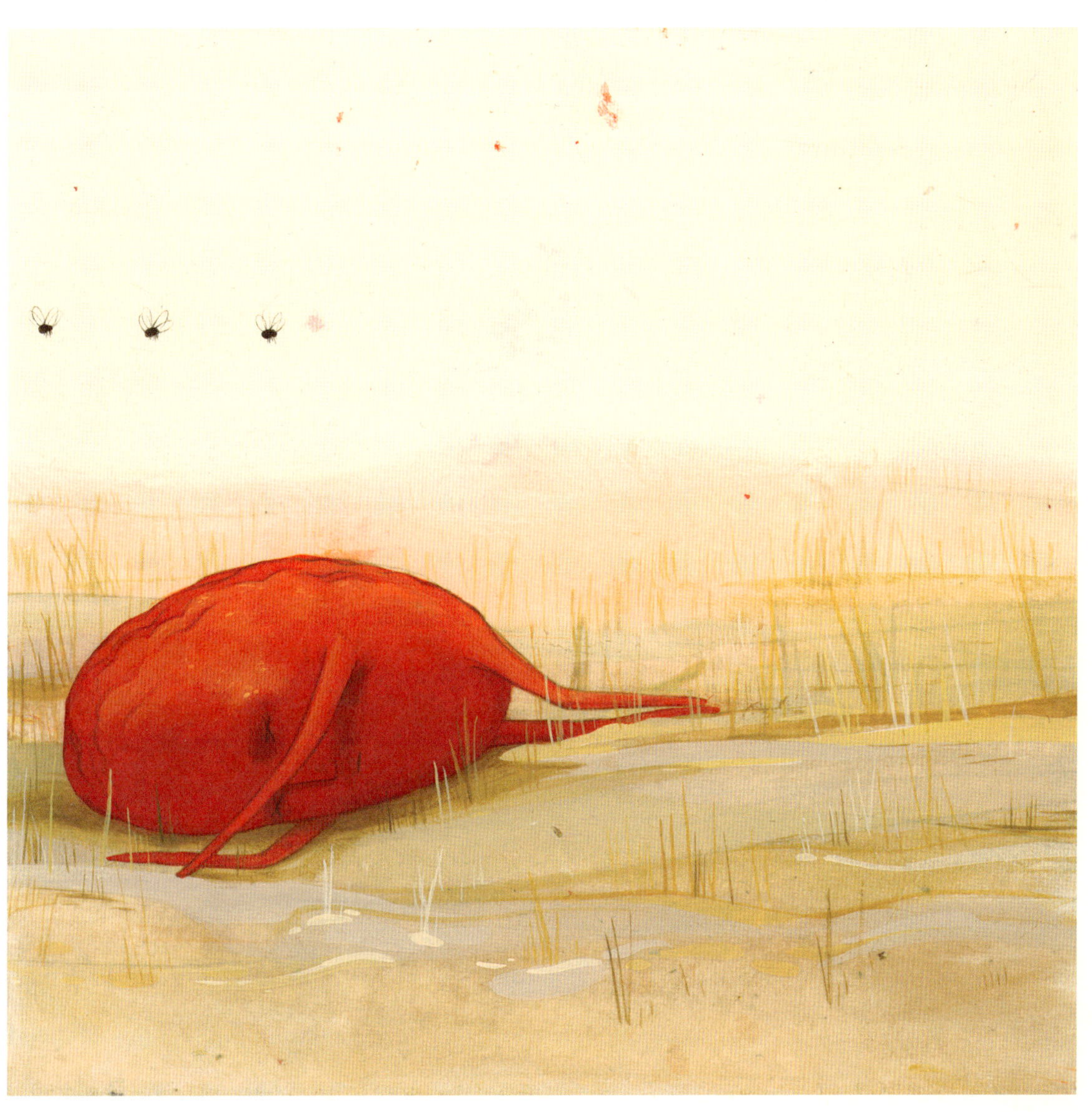

Falling to Circumstance
2006 — acrylic, collage on paper
6 x 6 in / 15.2 x 15.2 cm

River Run   2006 — acrylic, collage on paper
10 x 8 in / 25.4 x 20.3 cm

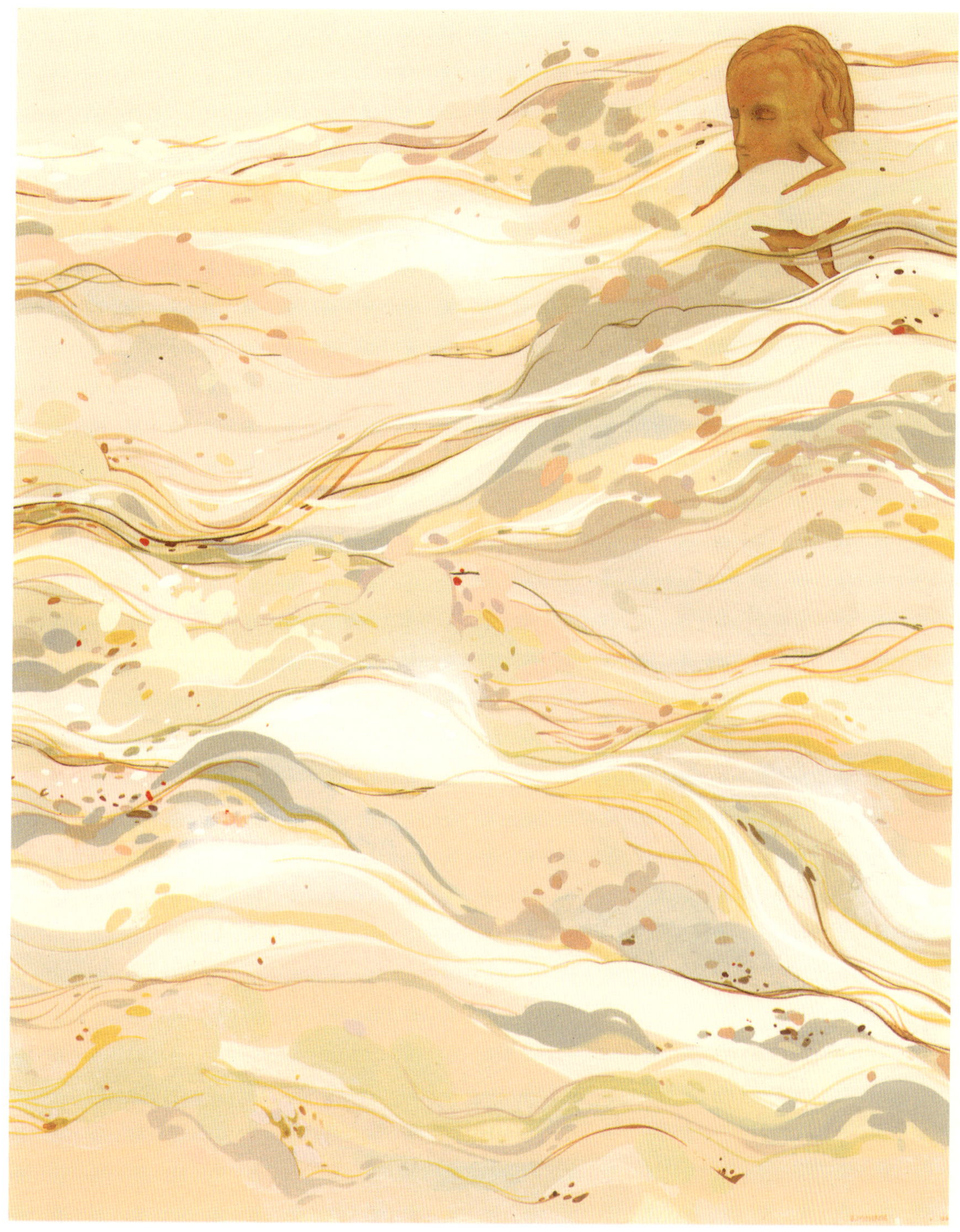

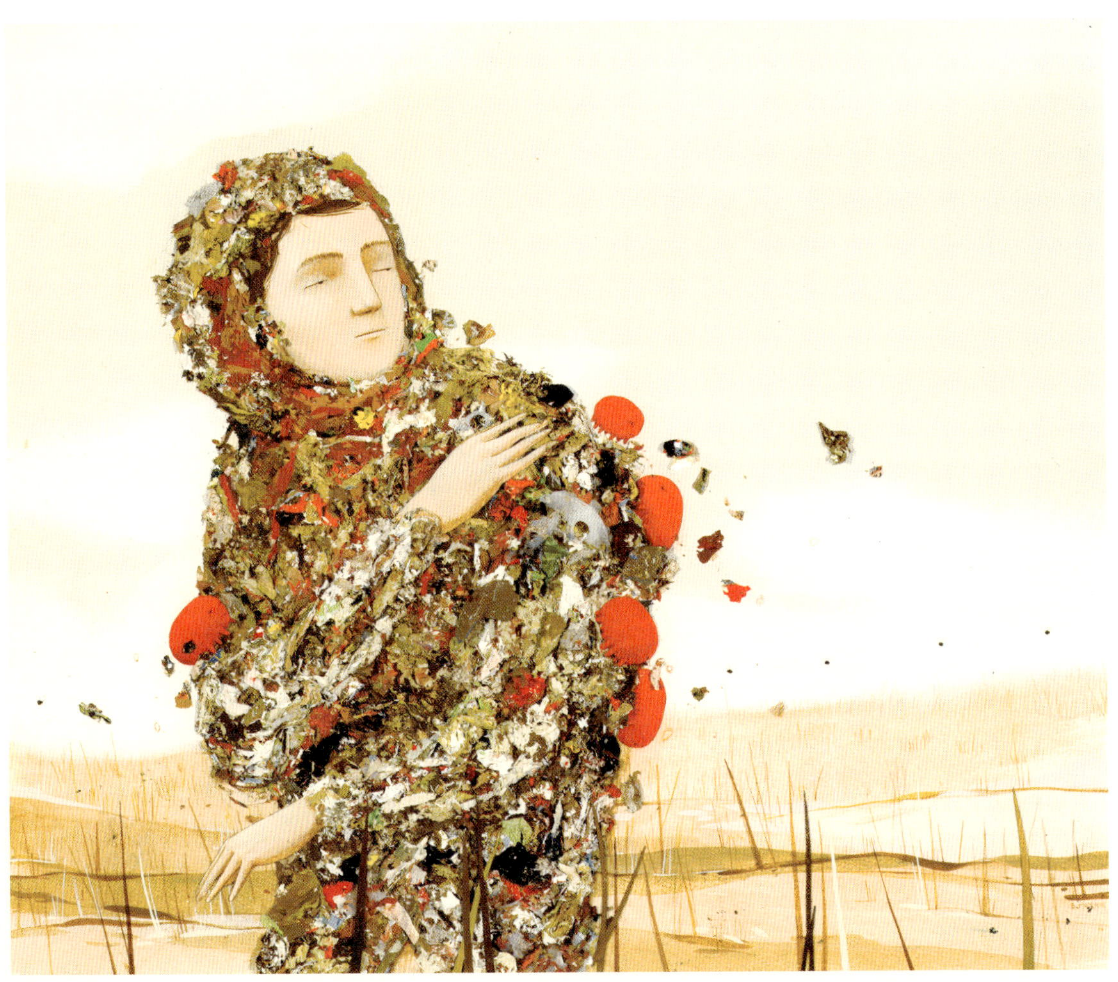

Suits Me   2006 — acrylic, collage [ps] on paper
14 x 14.5 in / 35.6 x 36.8 cm

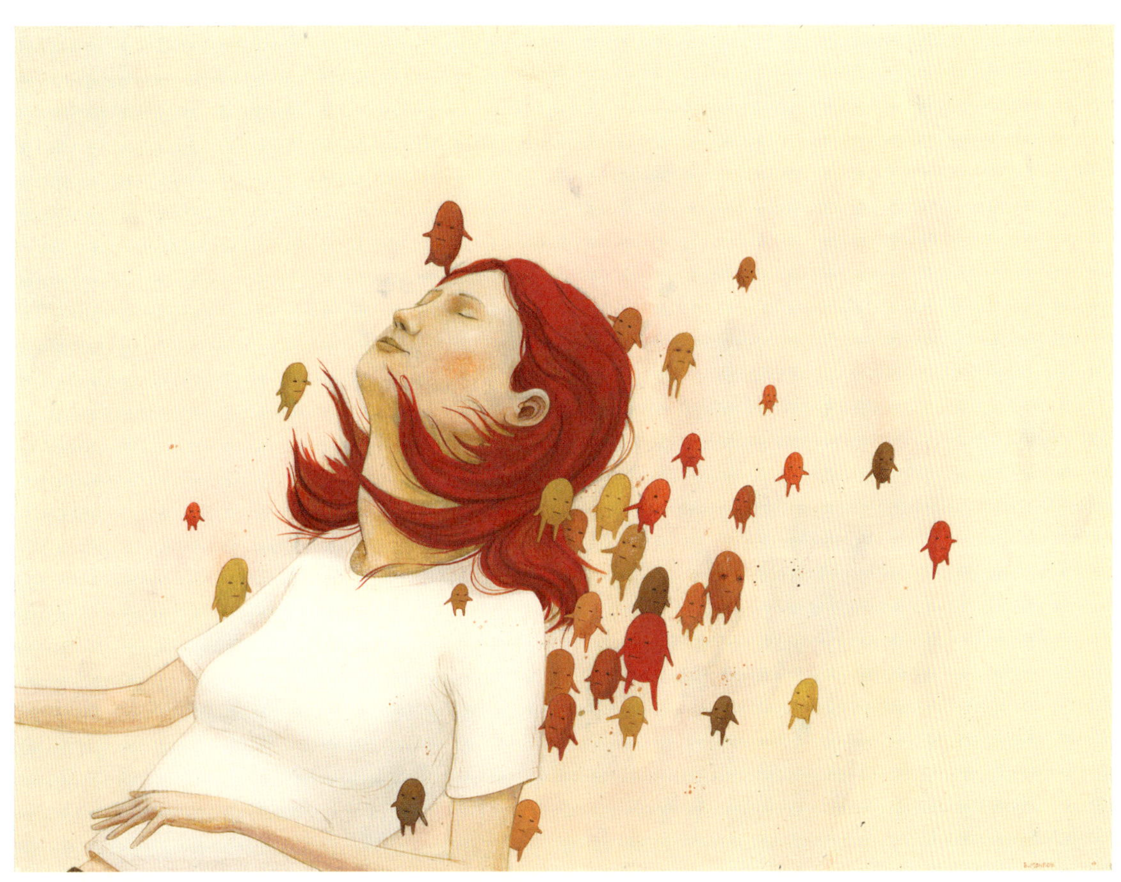

Taking Her Way 2006 — acrylic, collage on paper
8 x 10.75 in / 20.3 x 27.3 cm

(overleaf)
Land Inside 2006 — acrylic, collage on paper
26 x 40 in / 66 x 101.6 cm

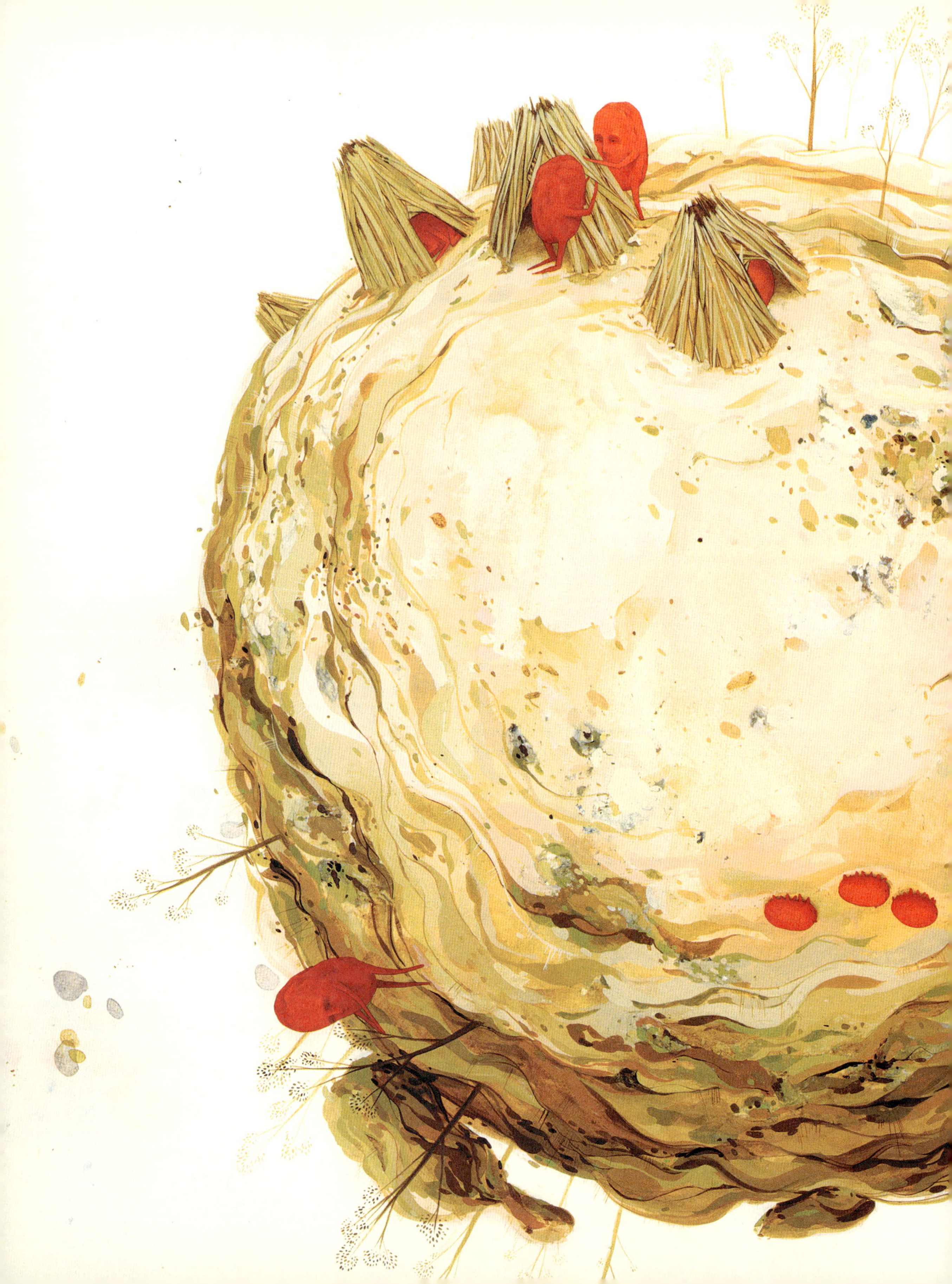

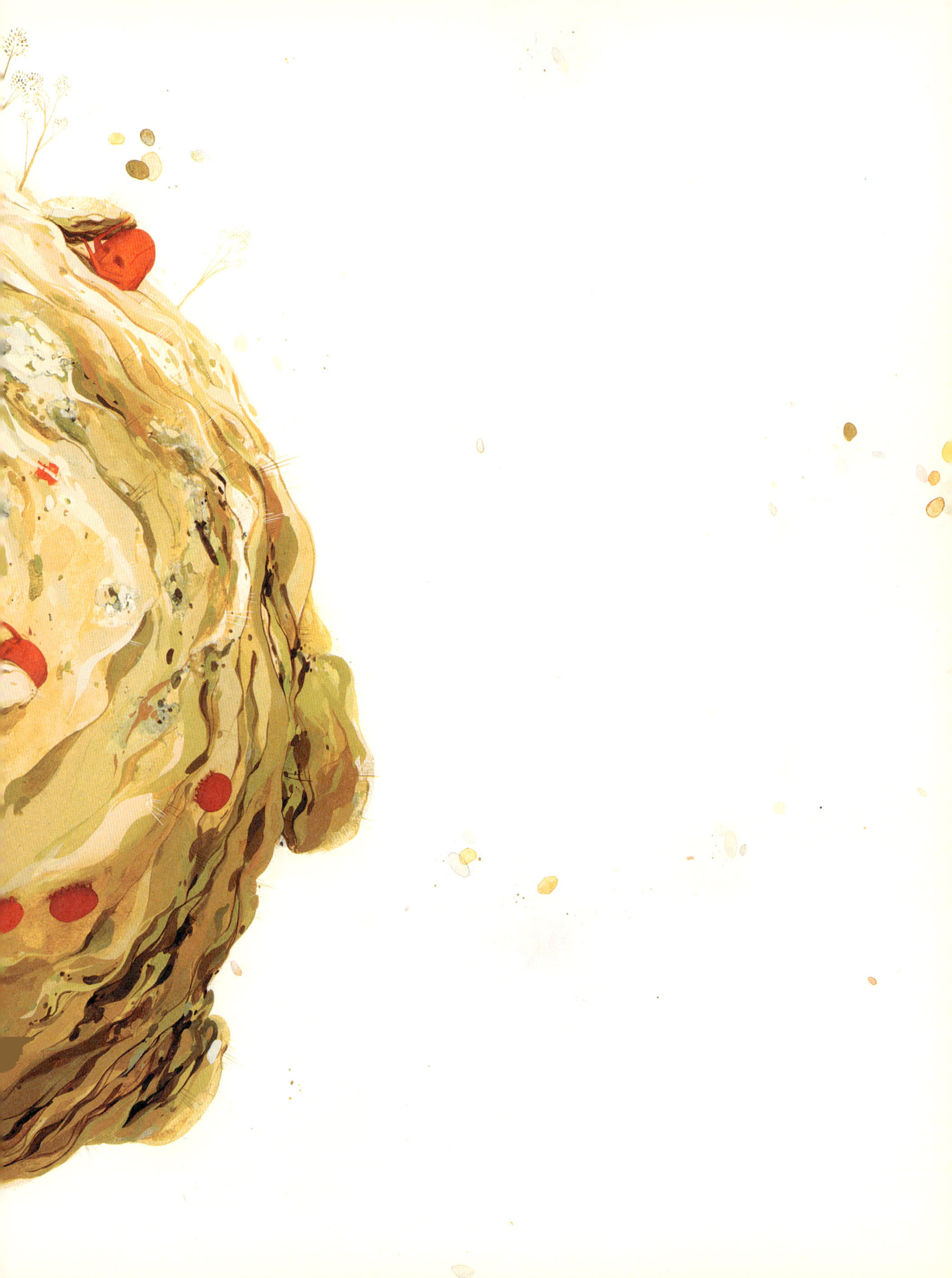

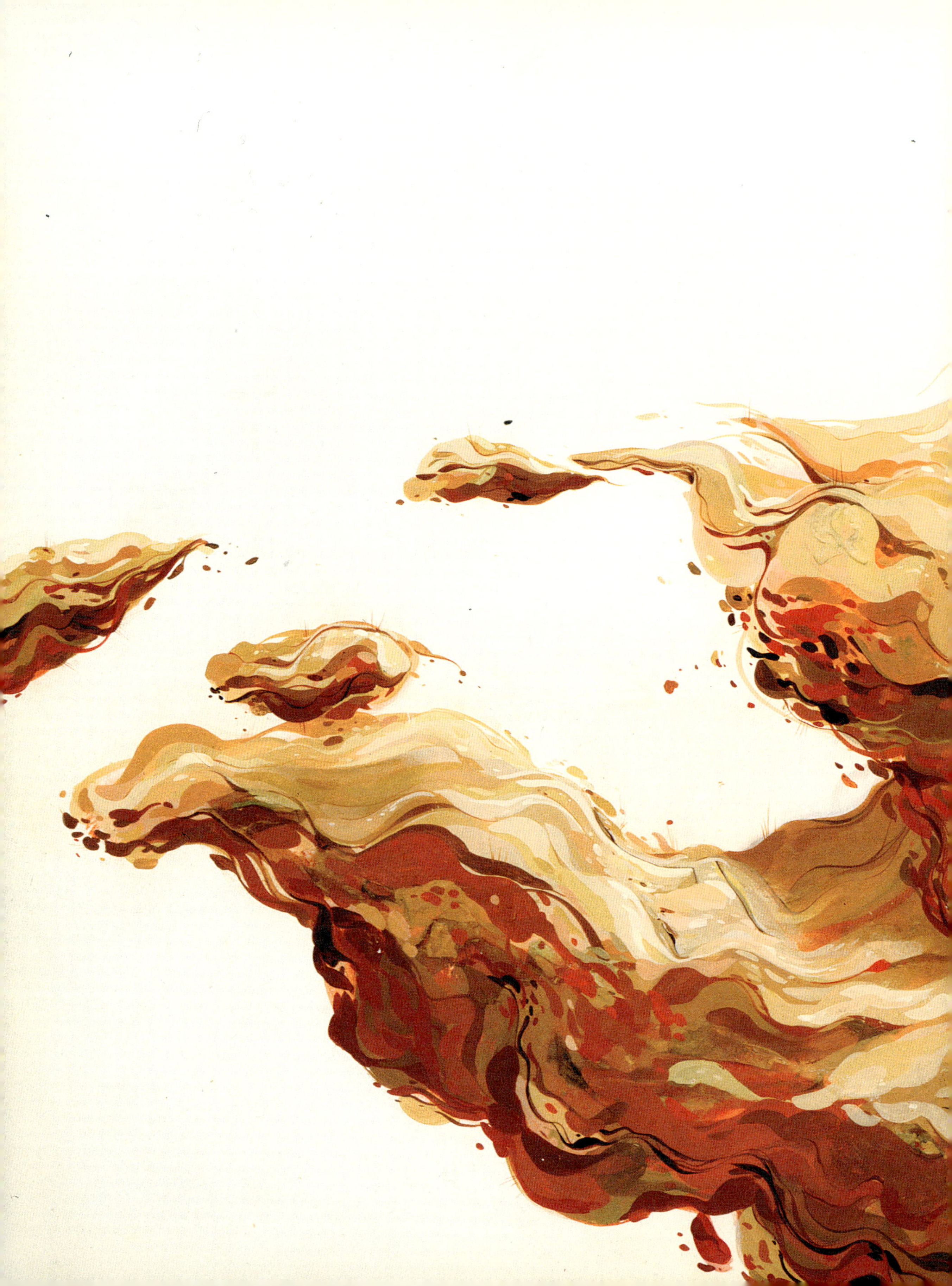

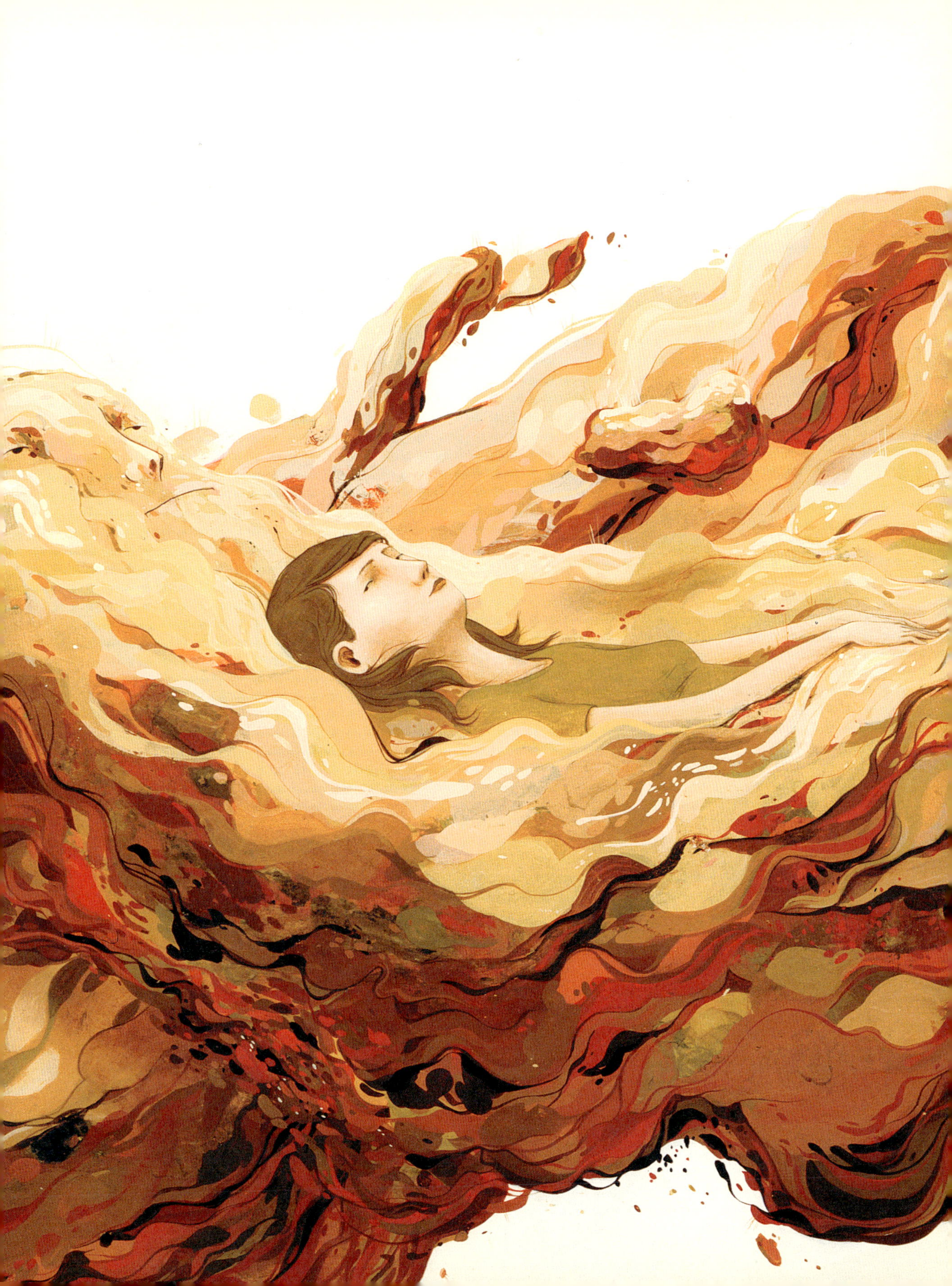

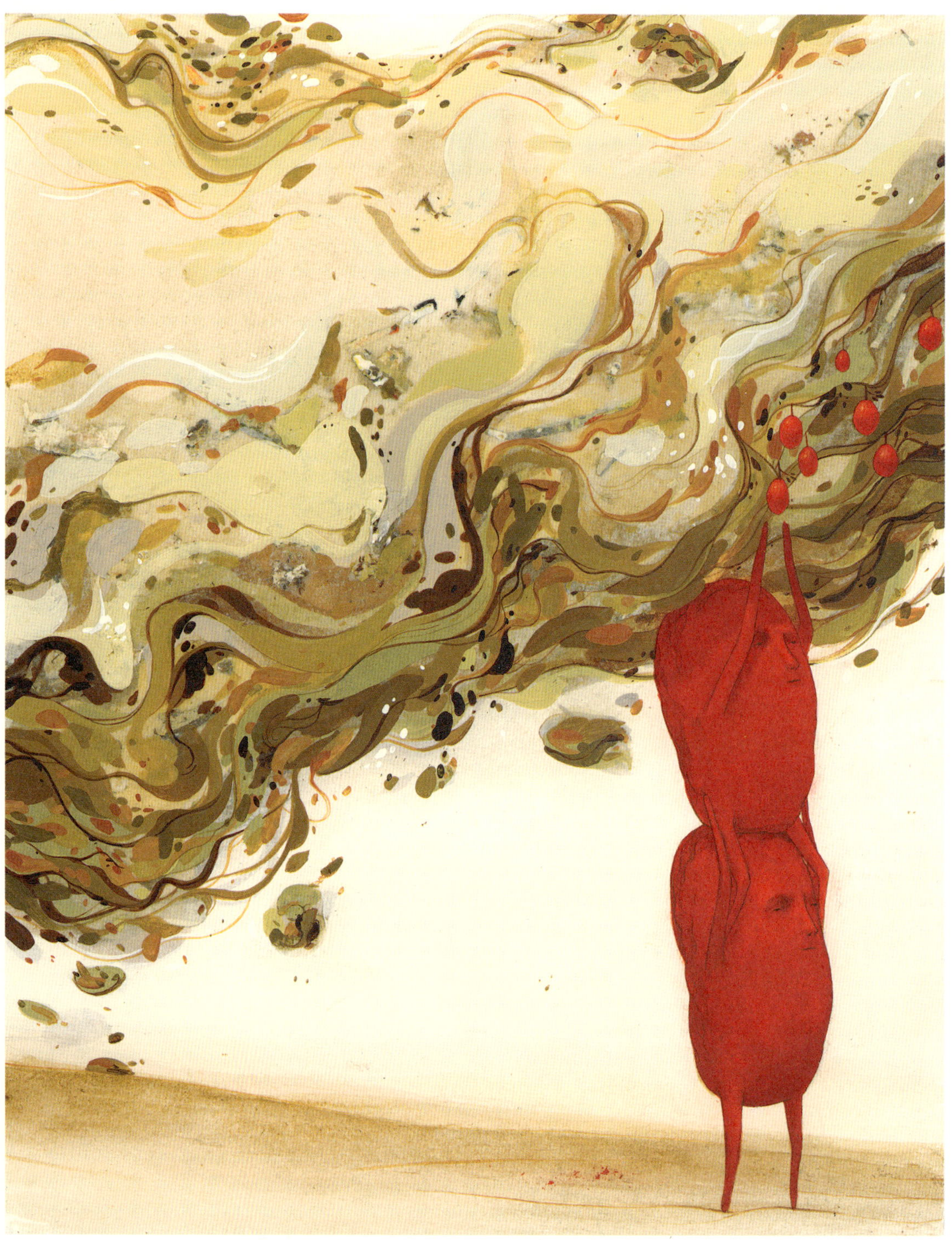

(overleaf)
**Blush from Side
to Side** 2006 — acrylic, collage on paper
26 x 40 in / 66 x 101.6 cm

Pick Me 2006 — acrylic, collage on paper
10.75 x 8.5 in / 27.3 x 21.6 cm

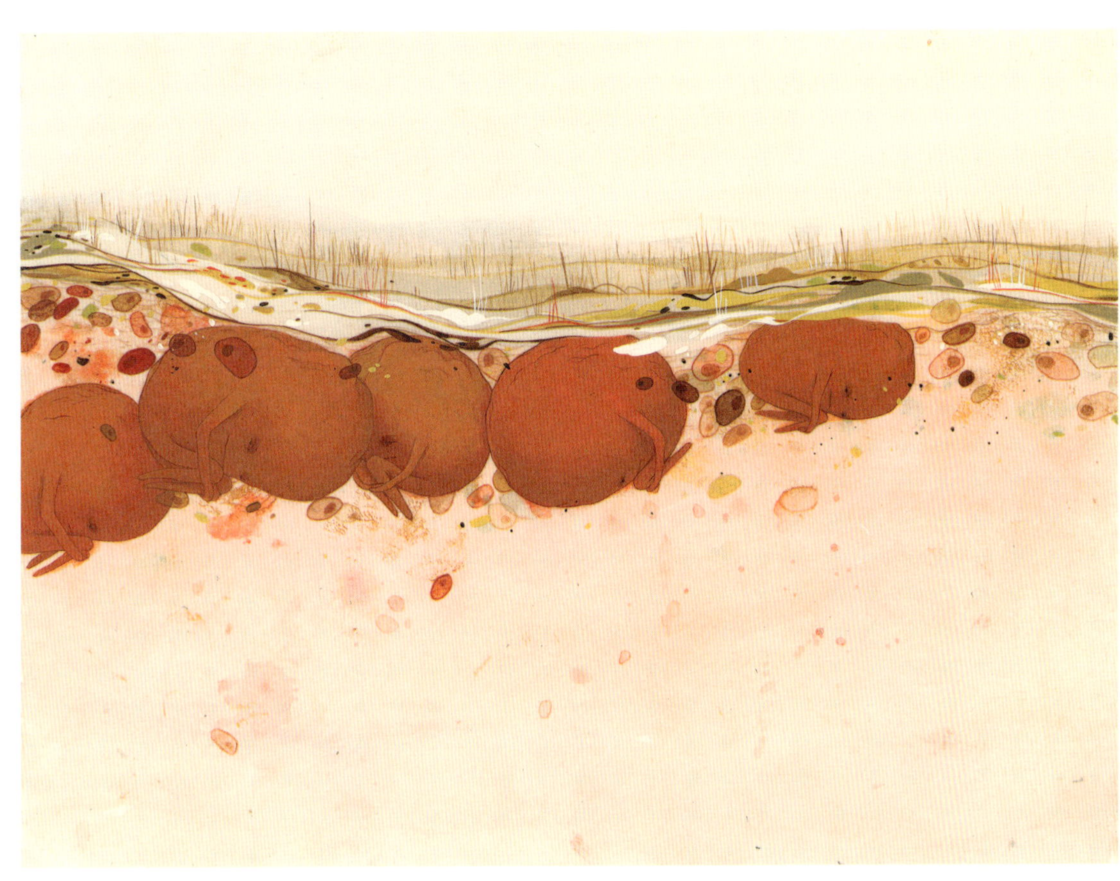

Seedlings   2006 — acrylic, collage on paper
                 8.75 x 10.75 in / 22.2 x 27.3 cm

33

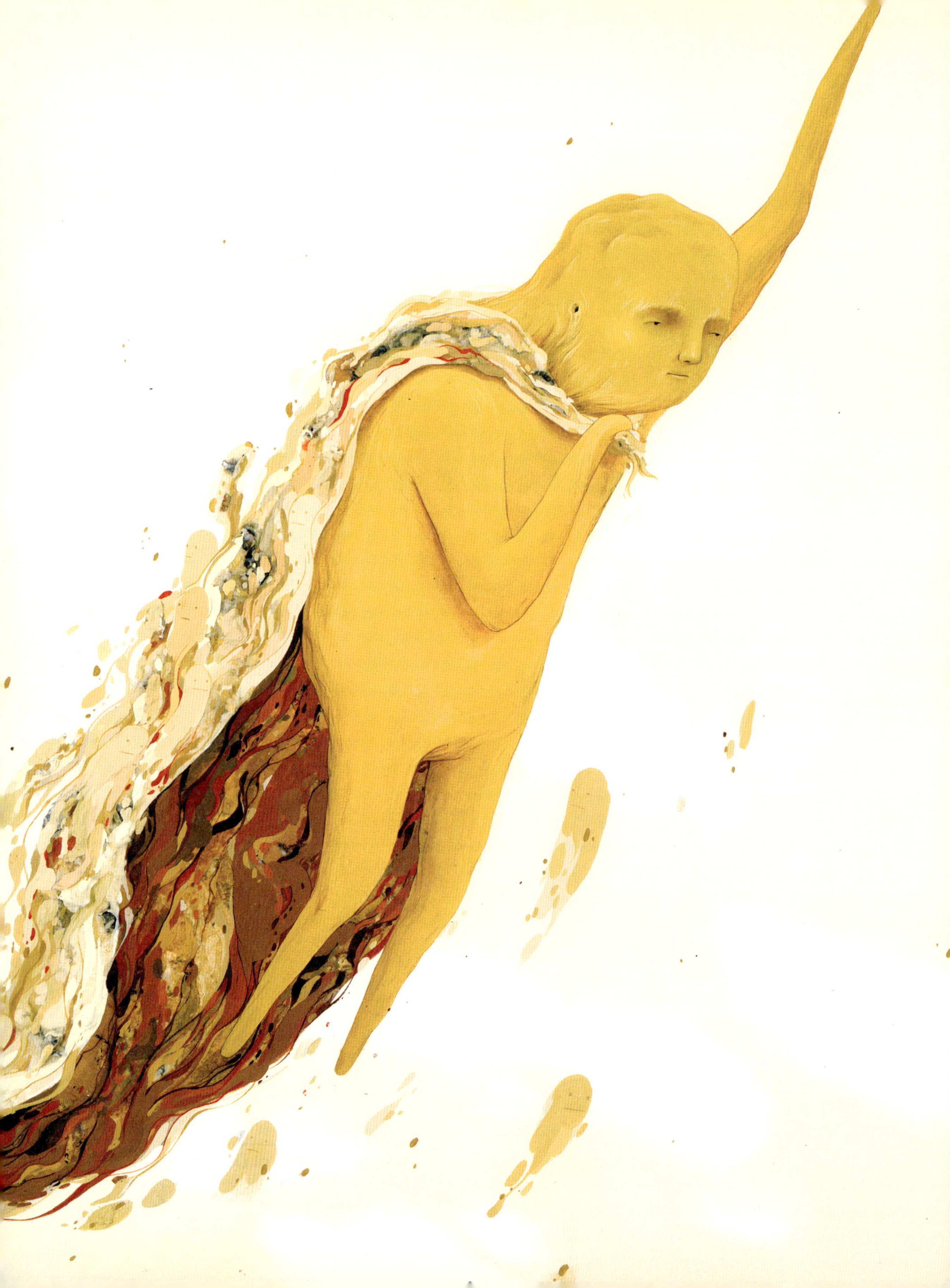

Blob Cape   2006 — acrylic, collage on paper
                   19 x 14 in / 48.3 x 35.6 cm

(overleaf)
Following Leaves   2006 — acrylic, collage on paper
                   56 x 66 in / 142.2 x 167.6 cm

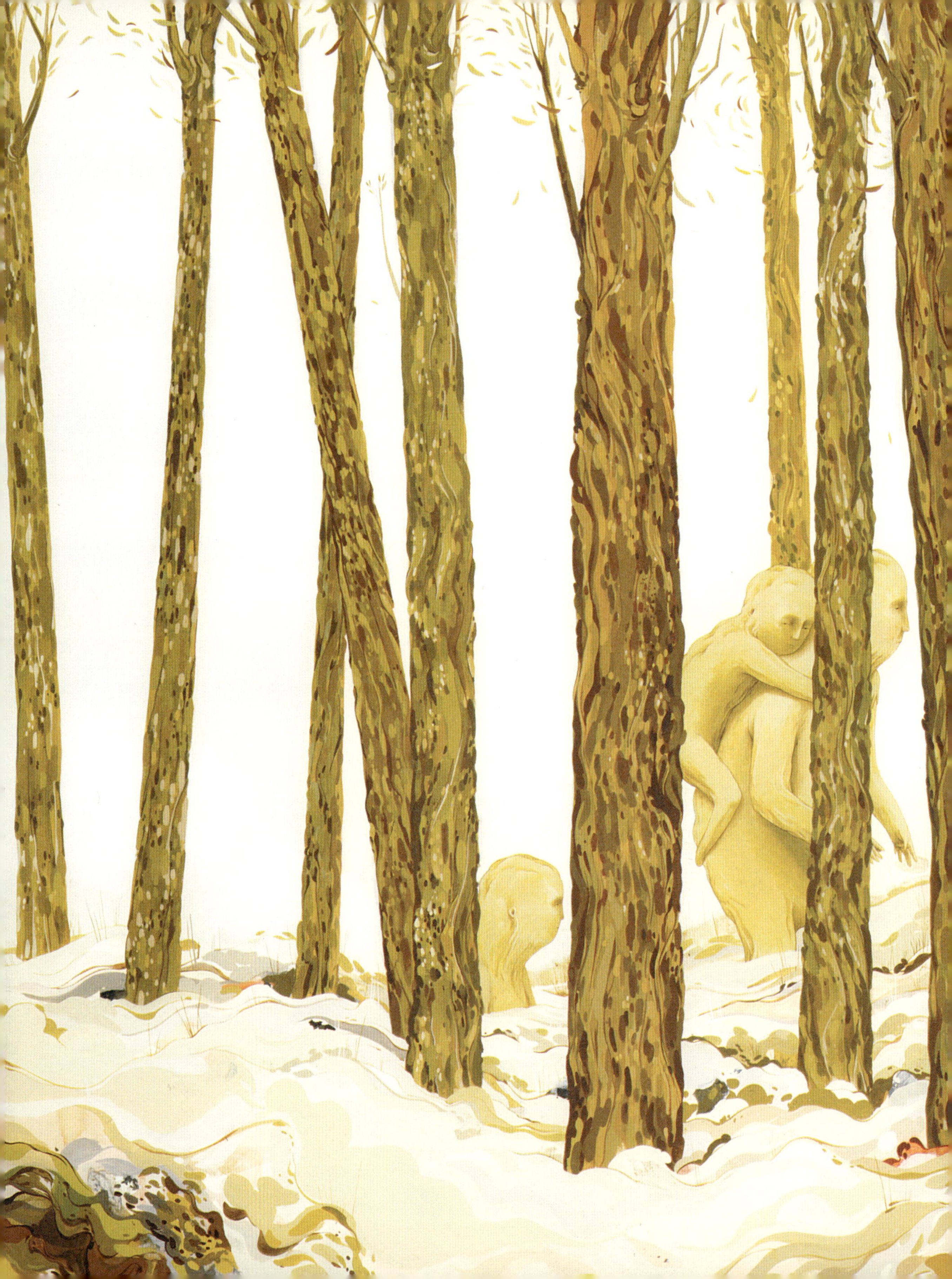

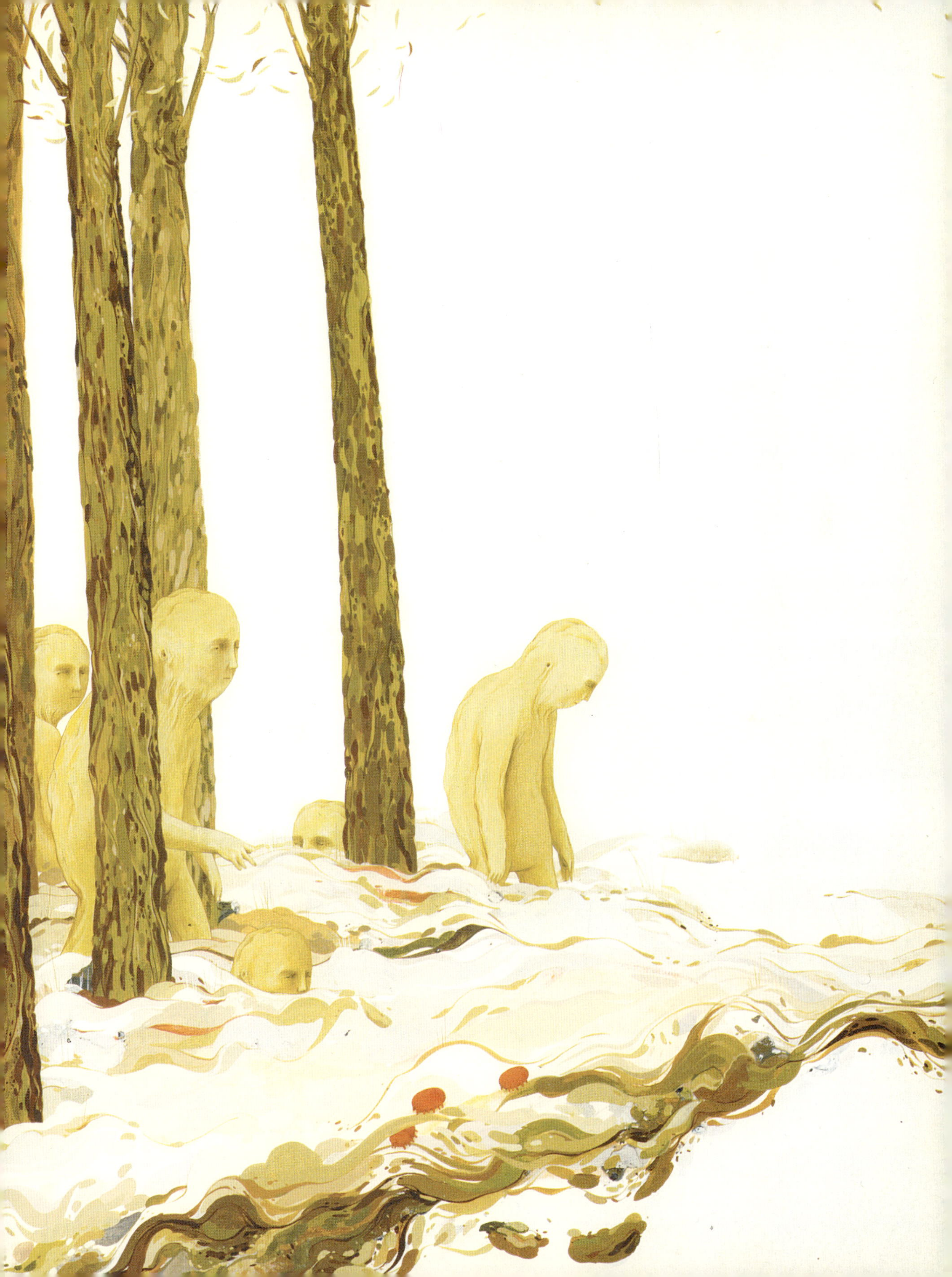

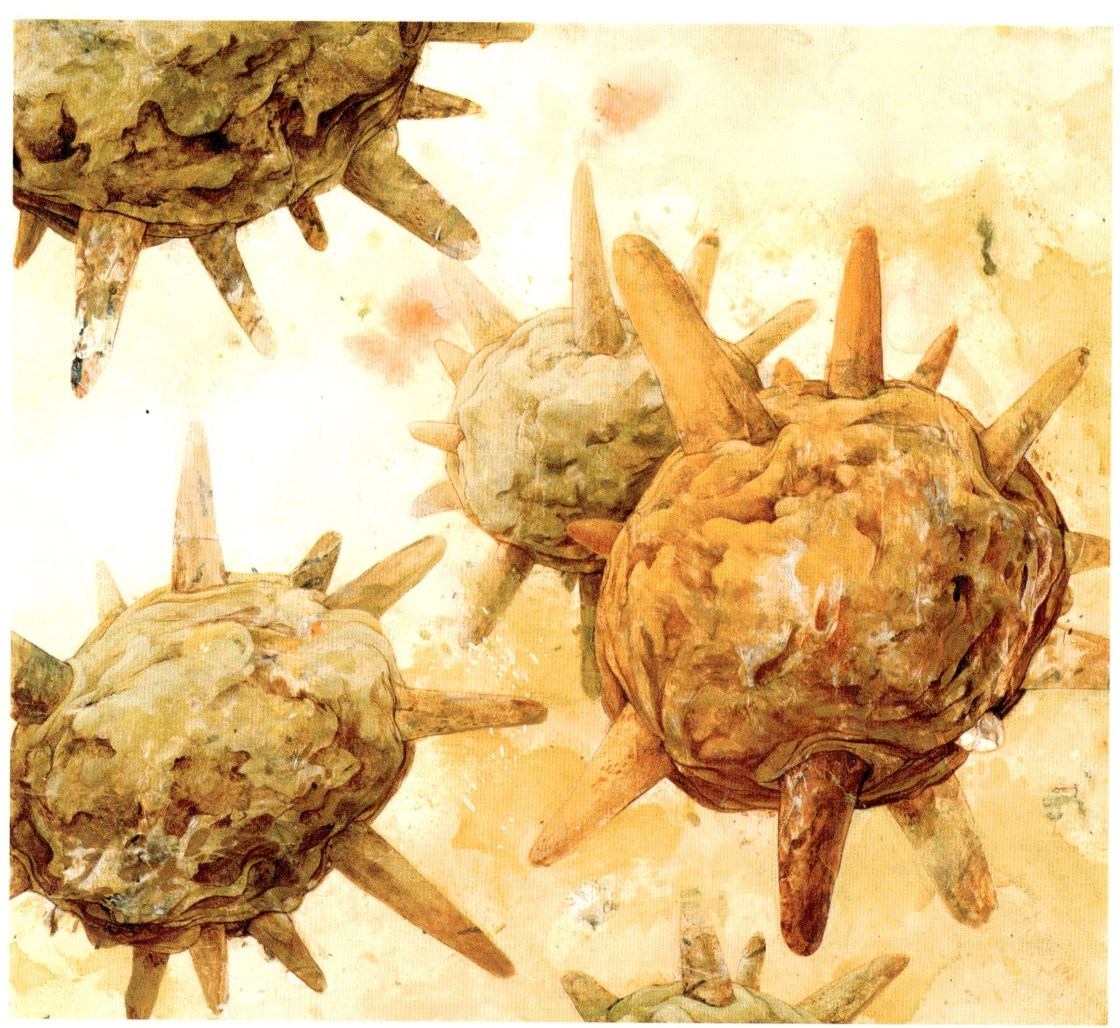

Orbits   2006 — acrylic, collage on paper
                10 x 11 in / 25.4 x 27.9 cm

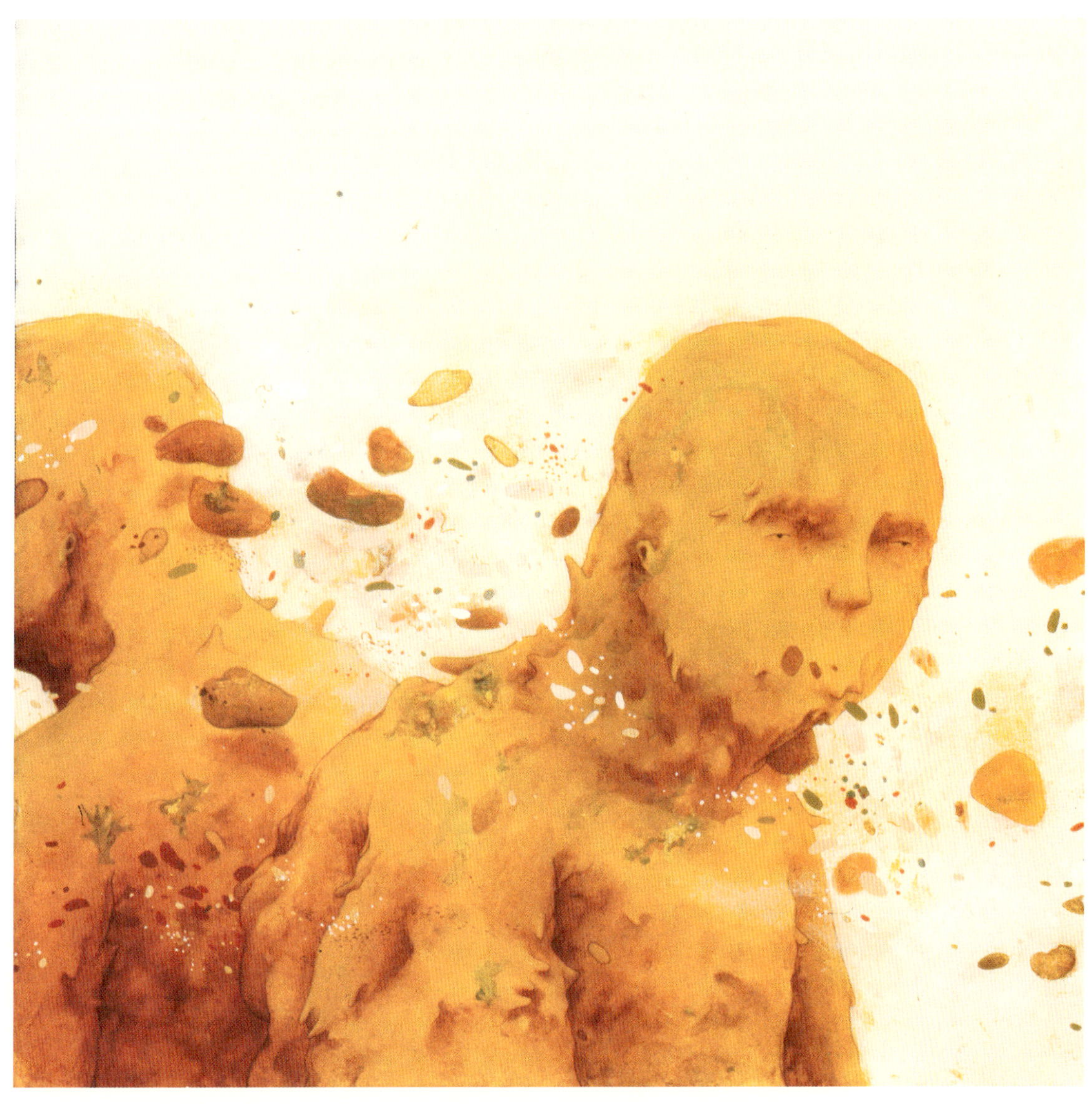

Self Poles   2006 — acrylic on paper
10 x 10 in / 25.4 x 25.4 cm

Growth of a Growth   2006 — acrylic, collage on paper
26 x 40 in / 66 x 101.6 cm

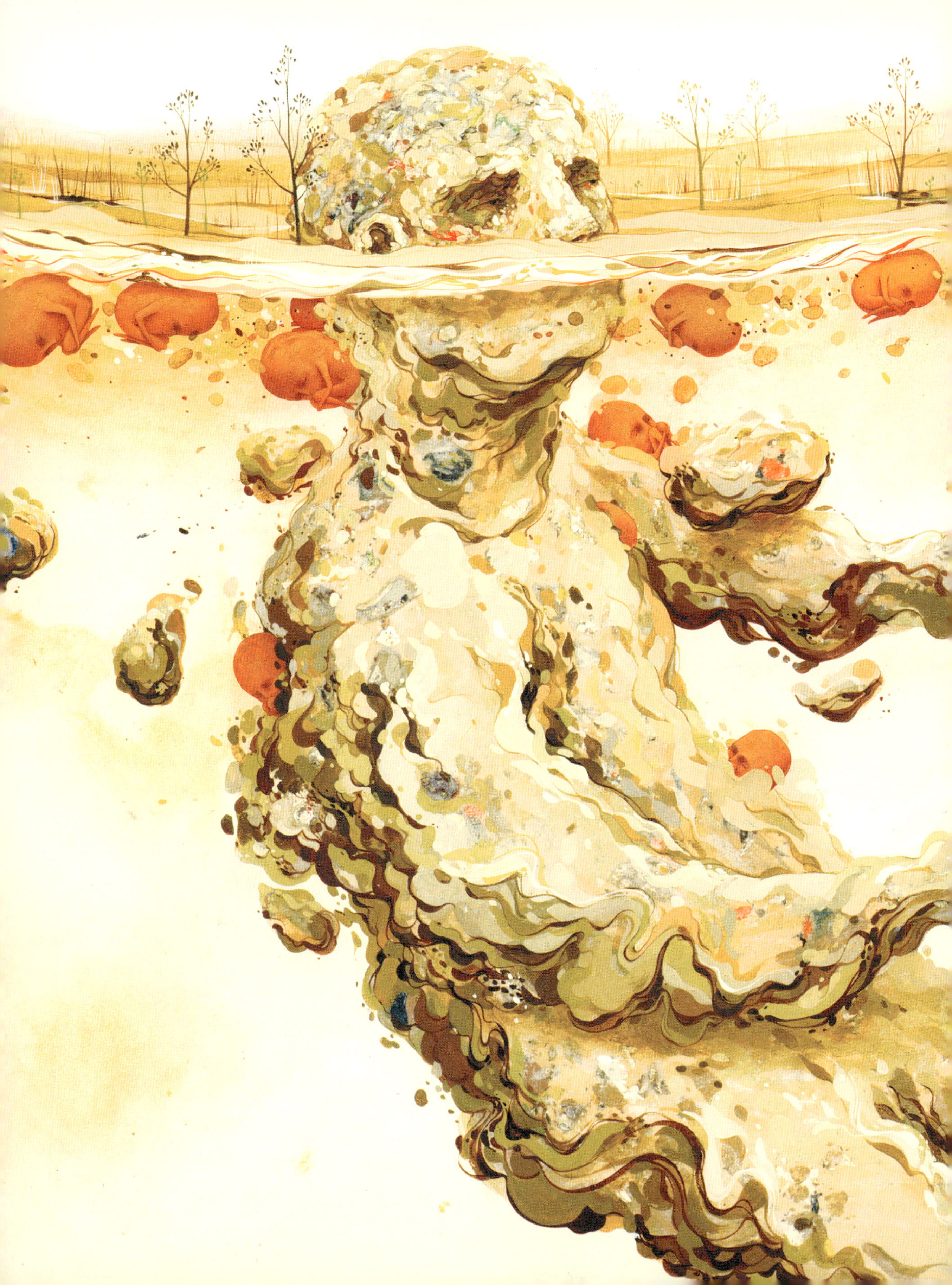

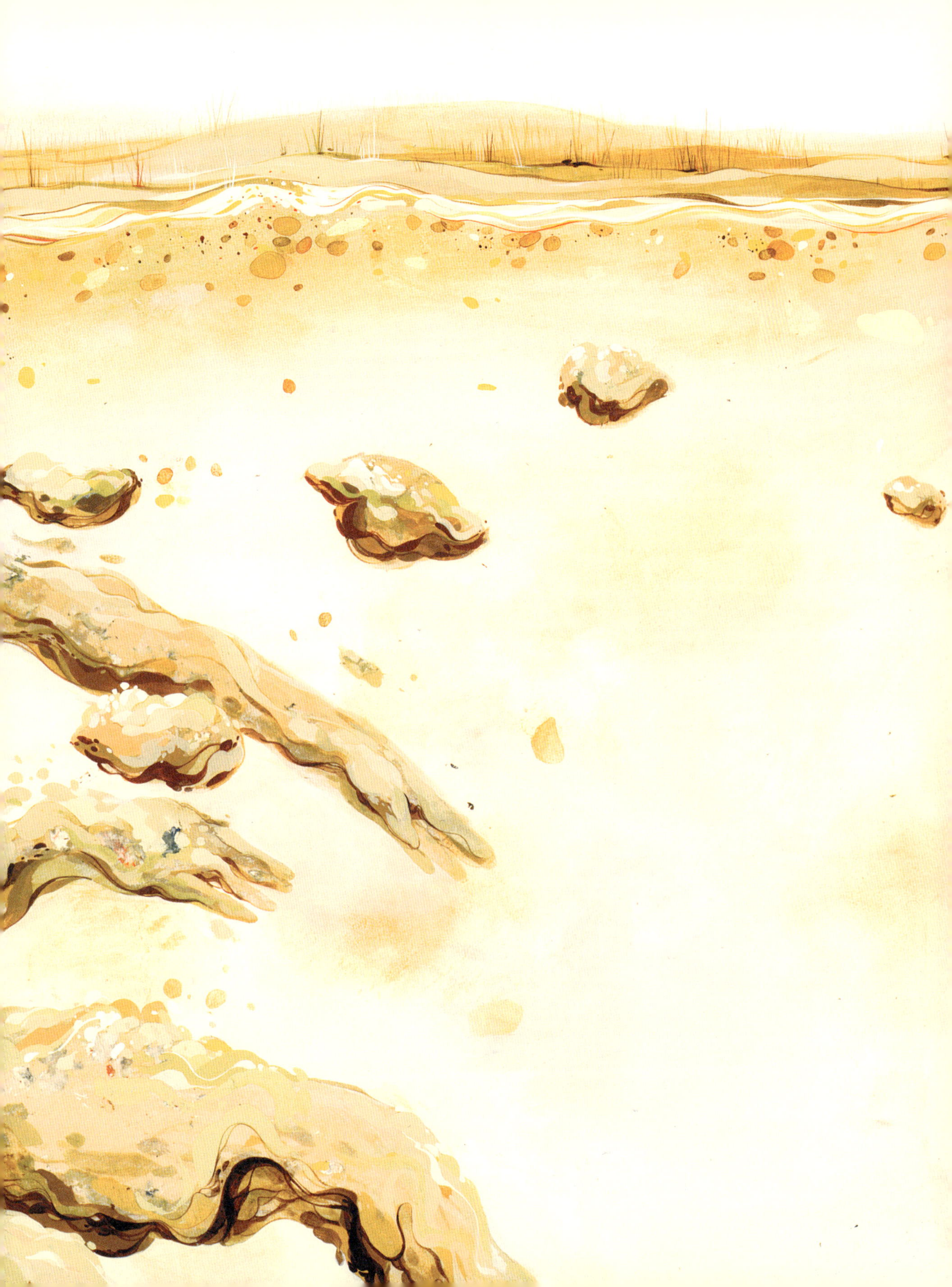

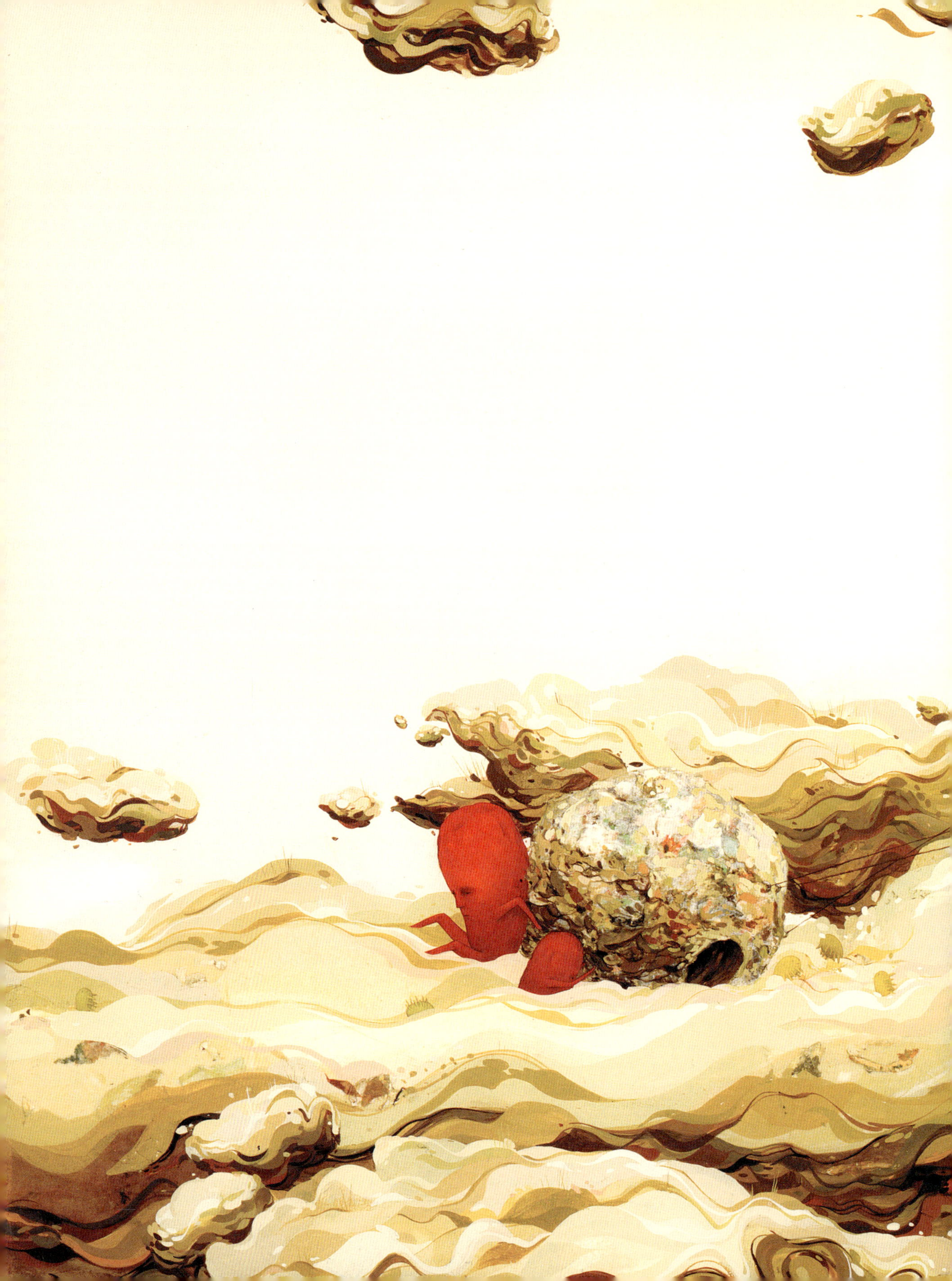

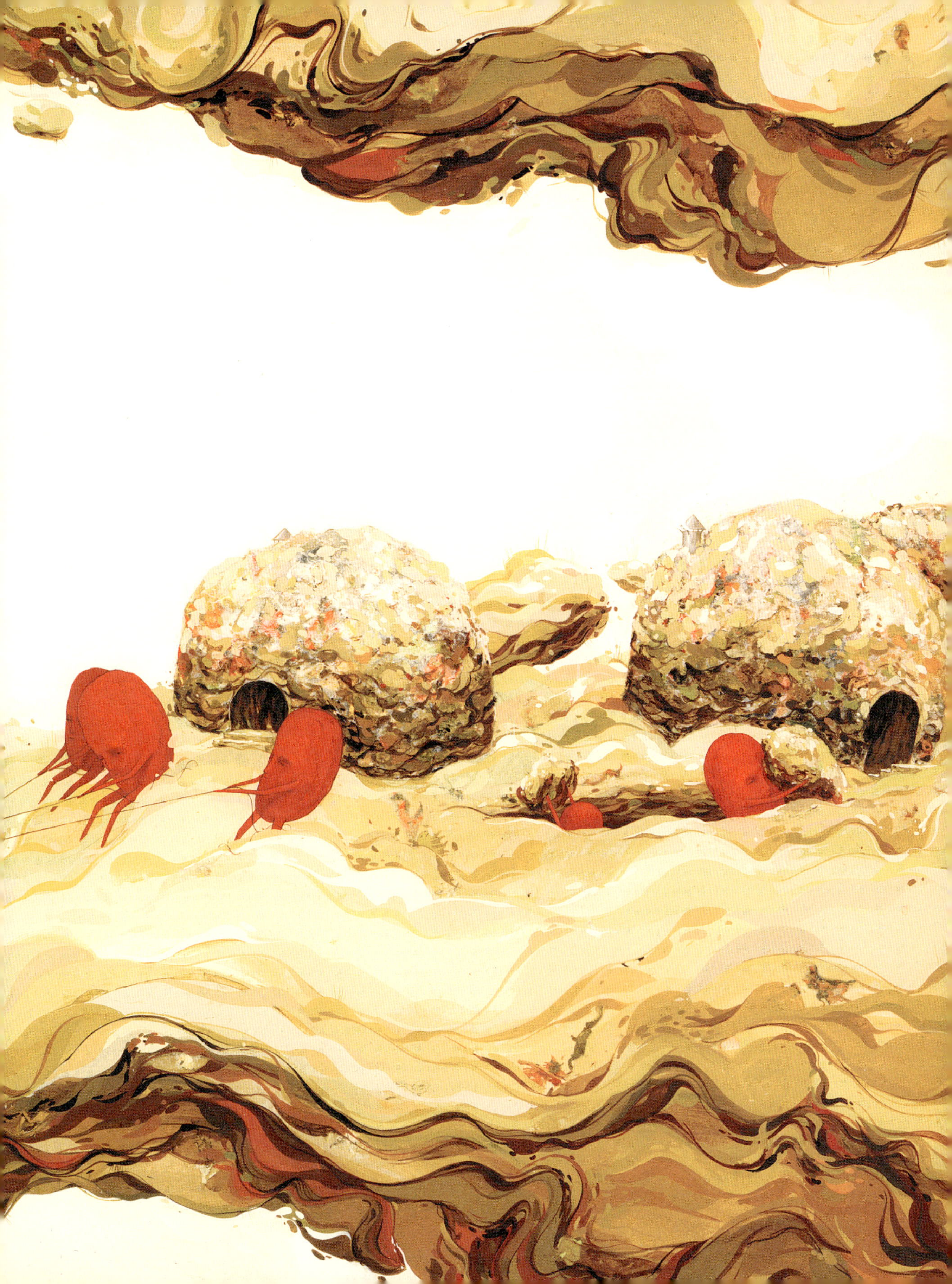

(overleaf)
Mobile Home   2006 — acrylic, collage on paper
26 x 40 in / 66 x 101.6 cm

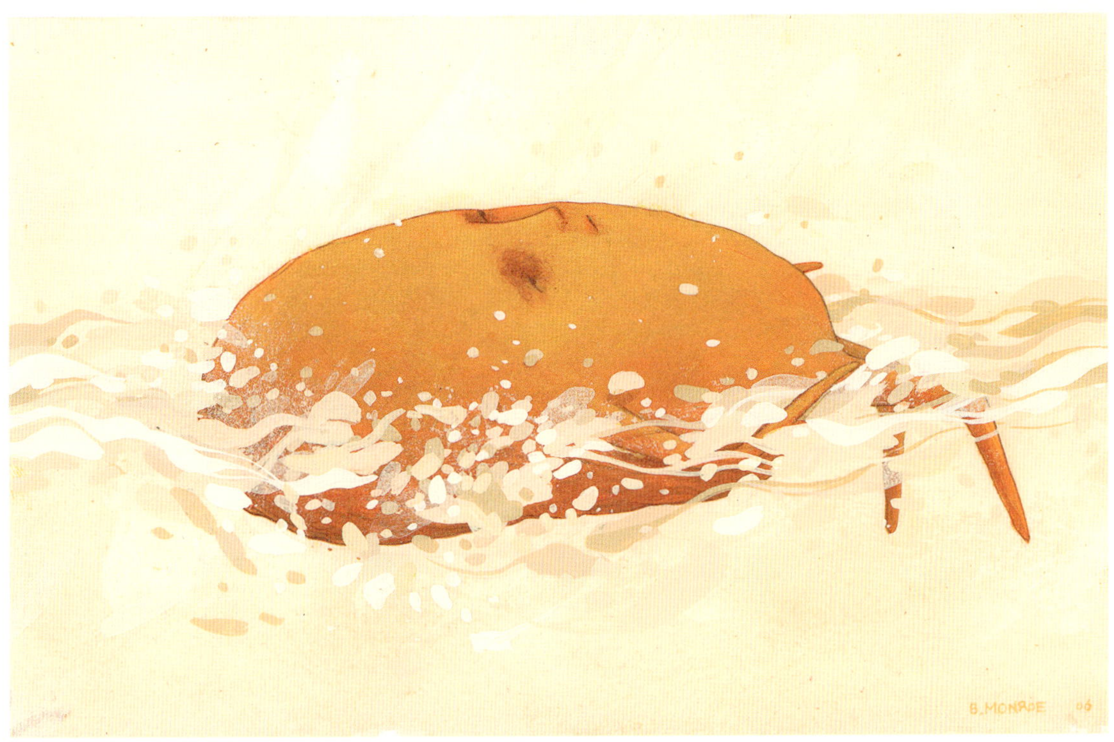

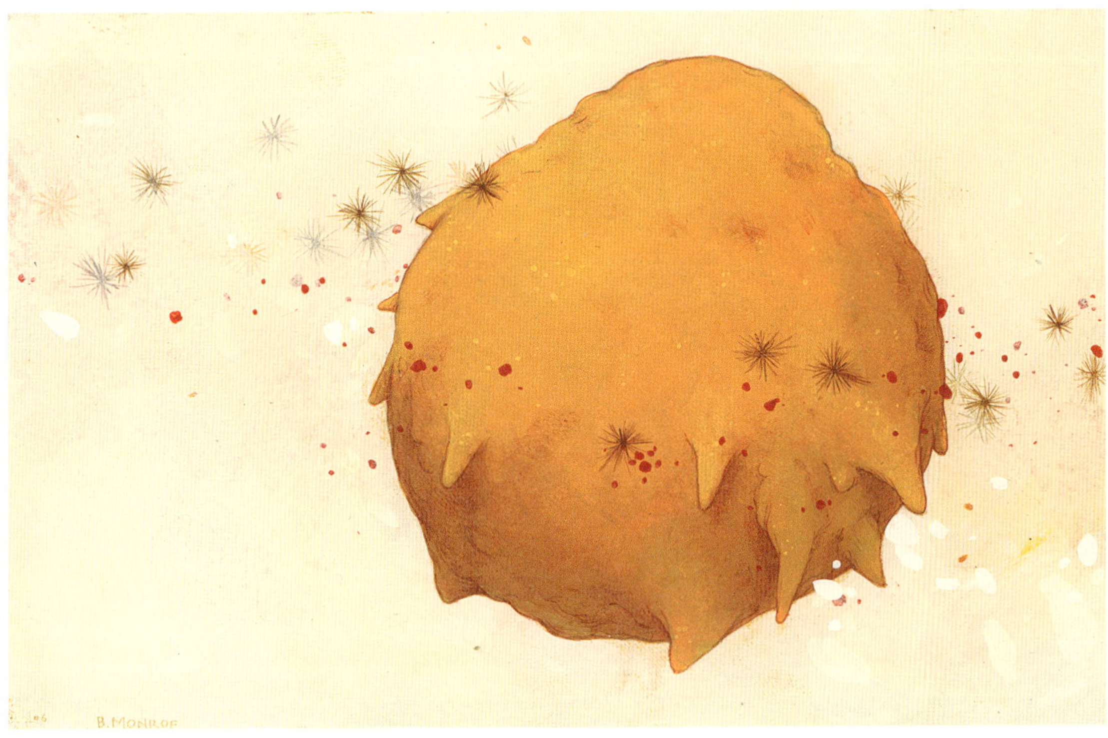

<table>
<tr><td>(top)
Thoughts Drifter</td><td>2006 — acrylic on paper
4 x 6 in / 10.2 x 15.2 cm</td><td>(bottom)
Simplicity</td><td>2006 — acrylic on paper
4 x 6 in / 10.2 x 15.2 cm</td></tr>
</table>

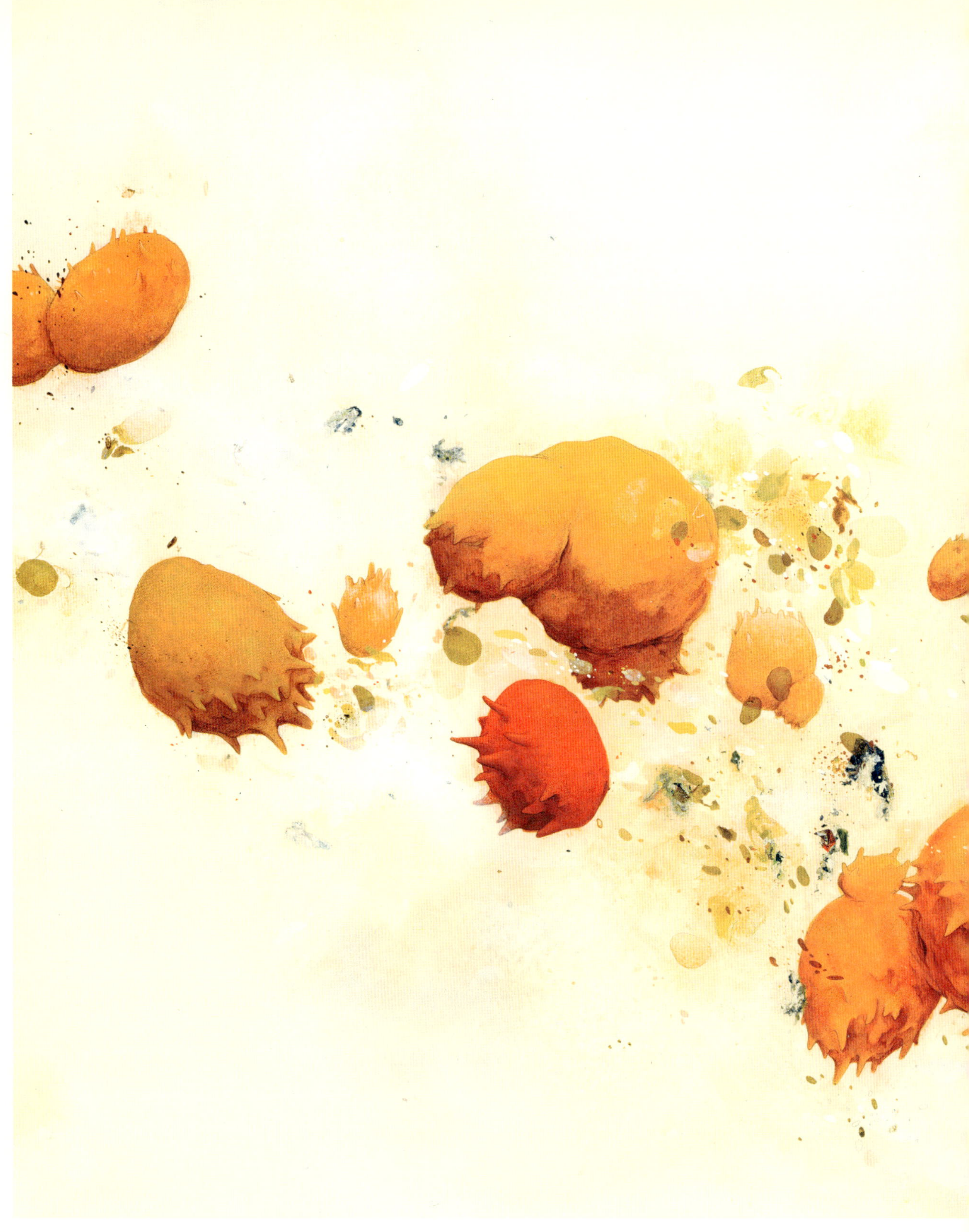

Orange Channel   2006 — acrylic on paper
                        14 x 19 in / 35.6 x 48.3 cm

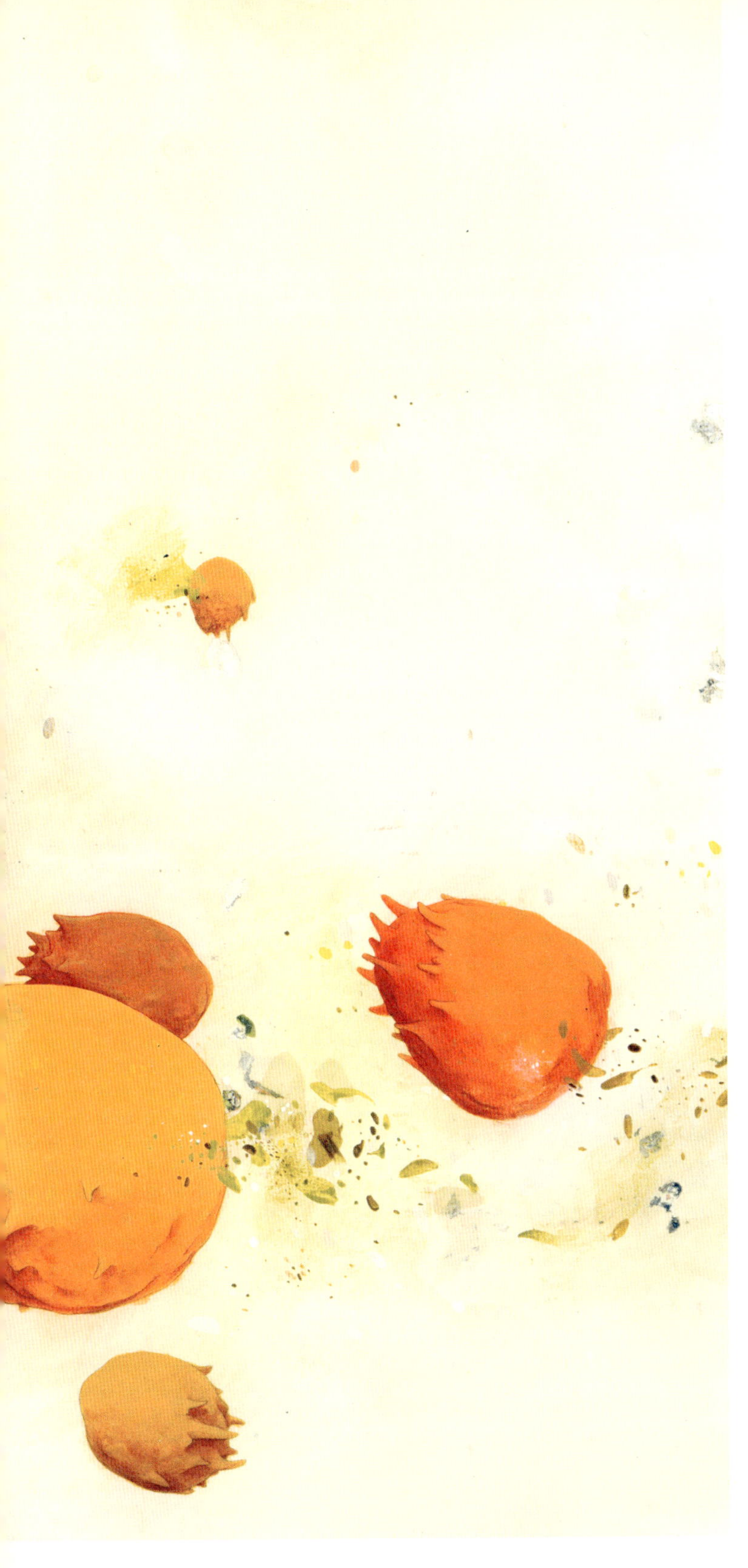

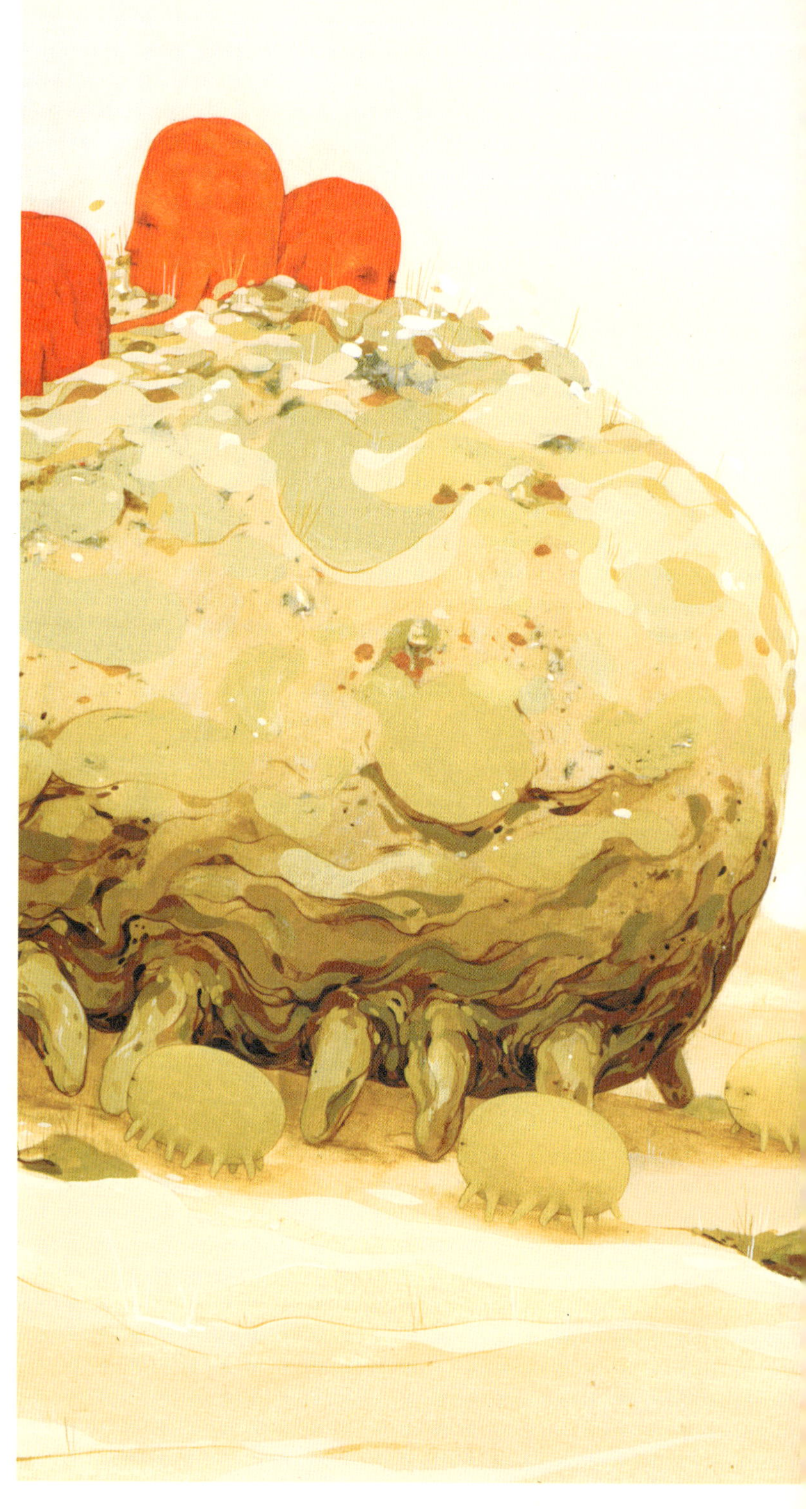

Crossing   2006 — acrylic, collage on paper
                20 x 23 in / 50.8 x 58.4 cm

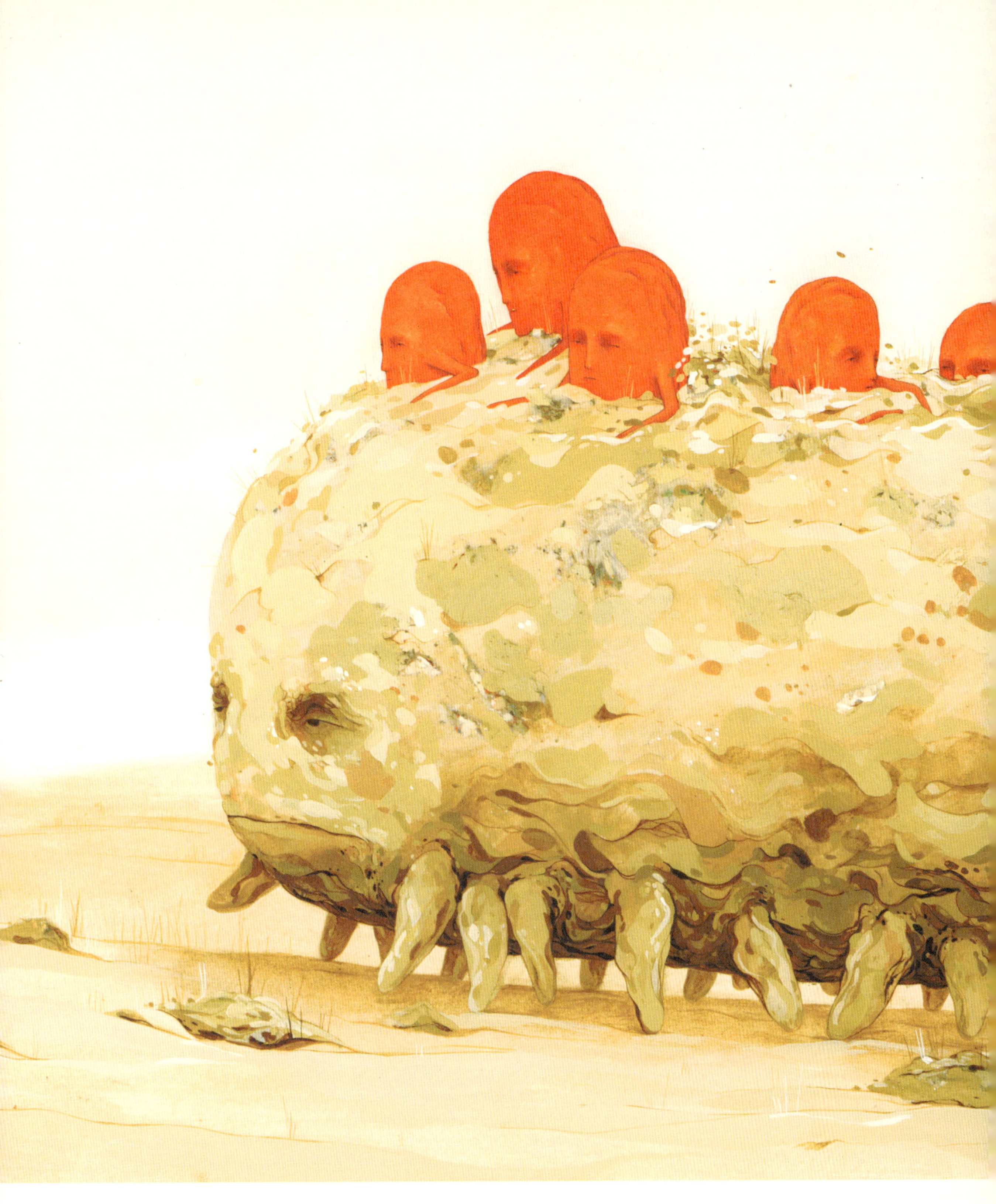

(overleaf)
Greater Mitosis   2006 — acrylic on paper
15 x 21 in / 38.1 x 53.3 cm

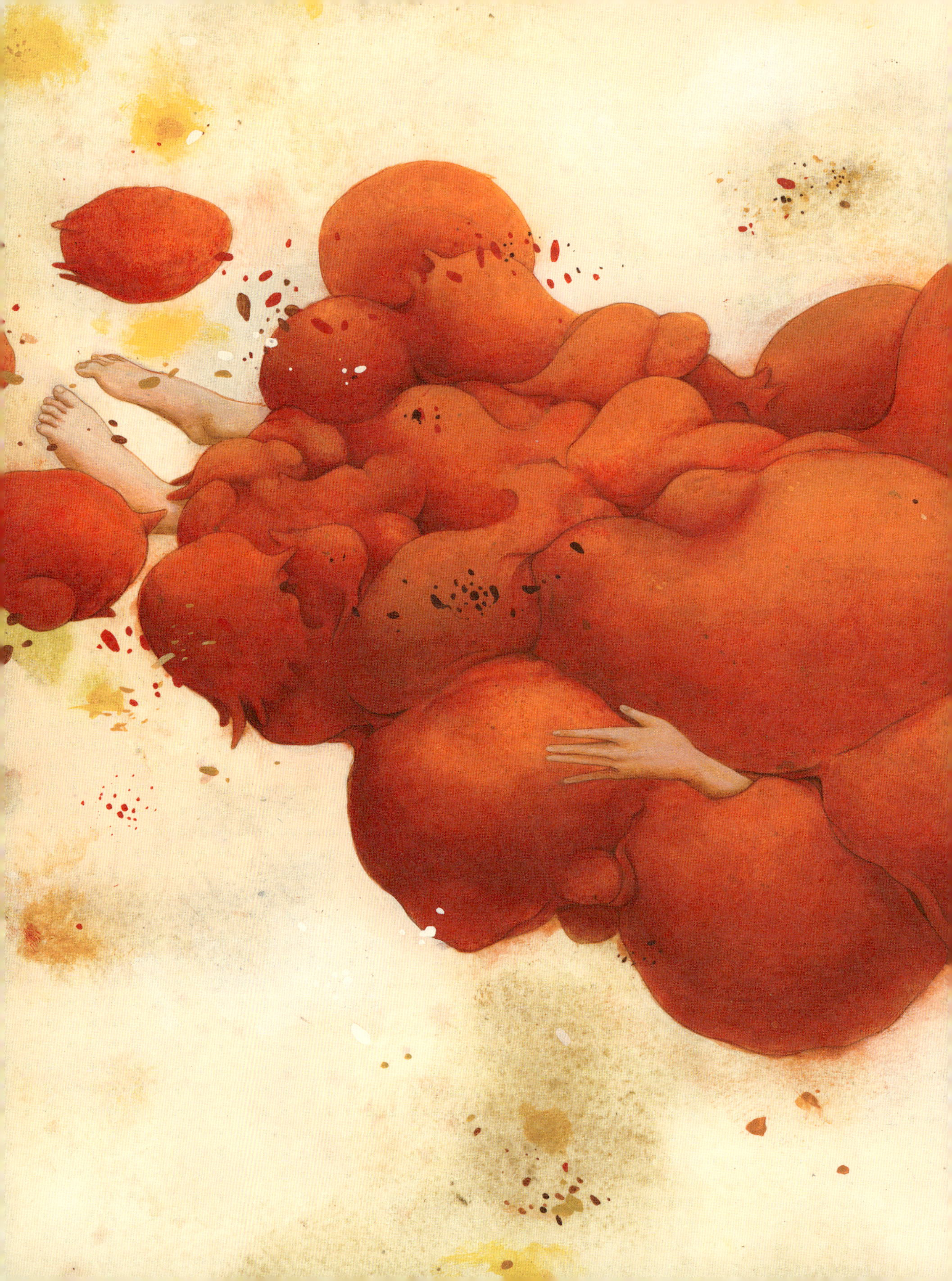

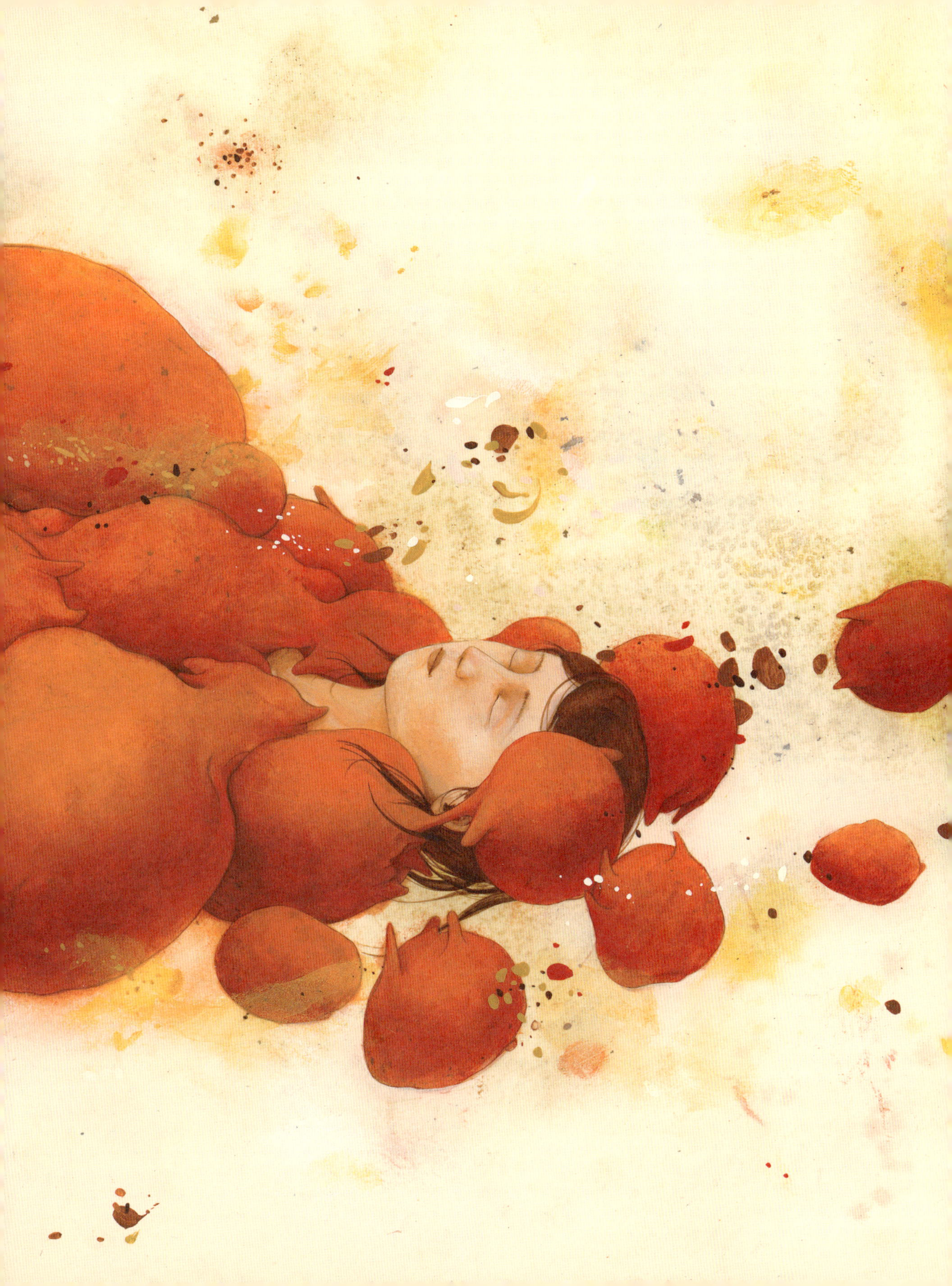

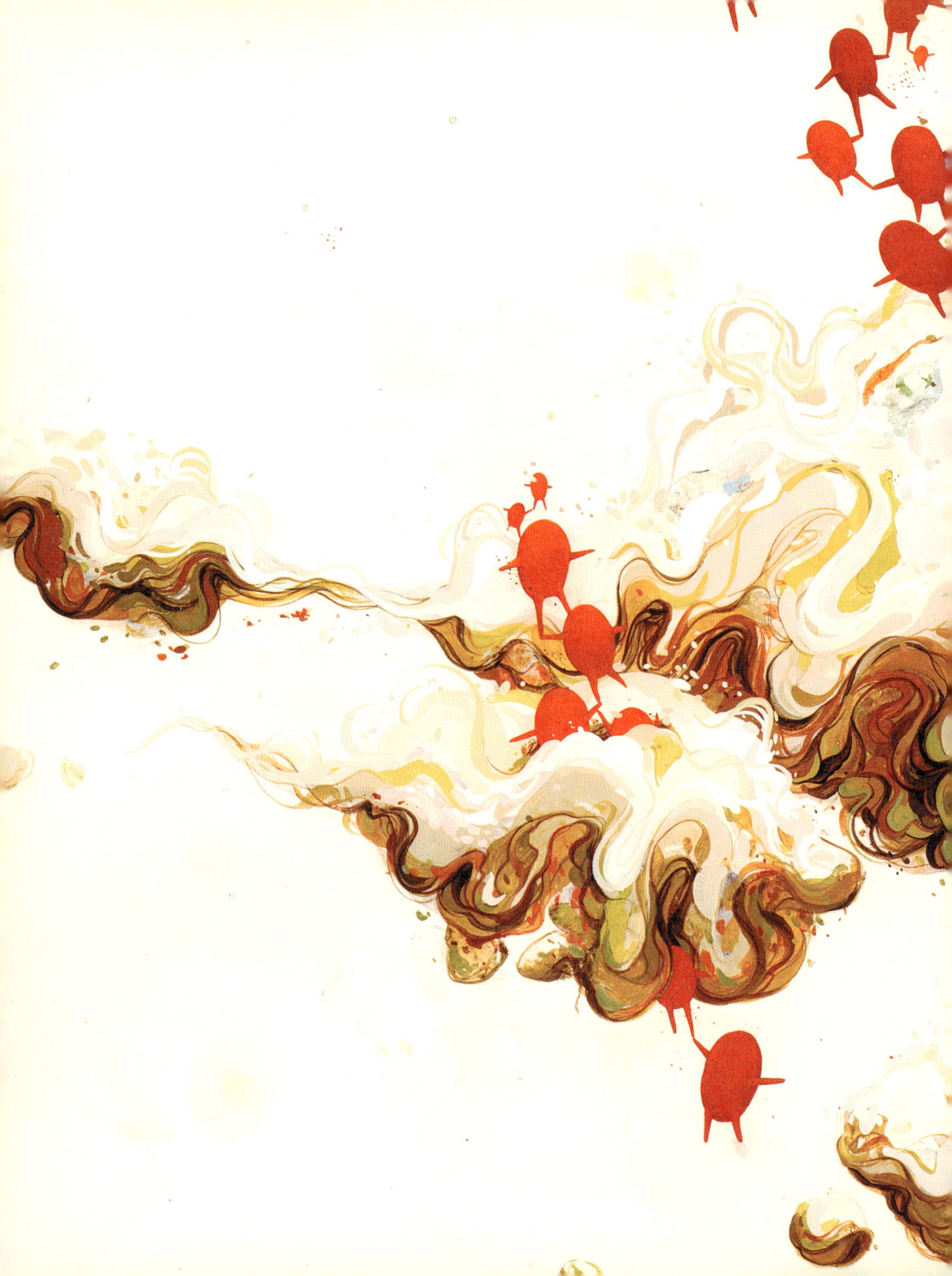

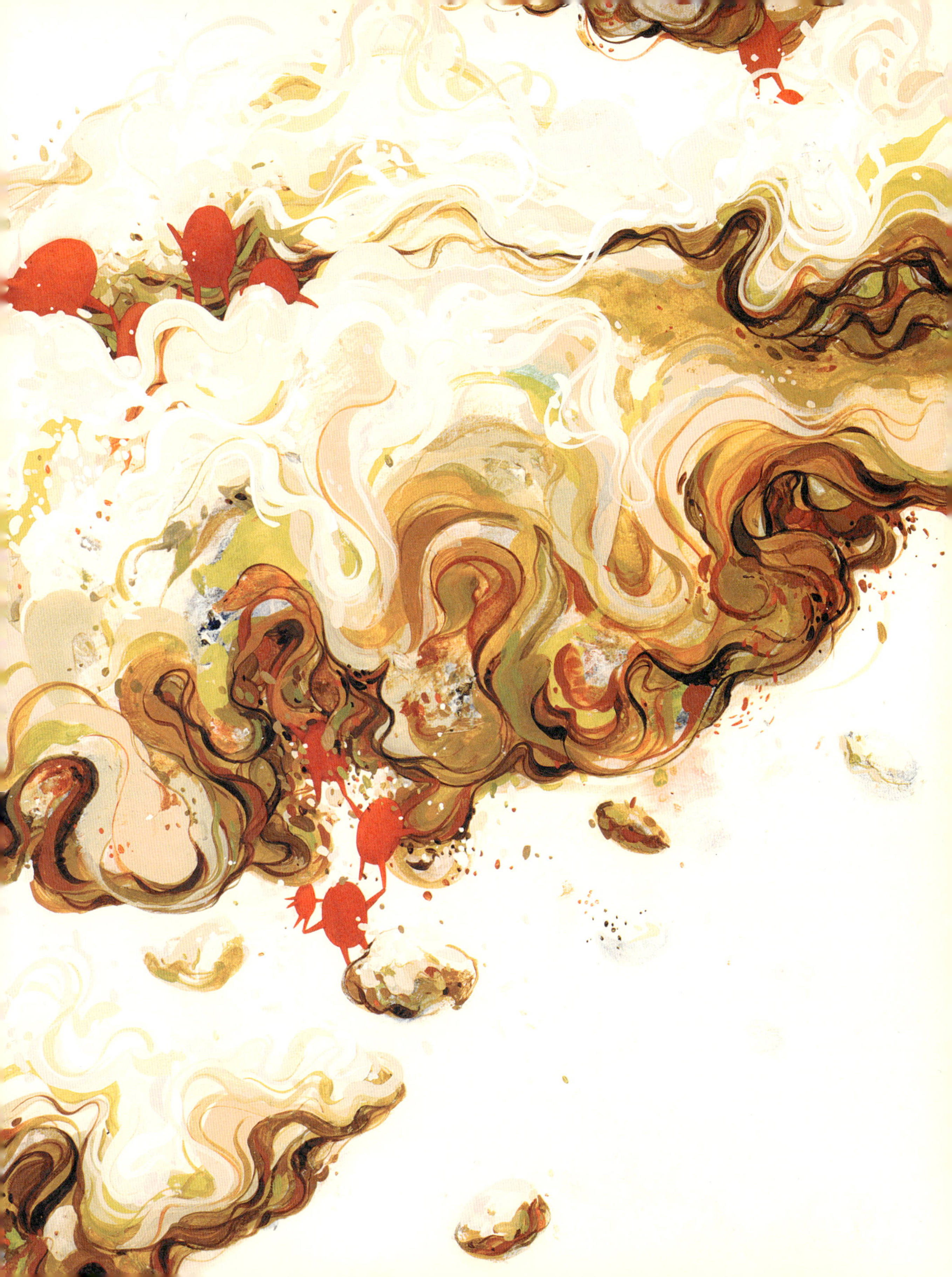

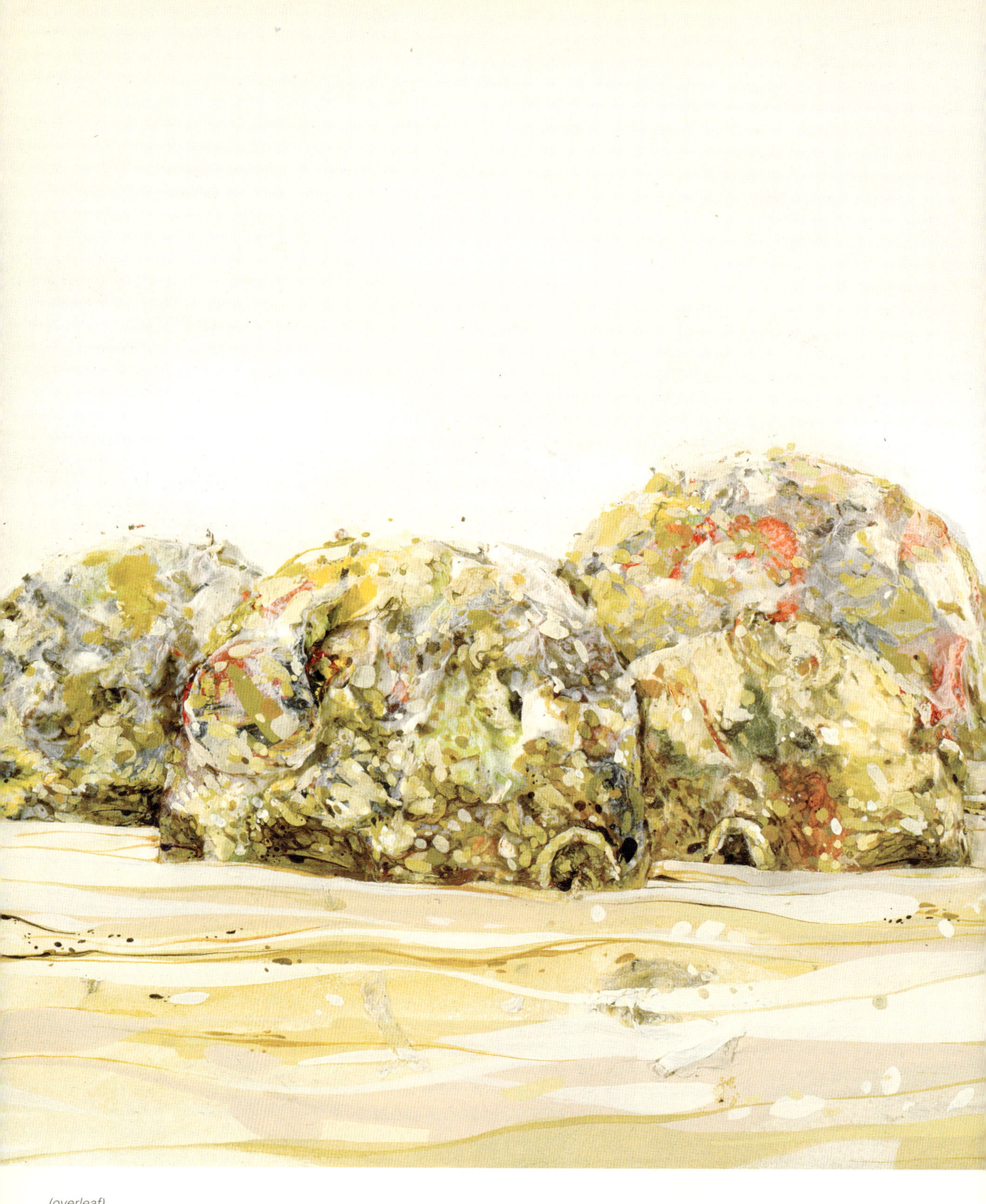

The Pull of Gravity 2007 — acrylic, collage on paper
19 x 26 in / 48.3 x 66 cm

Disguising as Rounded Mounds 2006 — acrylic, collage [ps] on paper
10 x 15 in / 25.4 x 38.1 cm

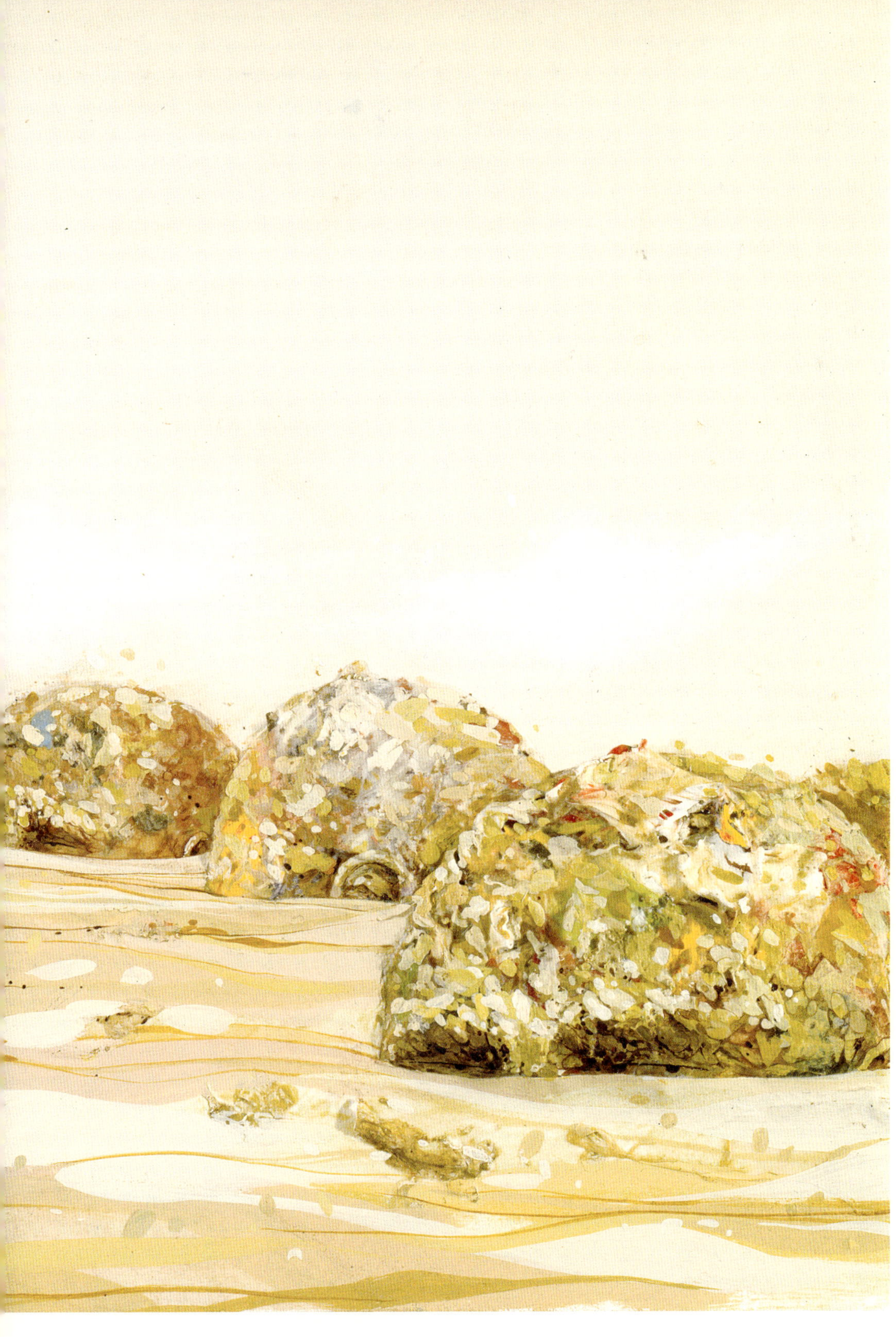

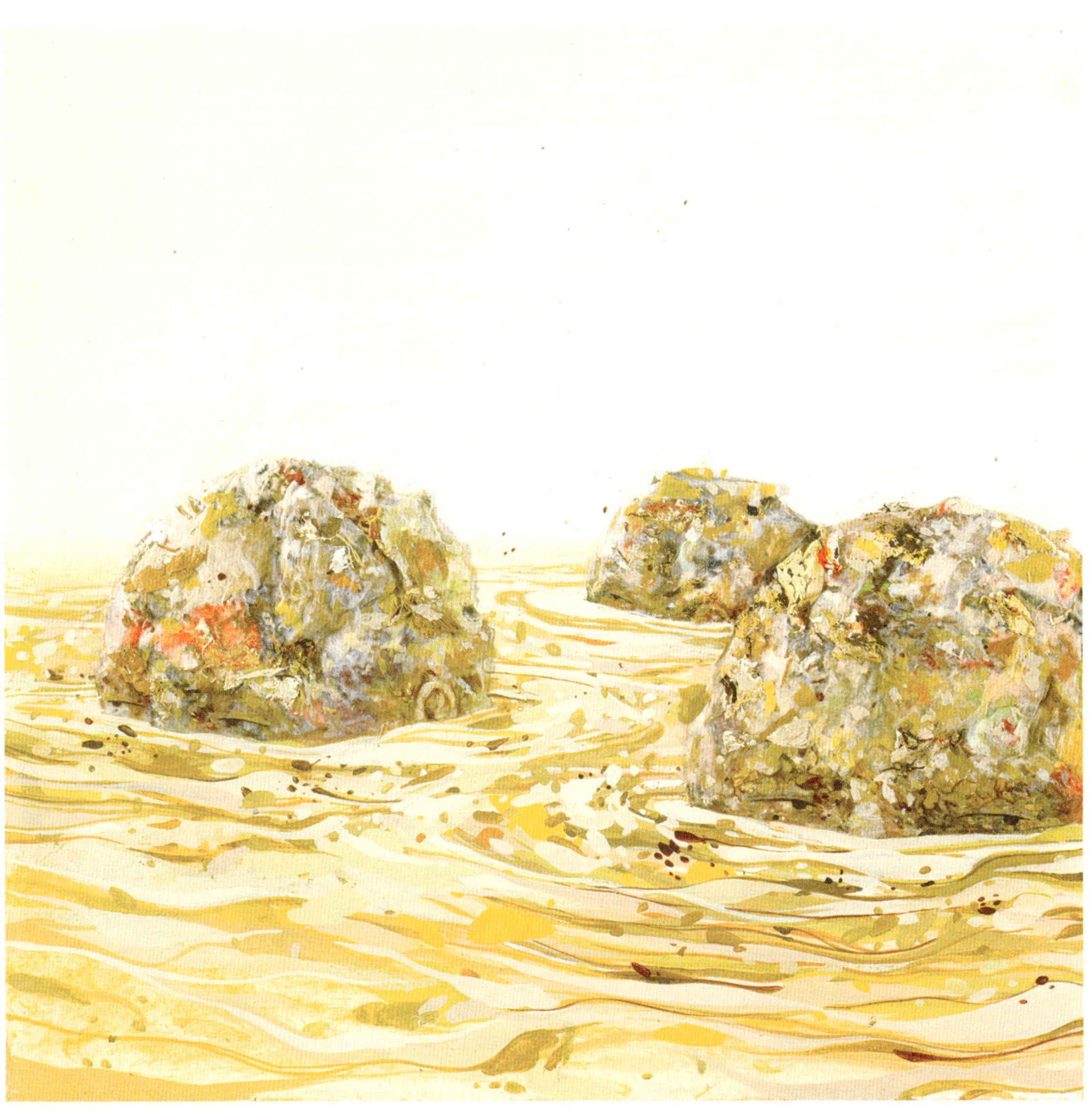

Suspicions   2006 — acrylic, collage [ps] on paper
7 x 7 in / 17.8 x 17.8 cm

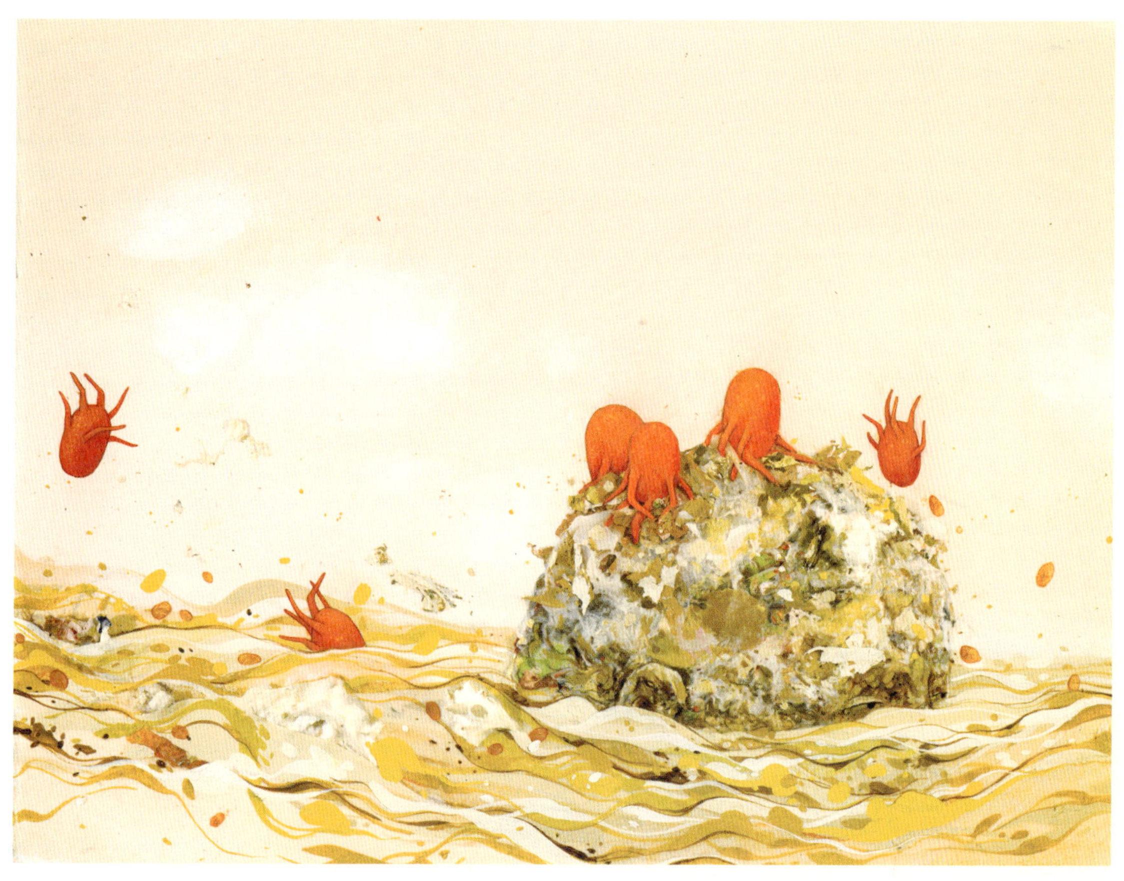

Traverse   2006 — acrylic, collage [ps] on paper   **A Sort of Blur**   2006 — acrylic, collage on paper
          8 x 10 in / 20.3 x 25.4 cm   26 x 38.5 in / 66 x 97.8 cm   57

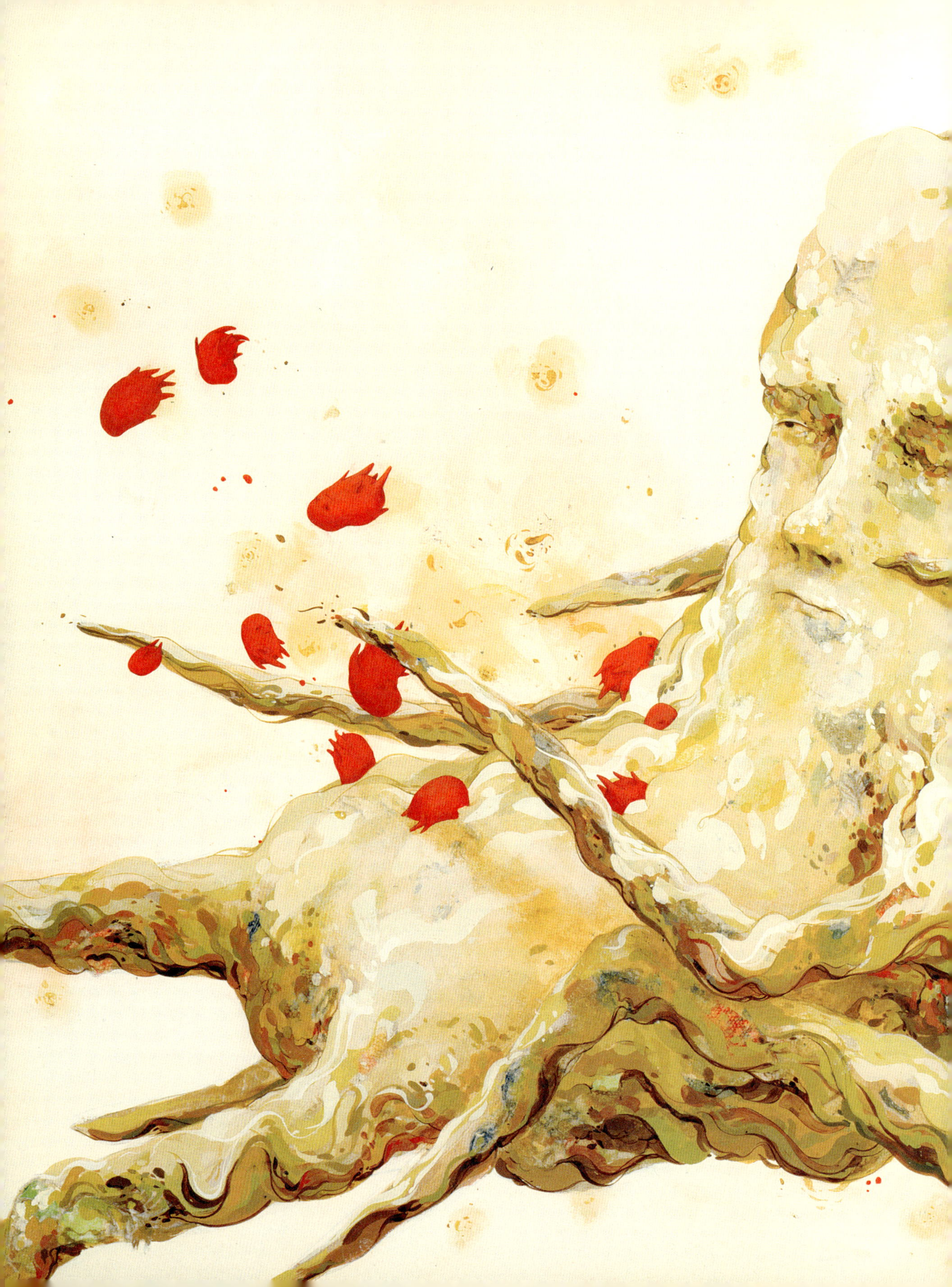

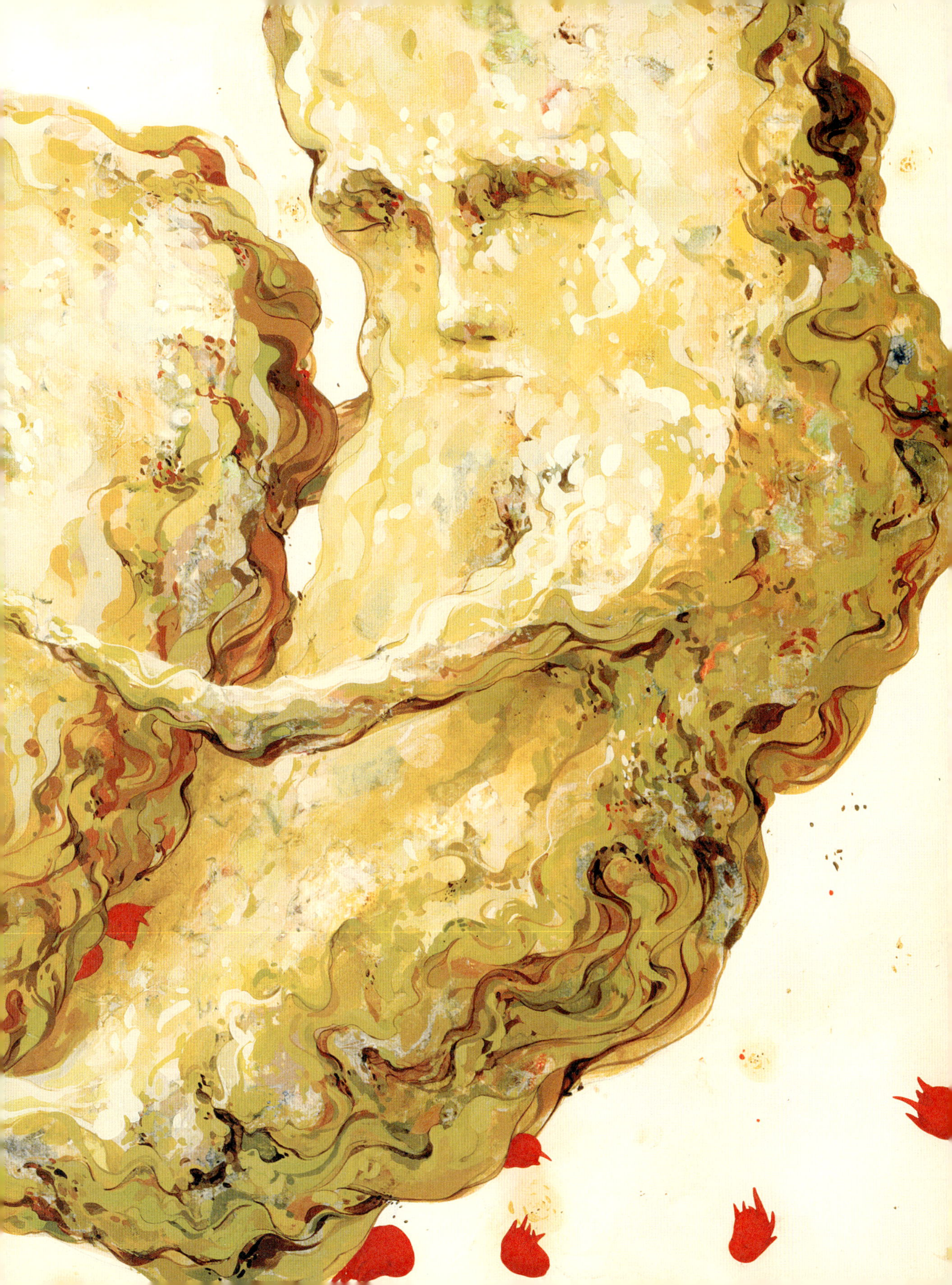

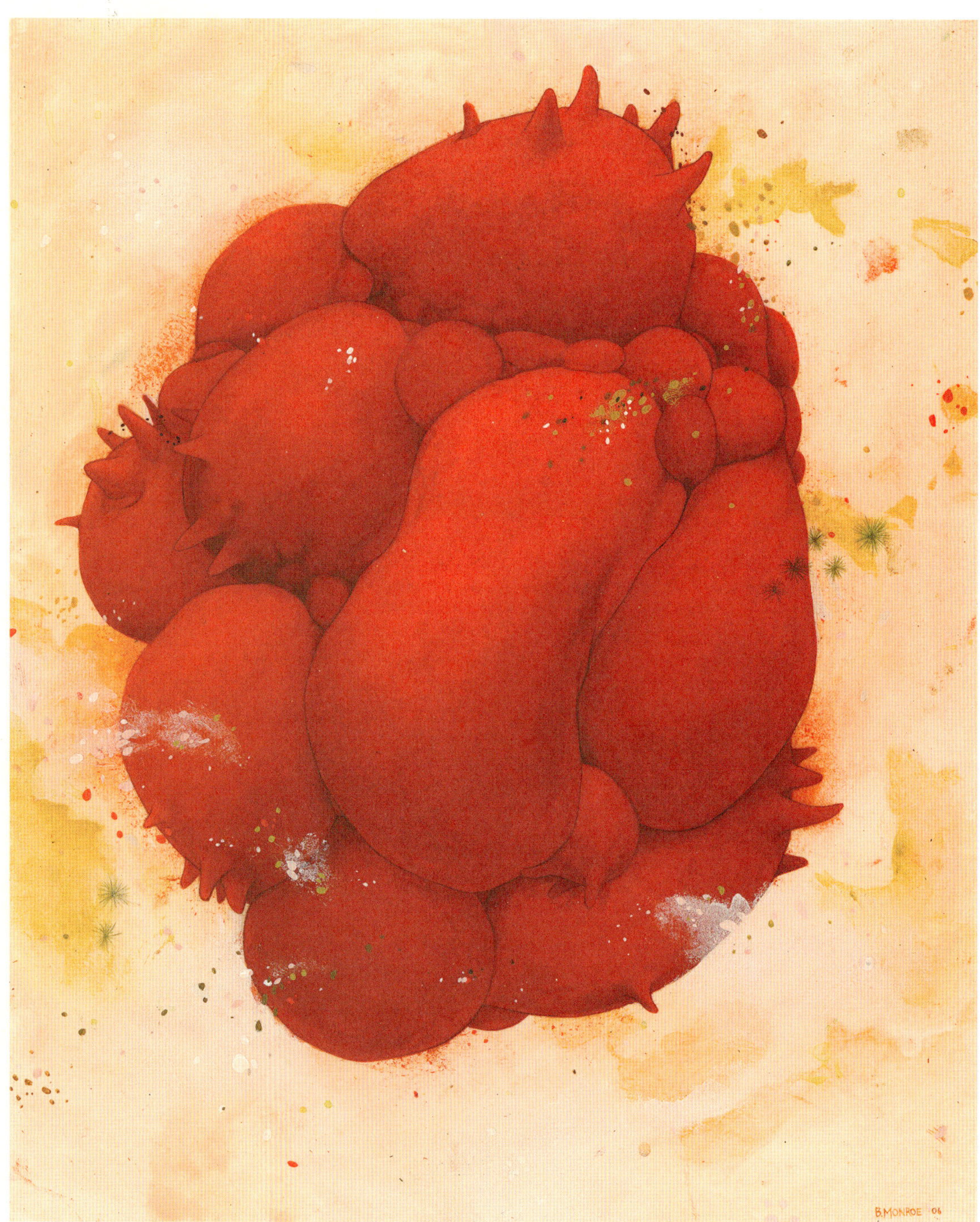

Redness   2006 — acrylic on paper
10 x 8 in / 25.4 x 20.3 cm

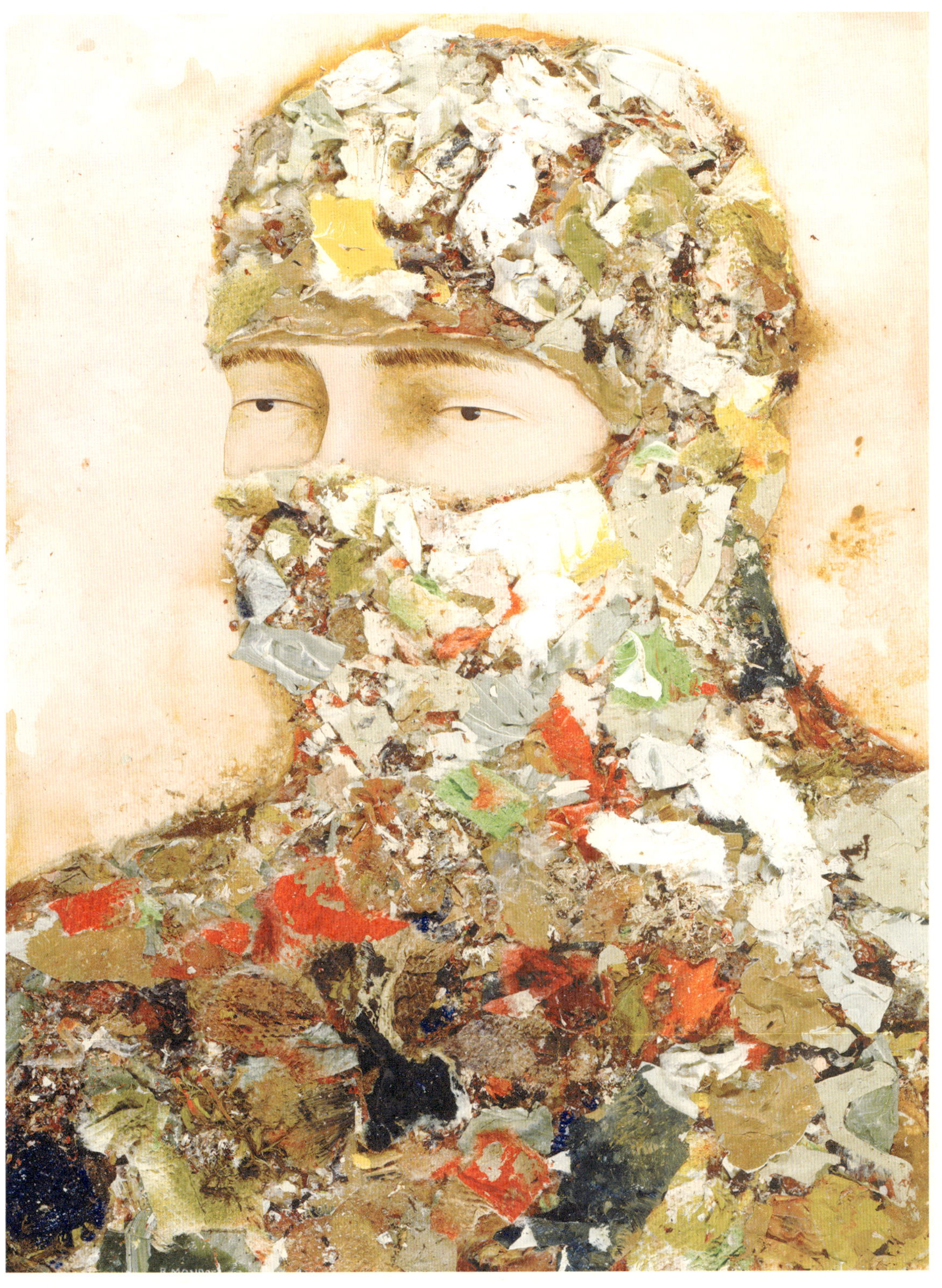

Personal Ninja   2007 — acrylic, collage [ps] on paper
11 x 8 in / 27.9 x 20.3 cm

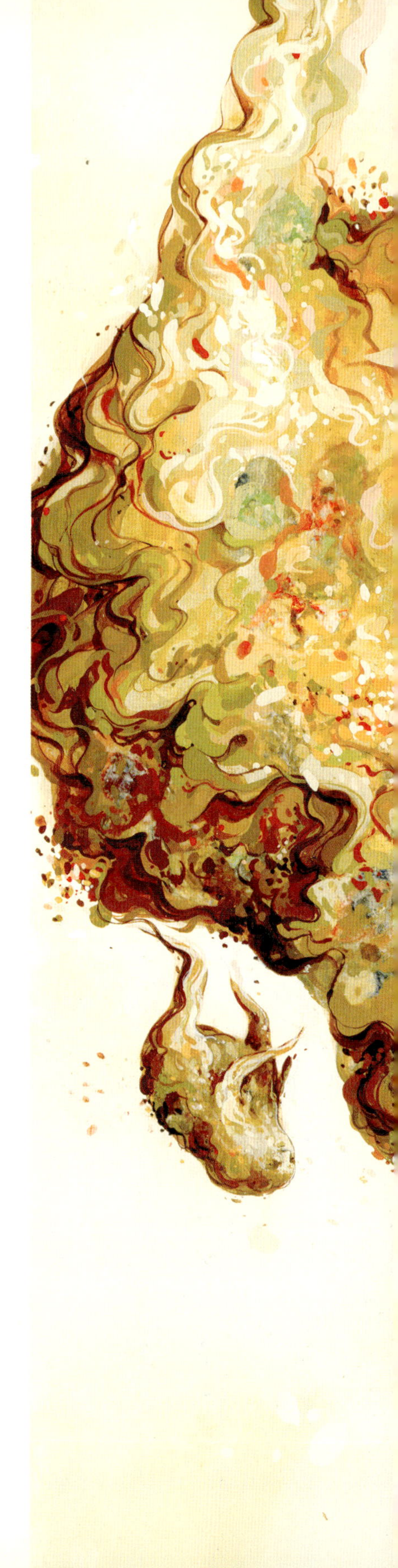

Swimming &
Sinking

2007 — acrylic, collage on paper
26 x 26 in / 66 x 66 cm

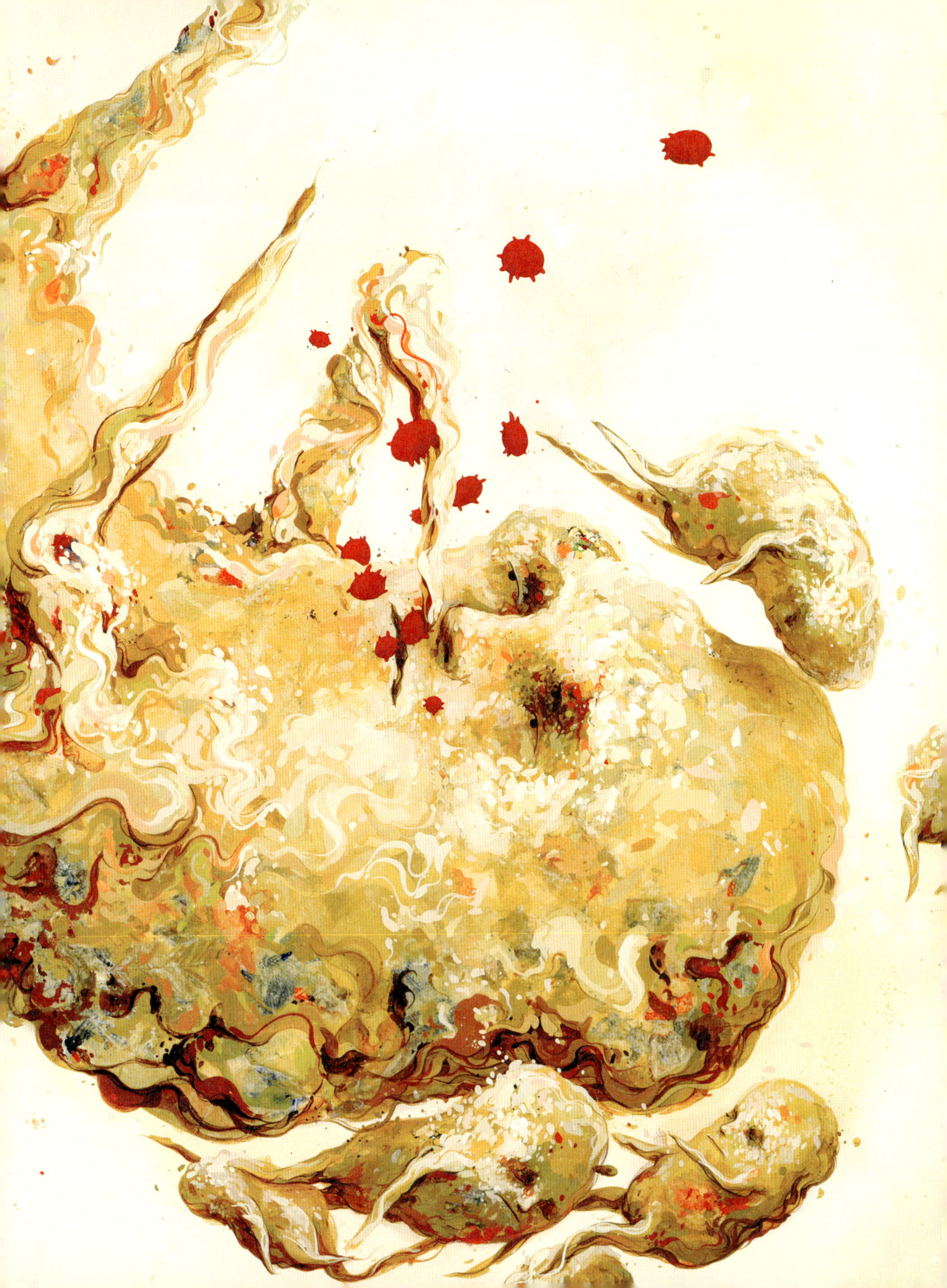

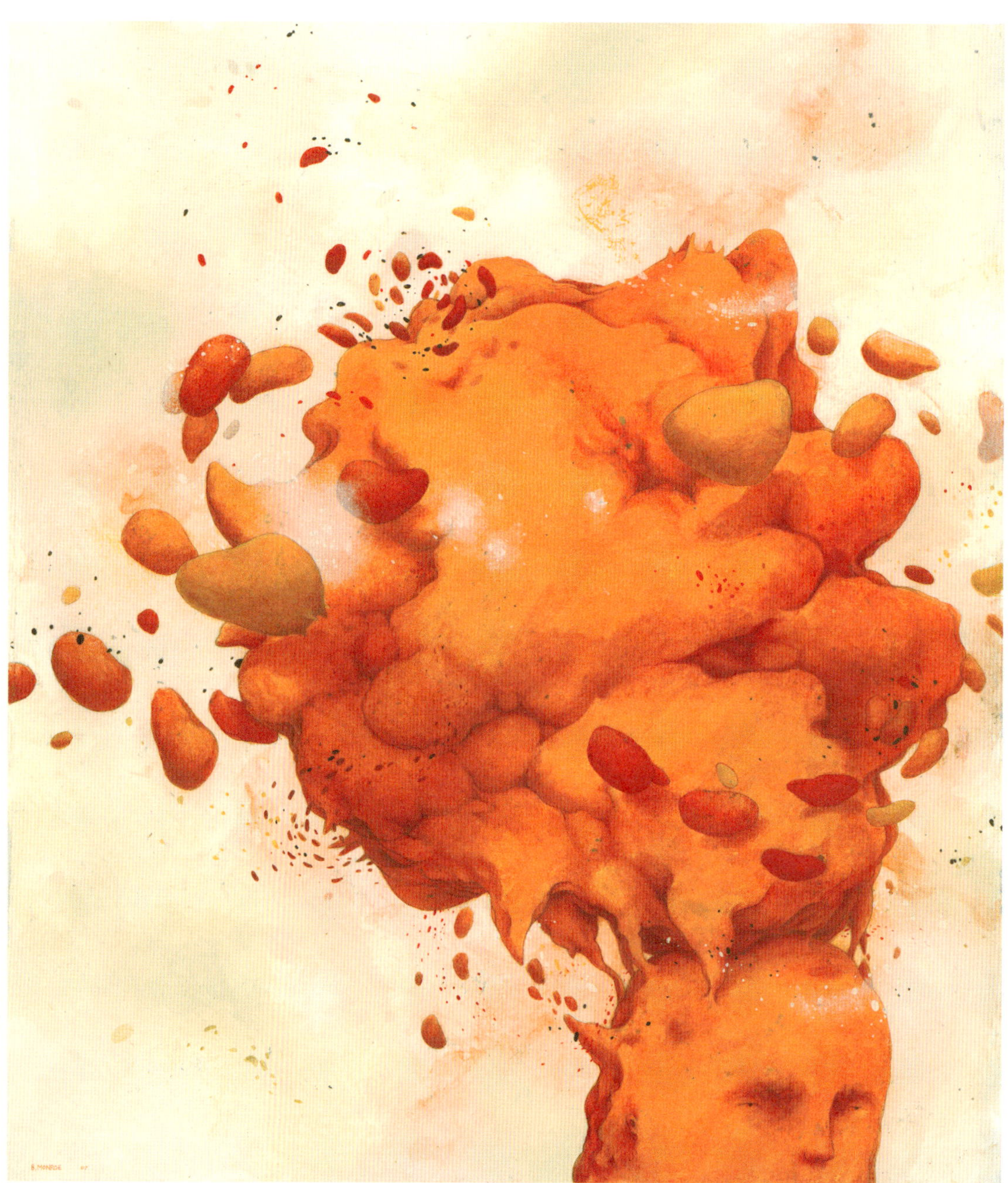

They Normally
Stay Inside

2007 — acrylic on paper
14 x 12 in / 35.6 x 30.5 cm

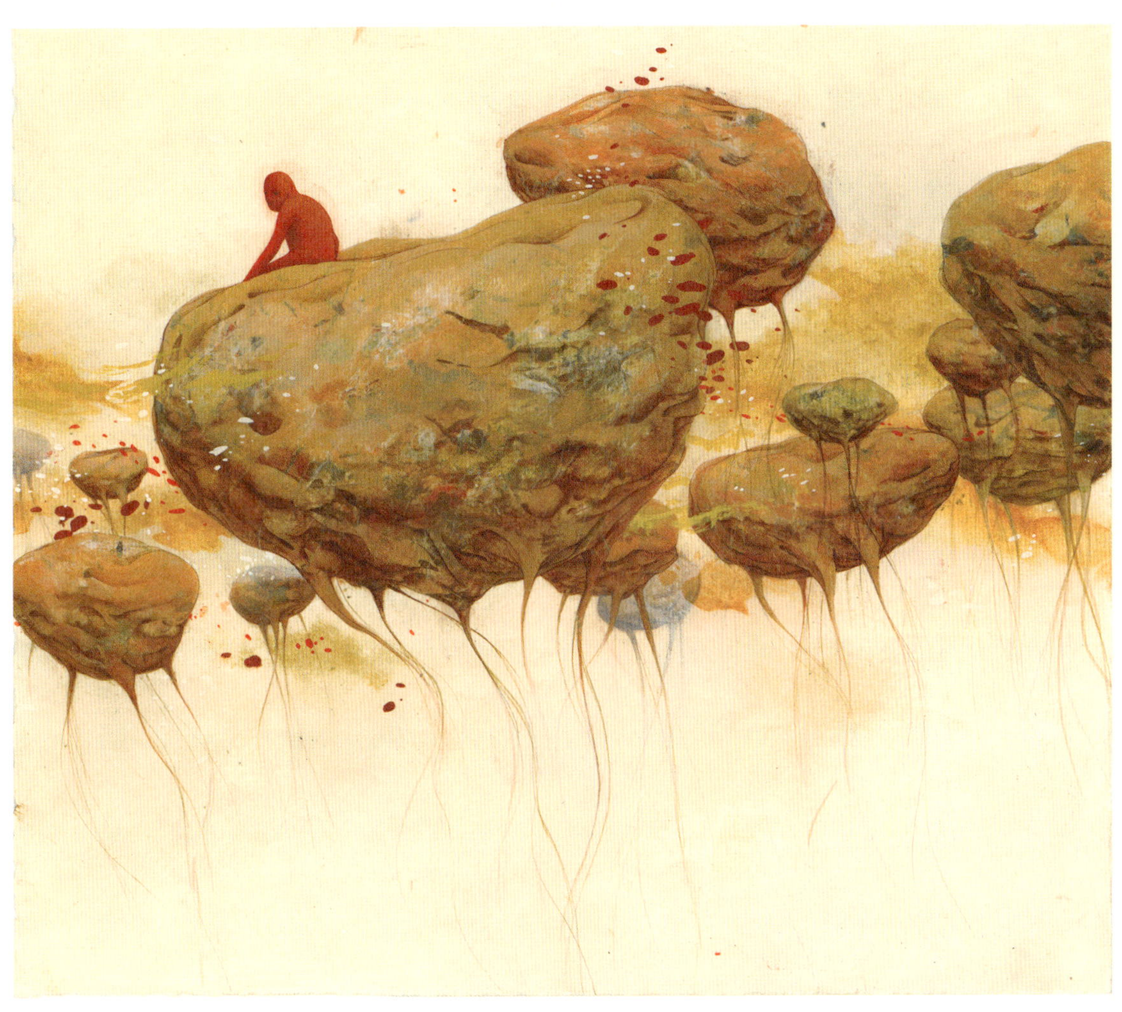

Lonesome   2007 — acrylic, collage on paper
13.5 x 15 in / 34.3 x 38.1 cm

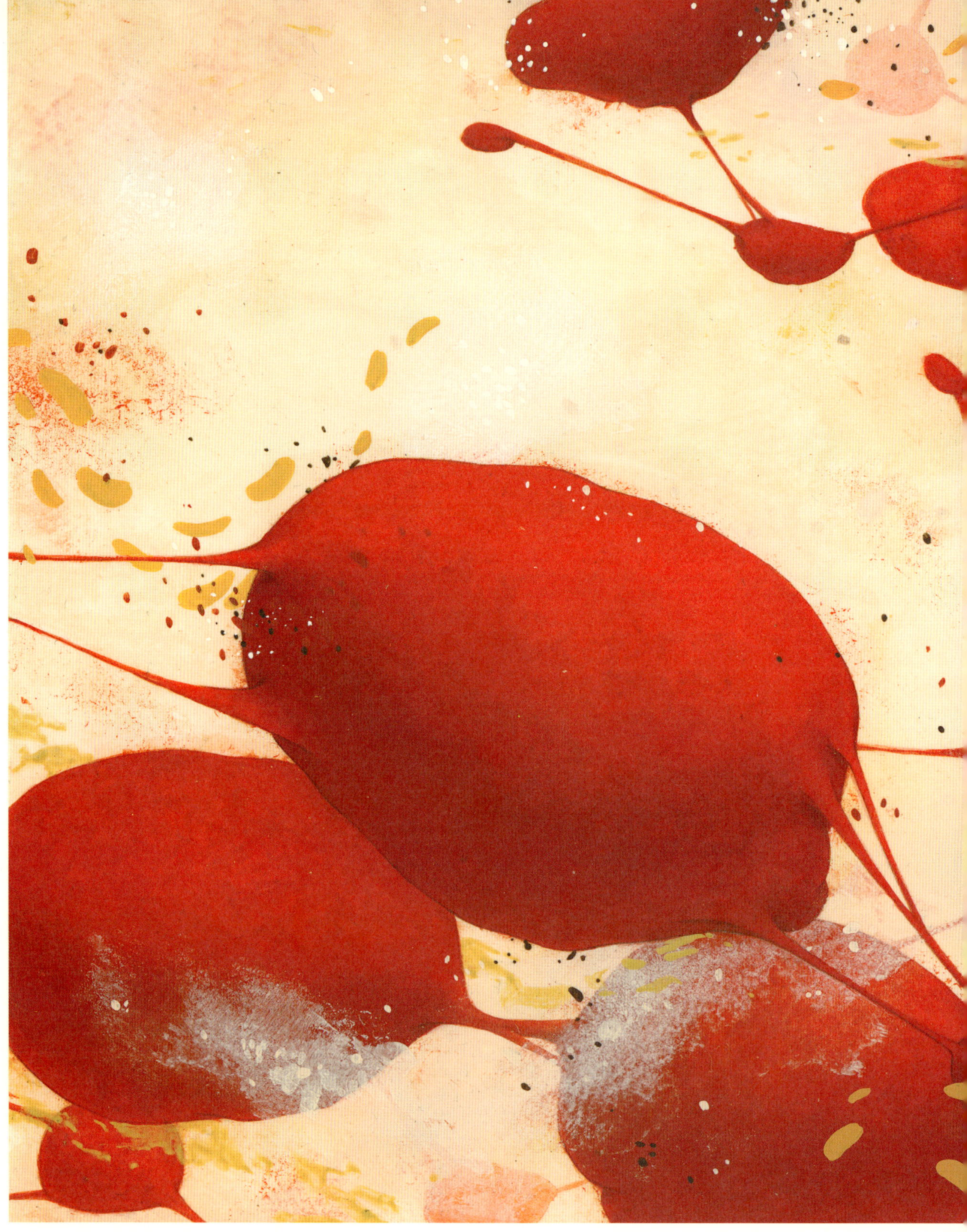

Neurons   2007 — acrylic, collage on paper
8 x 11.5 in / 20.3 x 29.2 cm

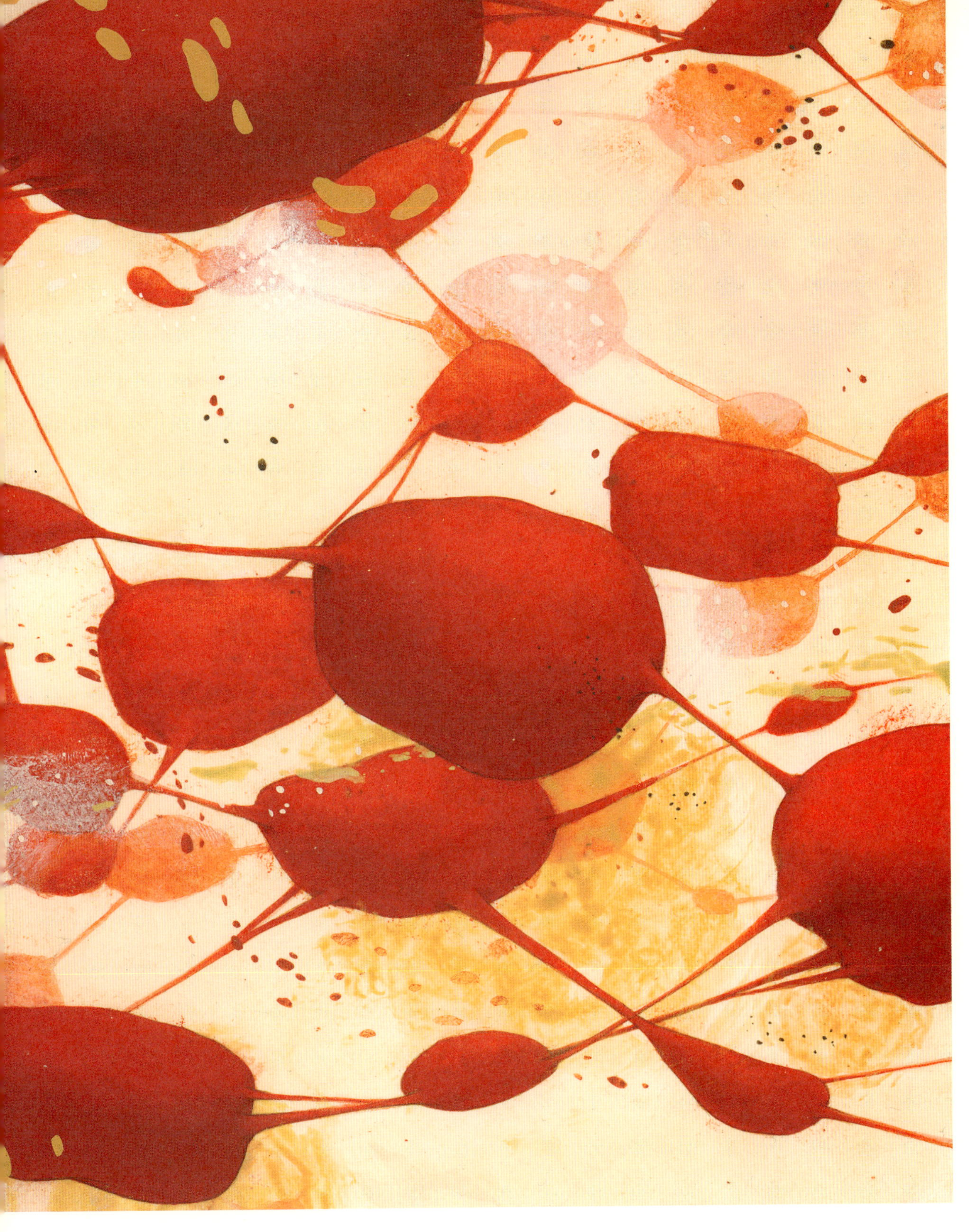

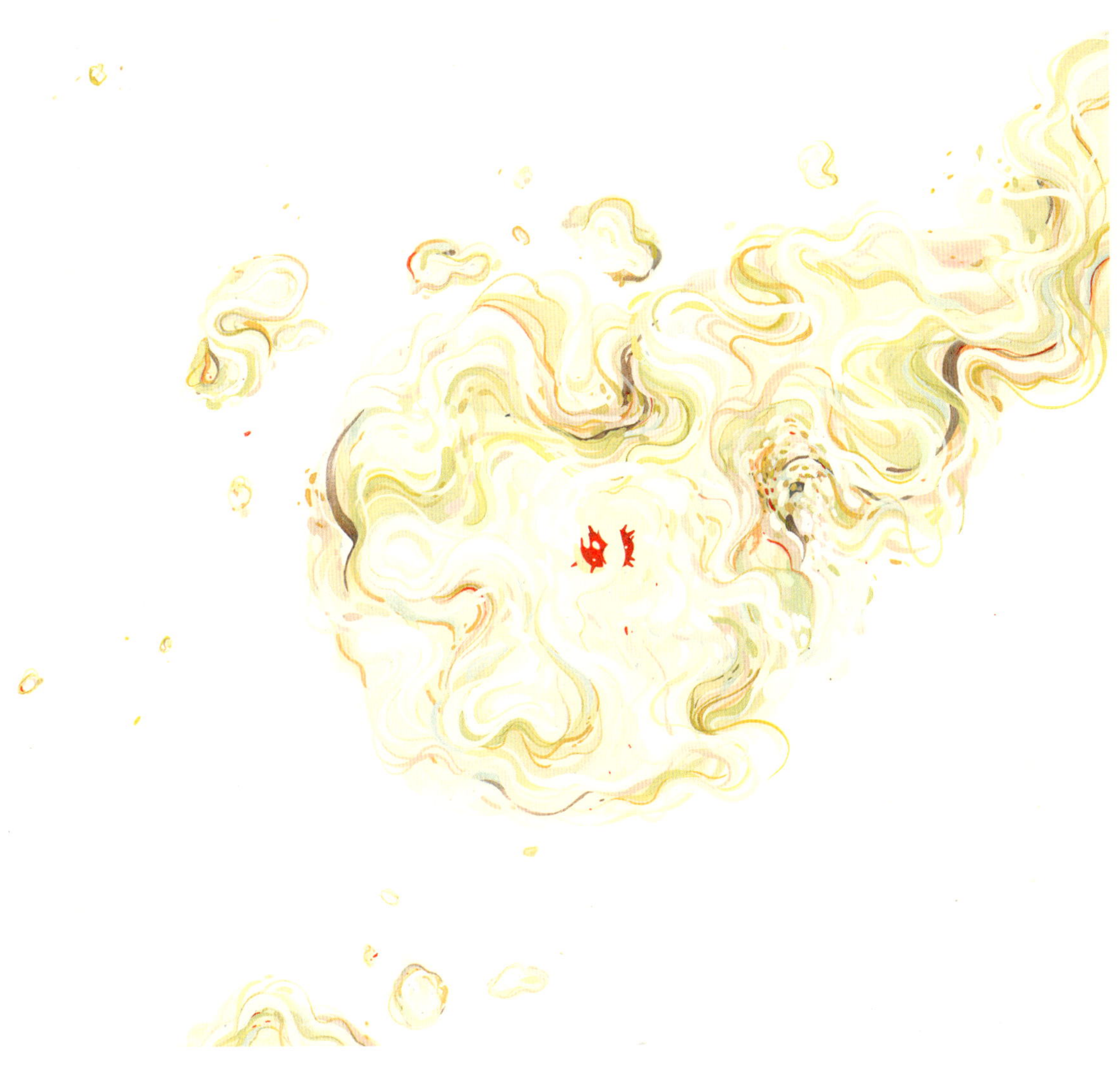

Cross Section 1   2007 — acrylic on paper
12 x 12 in / 30.5 x 30.5 cm

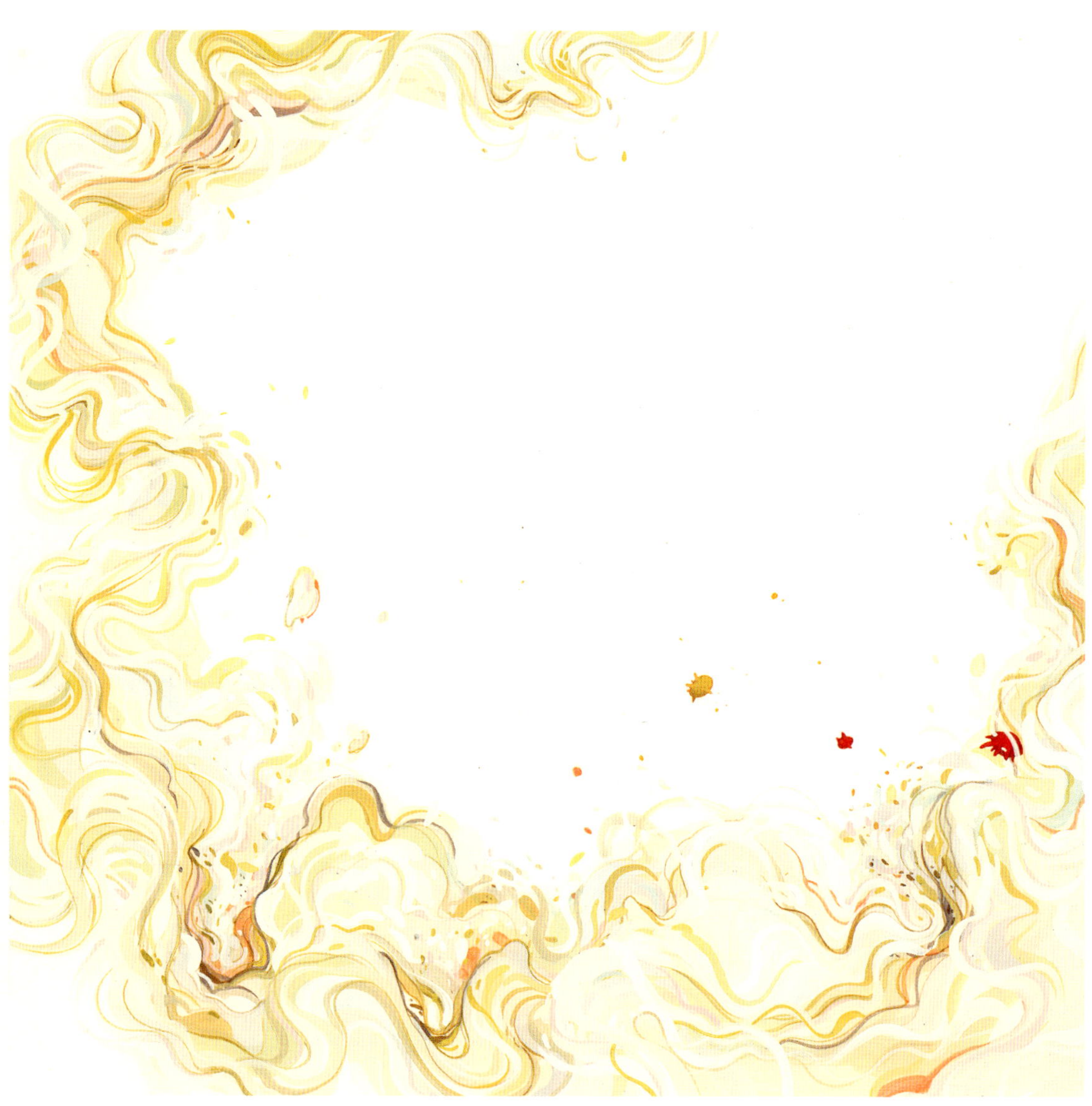

Cross Section 2   2007 — acrylic on paper
12 x 12 in / 30.5 x 30.5 cm

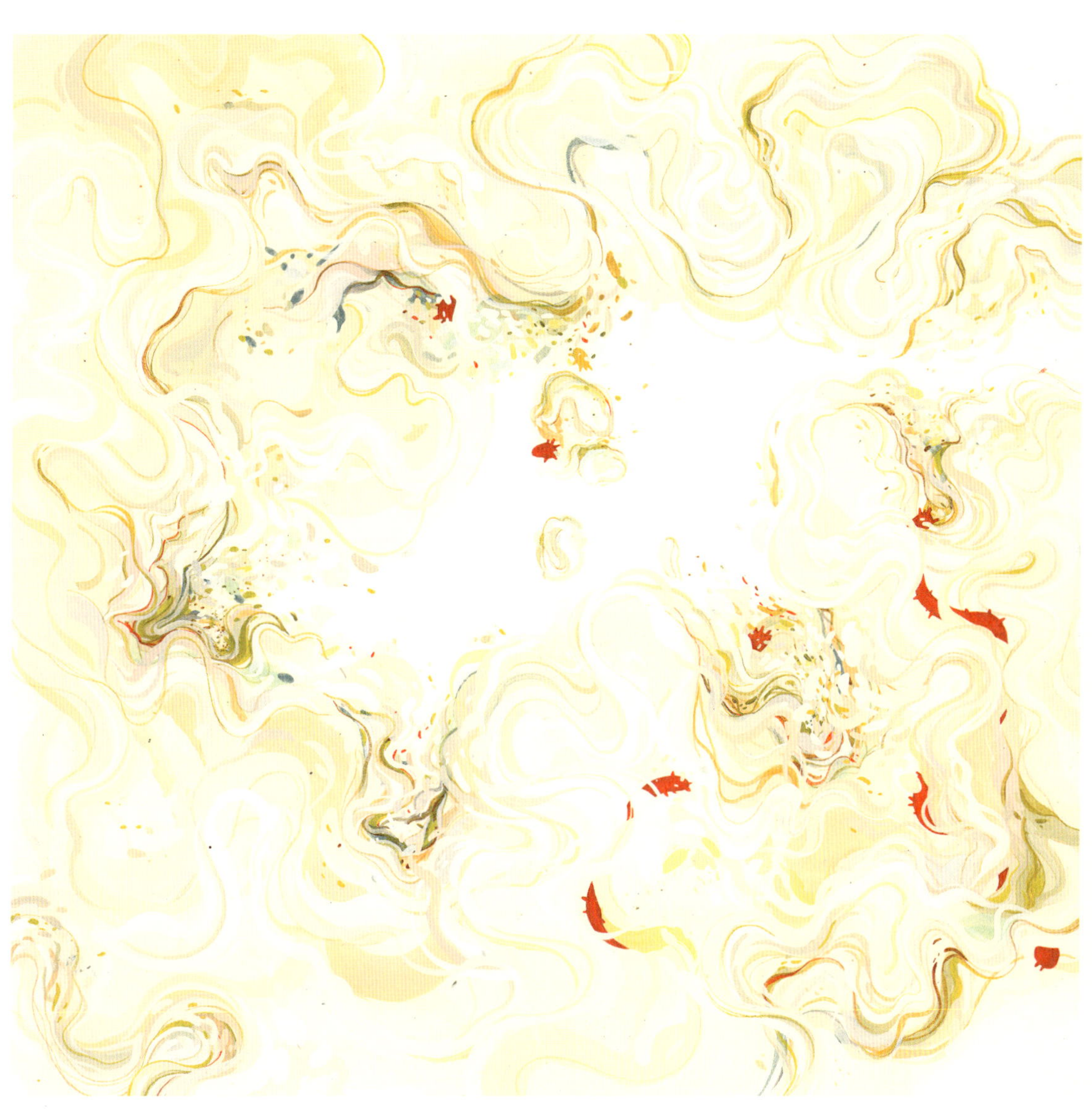

Cross Section 3 2007 — acrylic on paper
12 x 12 in / 30.5 x 30.5 cm

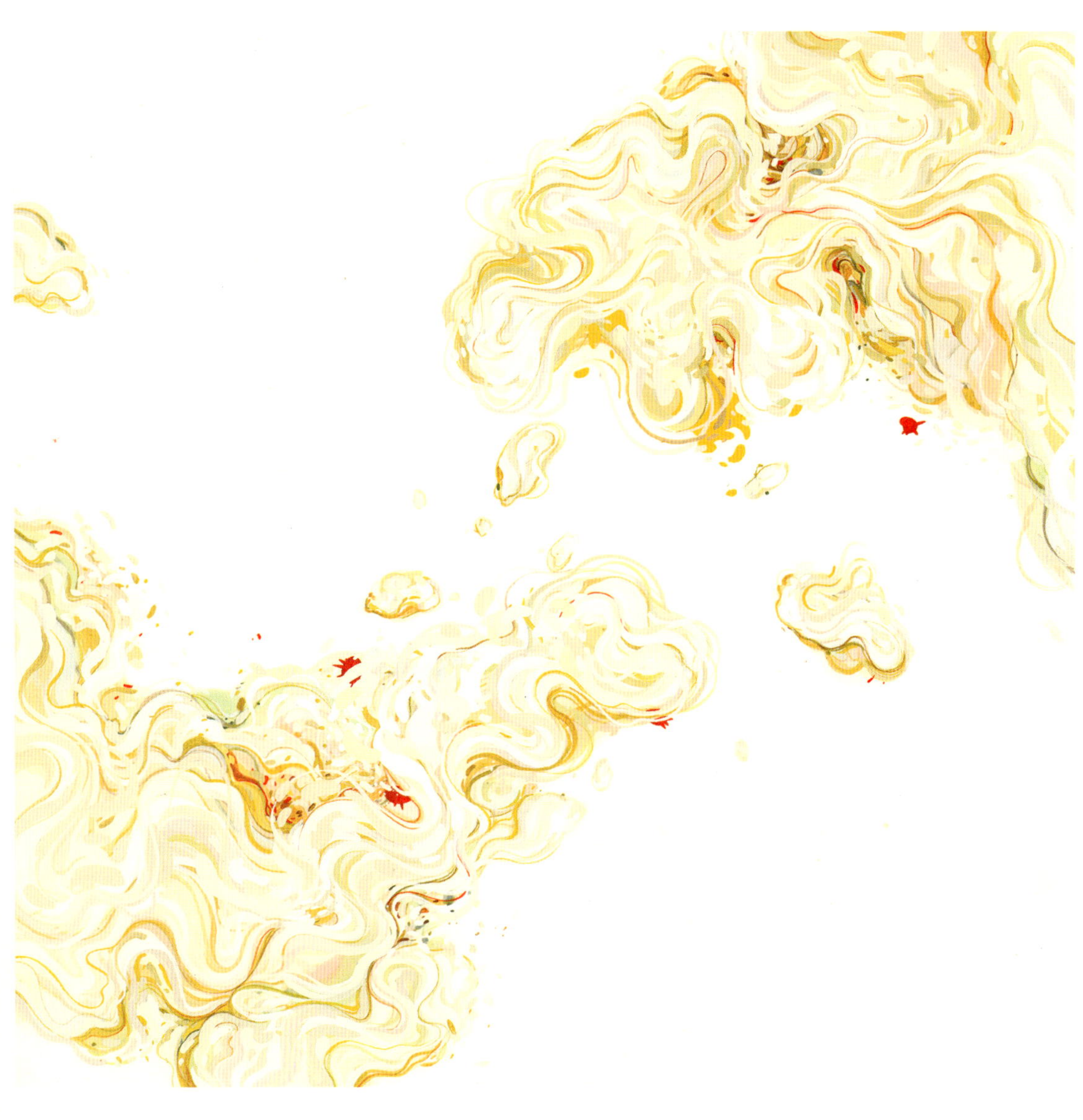

Cross Section 4   2007 — acrylic on paper
12 x 12 in / 30.5 x 30.5 cm

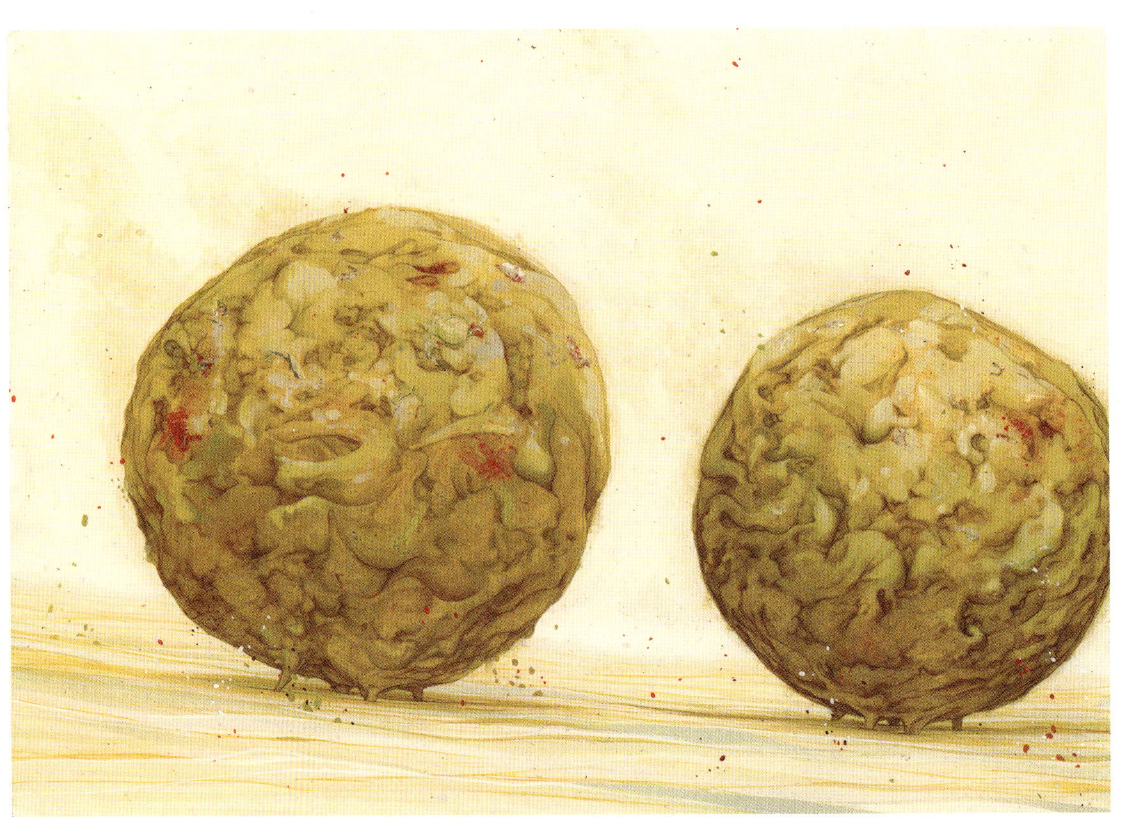

Holding Fast 2007 — acrylic on paper
11.5 x 16 in / 29.2 x 40.6 cm

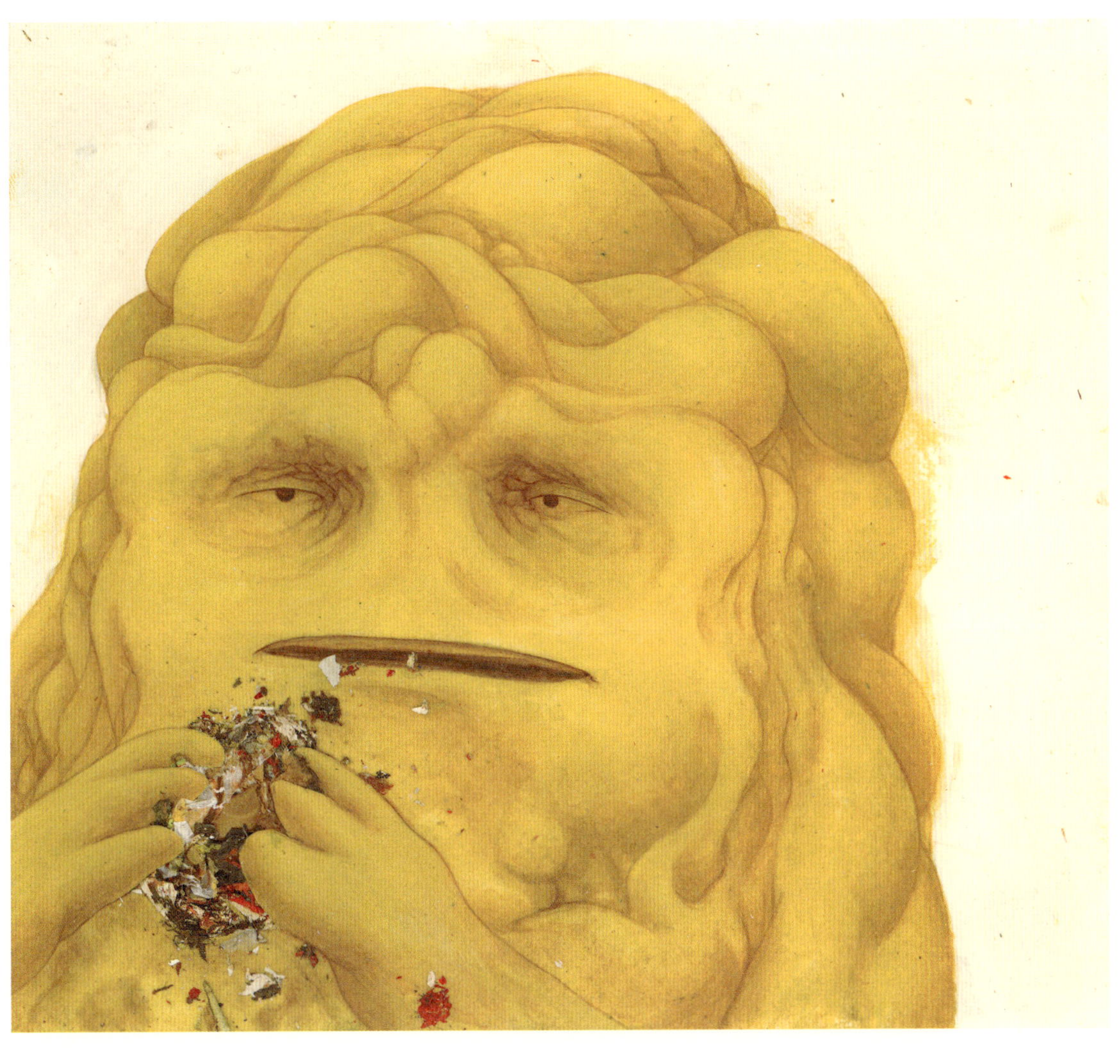

Eating Shit 2007 — acrylic, collage [ps] on paper
5.5 x 6 in / 14 x 15.2 cm

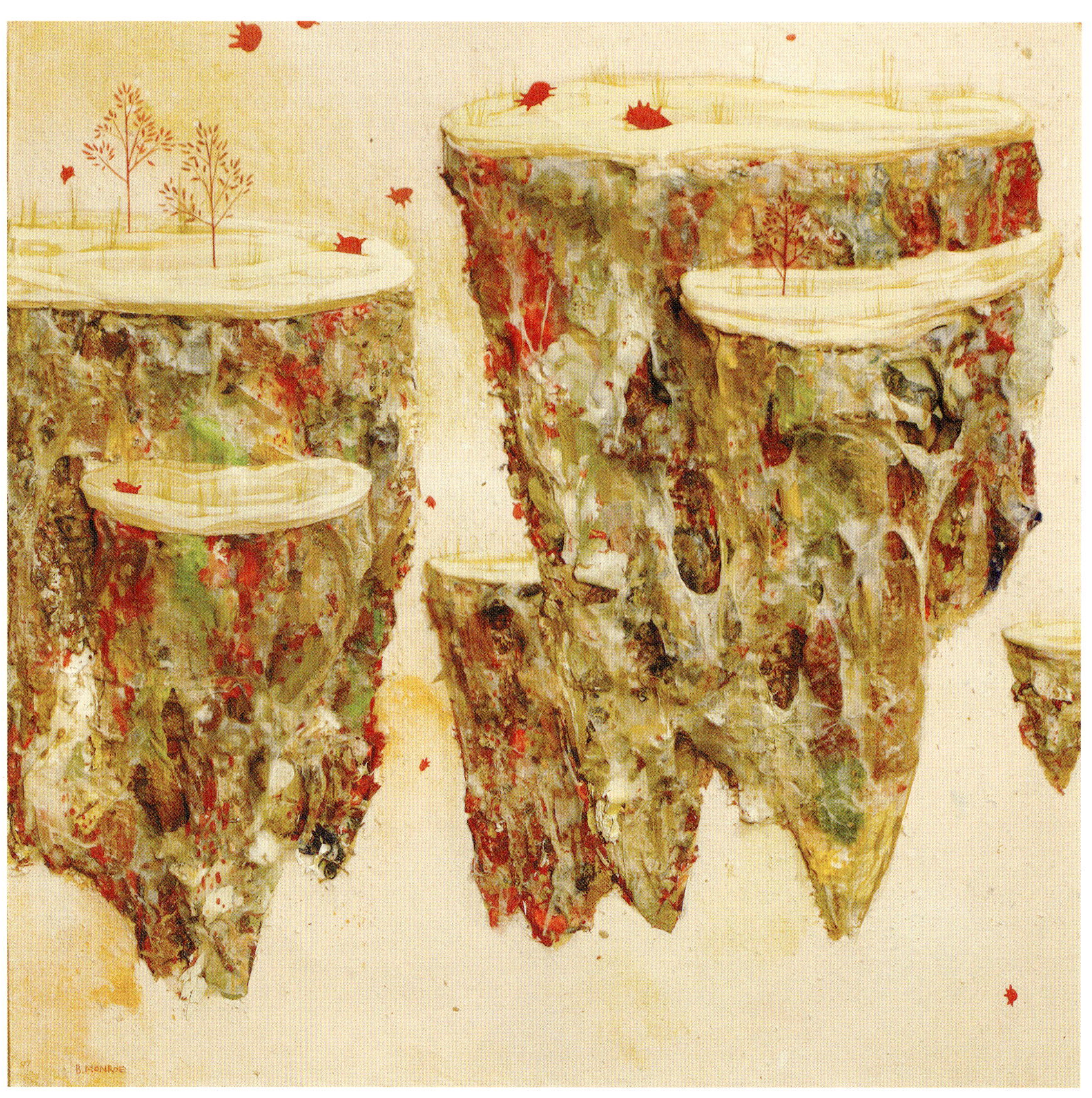

Tooth Dreams   2007 — acrylic, collage [ps] on paper
8 x 8 in / 20.3 x 20.3 cm

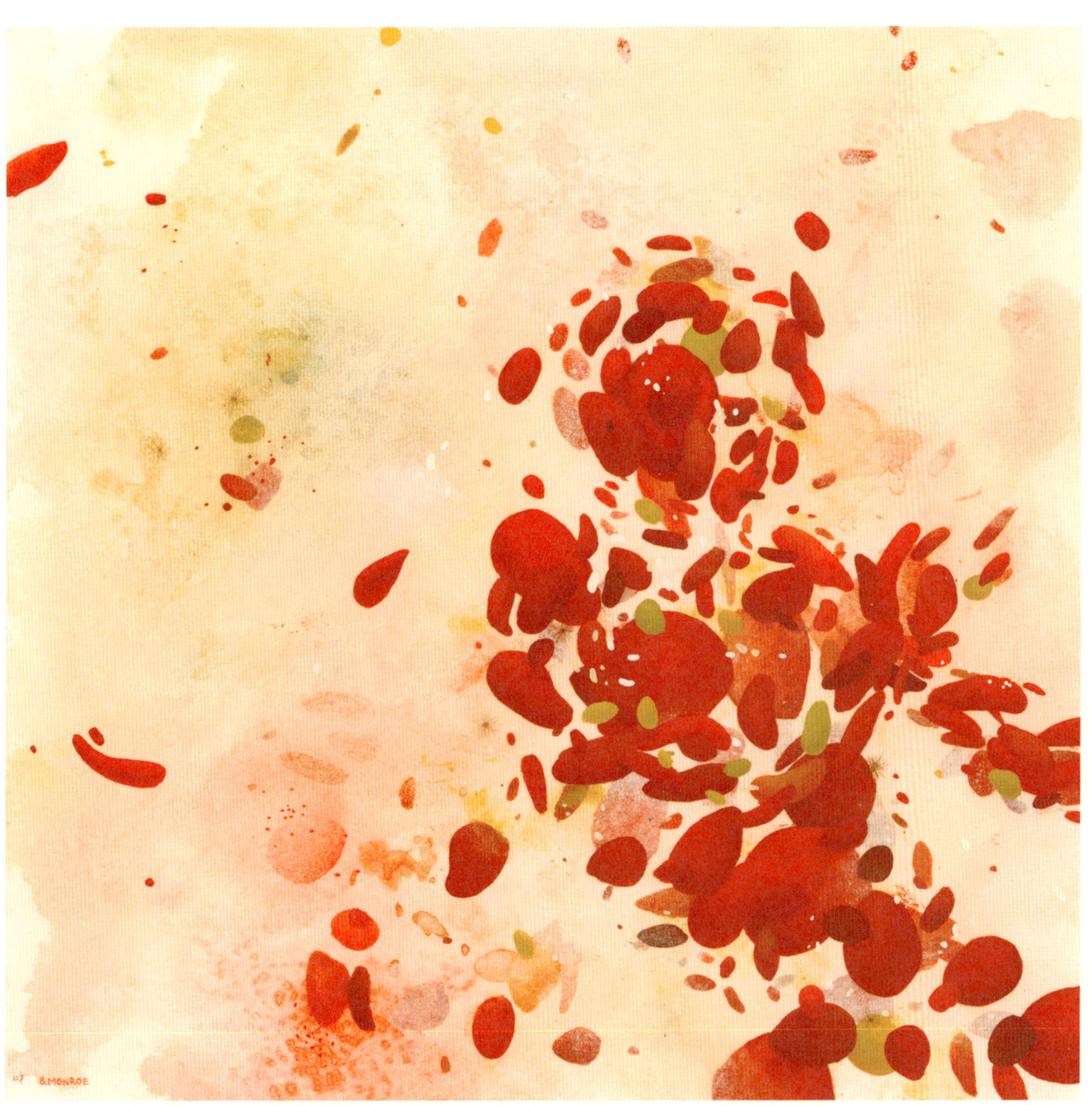

Organizing
Larger Forms

2007 — acrylic on paper
8 x 8 in / 20.3 x 20.3 cm

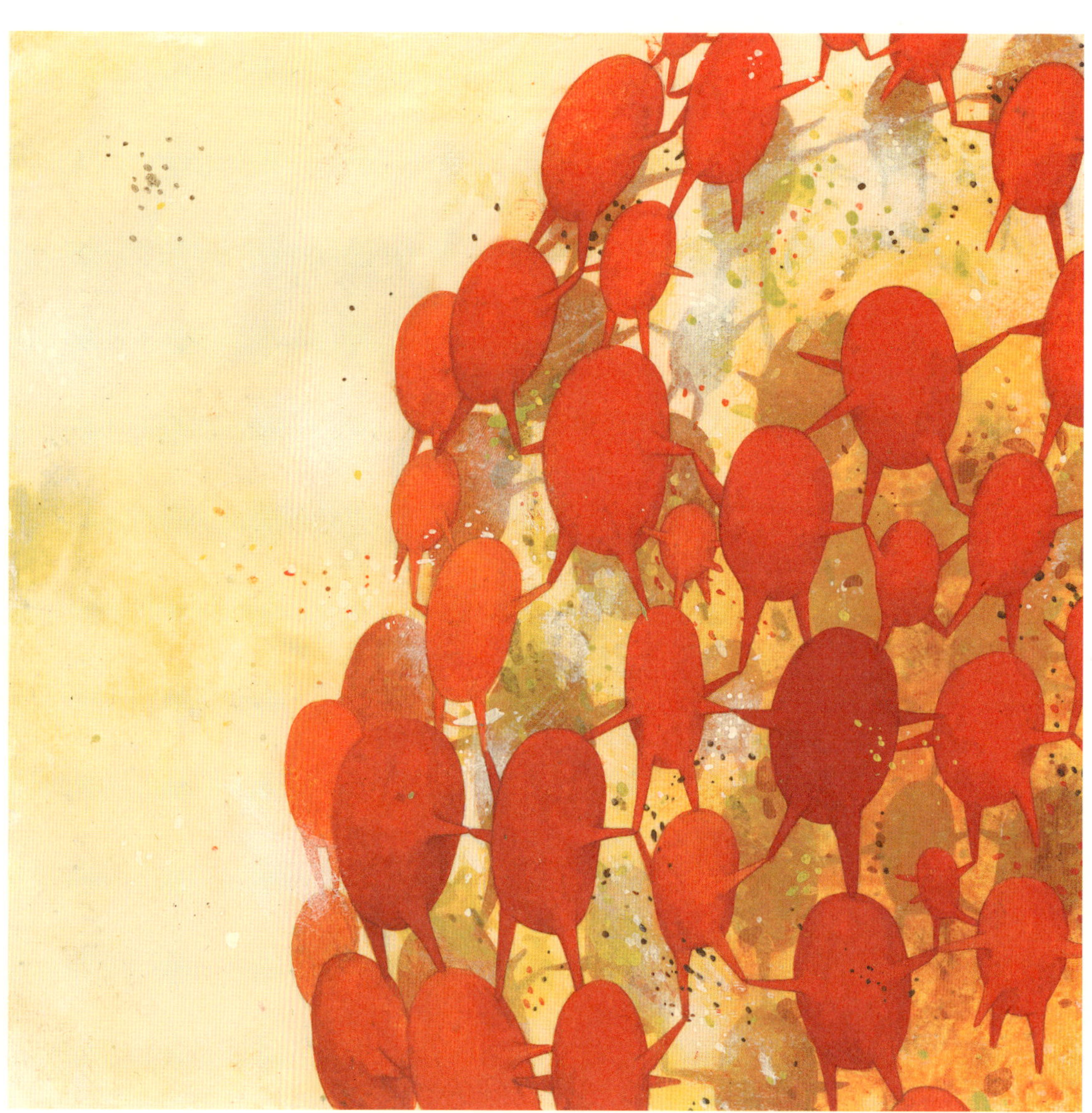

Containing Gasses
(diptych)
2007 — acrylic, collage on paper
8 x 8 in / 20.3 x 20.3 cm *(each)*

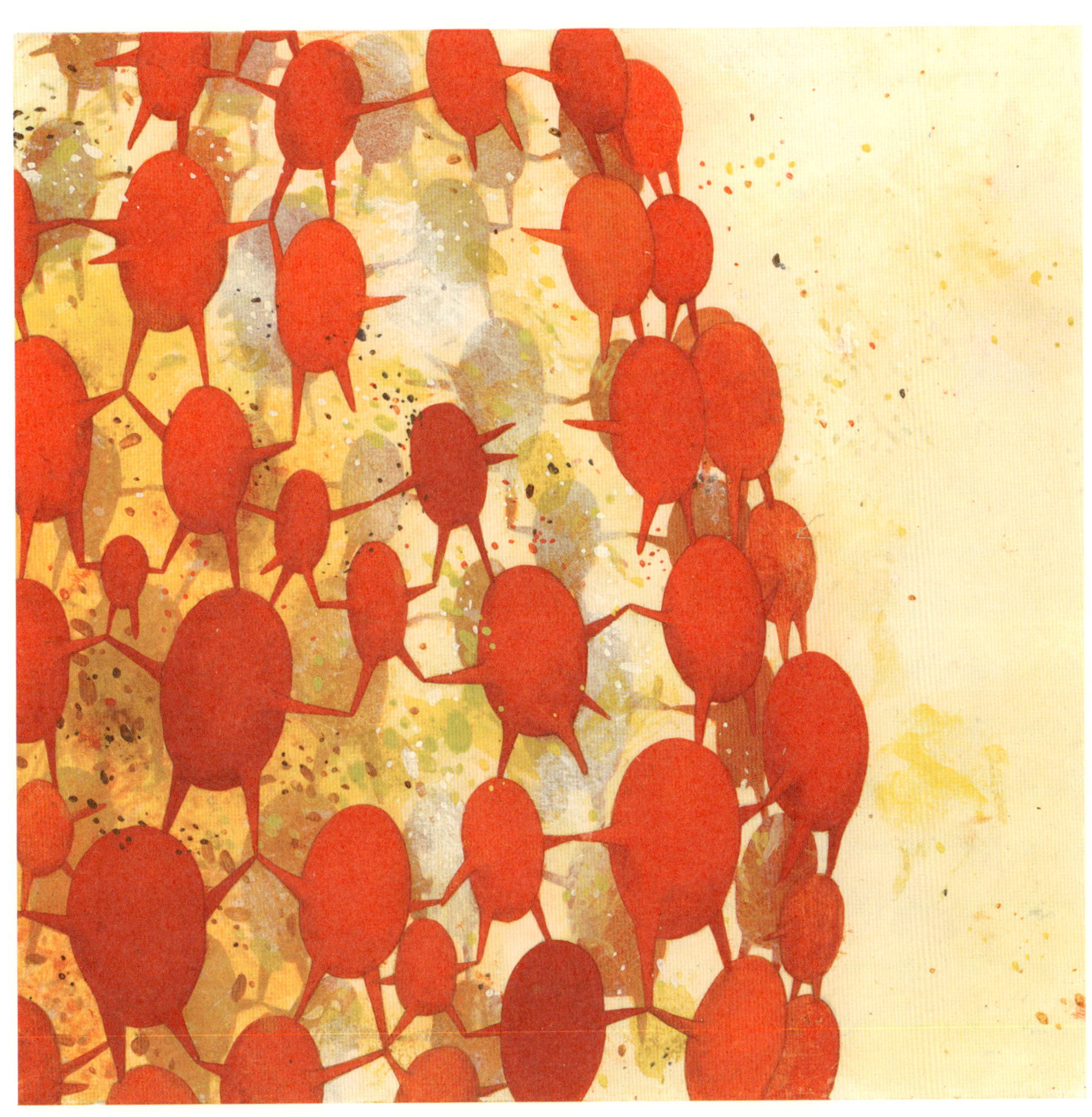

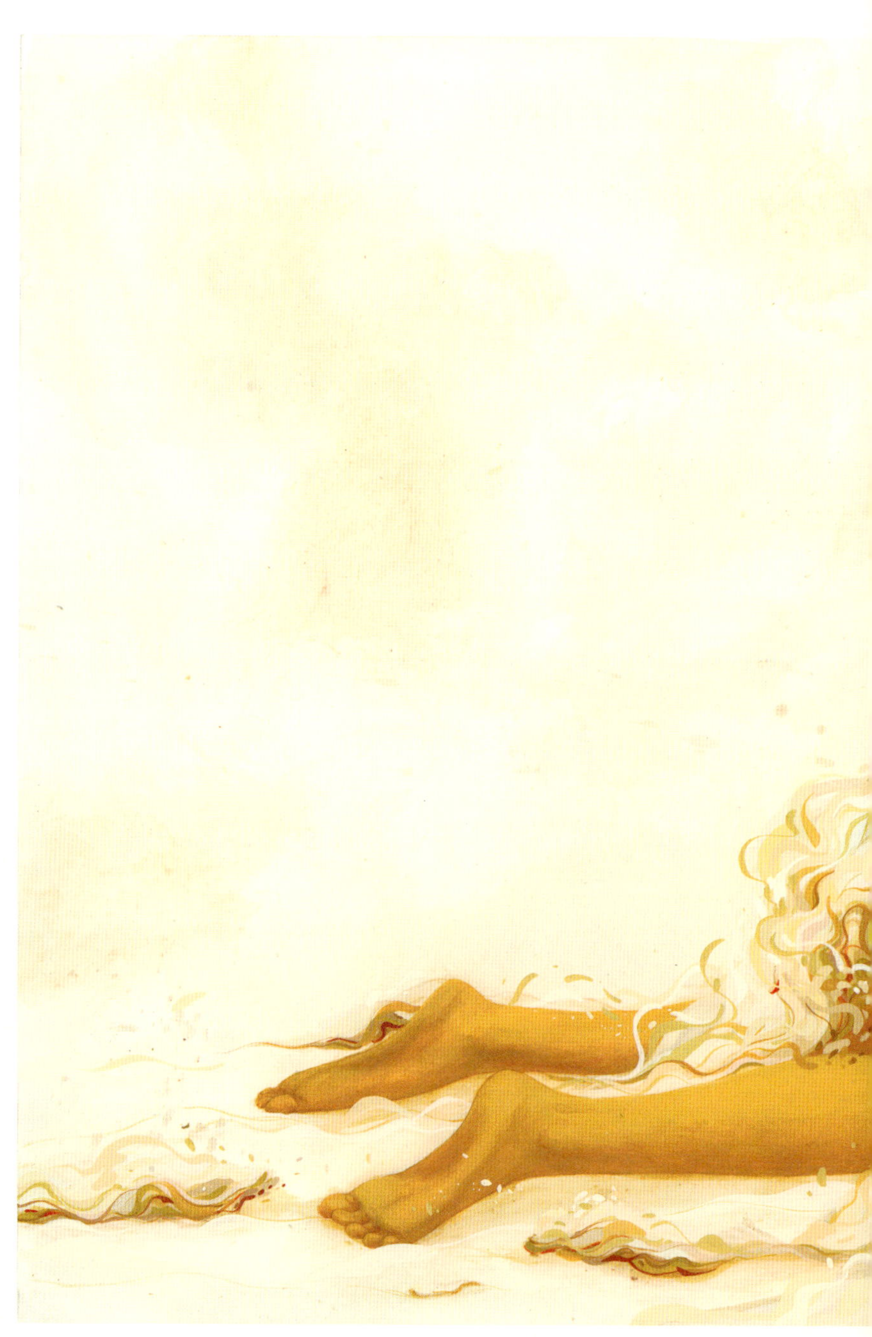

Searching   2007 — acrylic on paper
              14 x 26 in / 35.6 x 66 cm

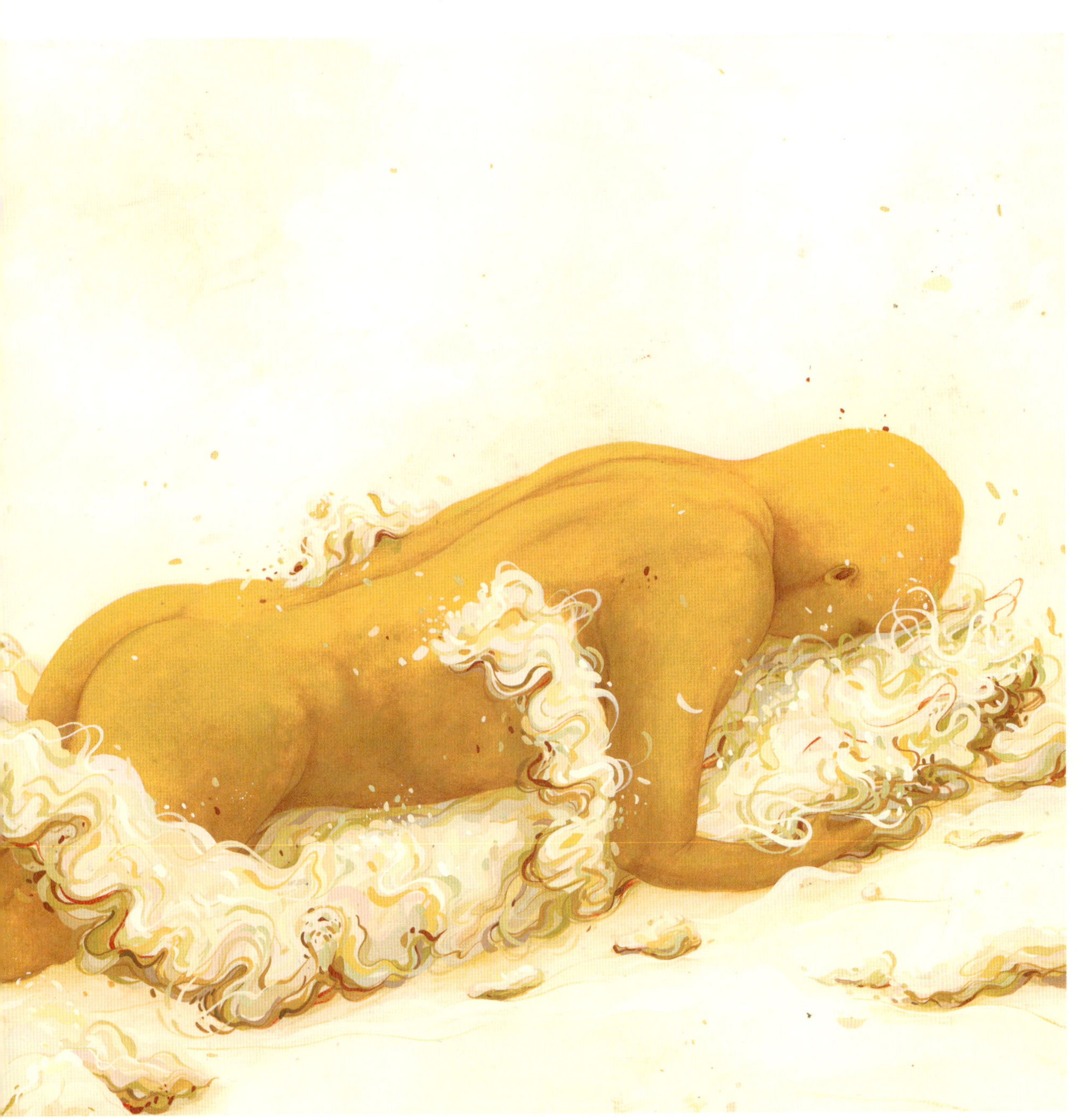

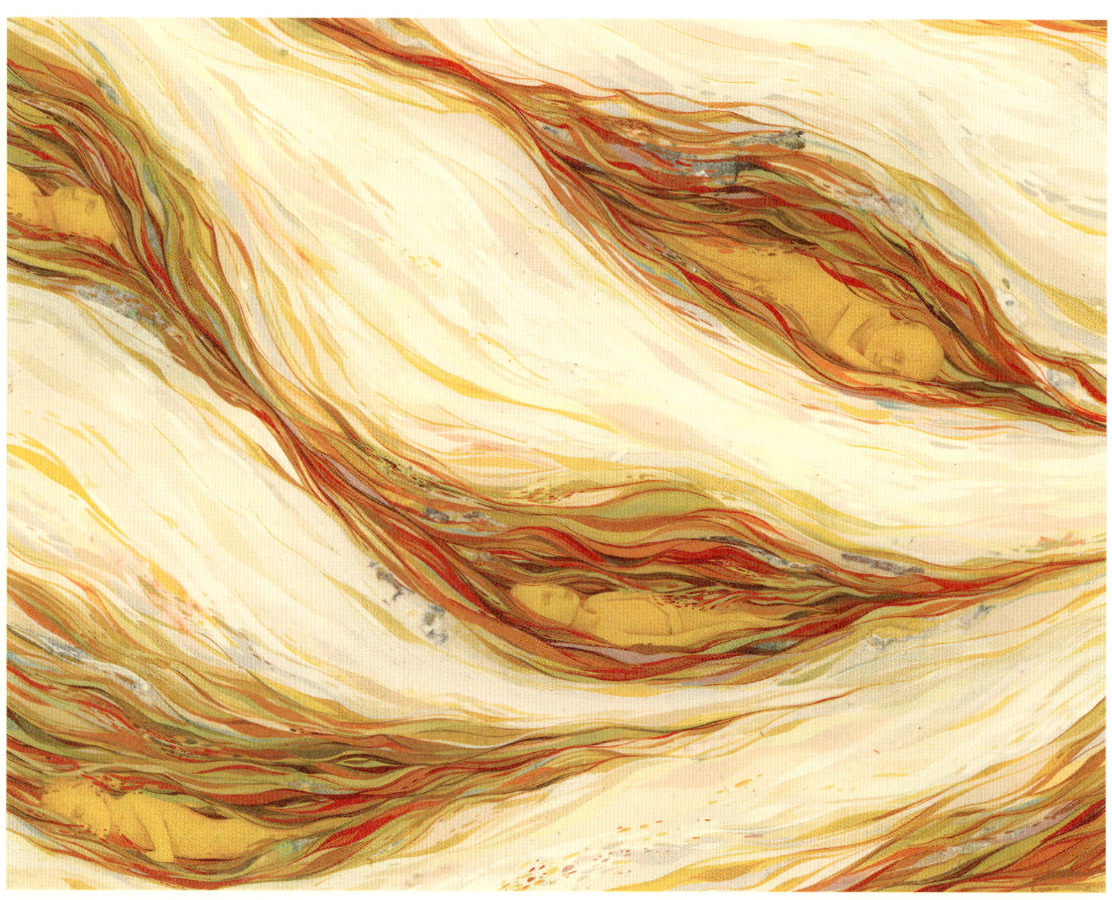

Resting   2007 — acrylic, collage on paper
14.5 x 17.75 in / 36.8 x 45.1 cm

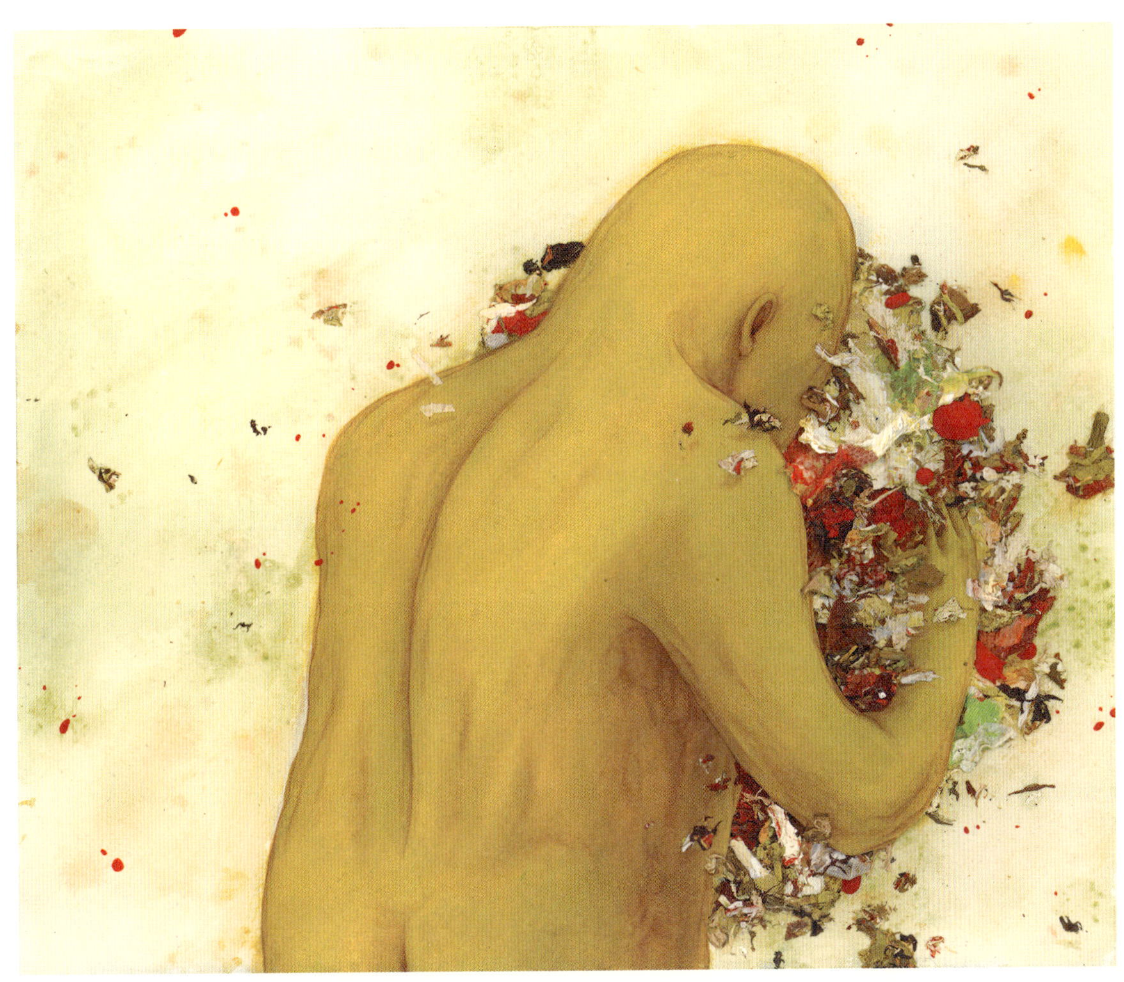

The Goods   2007 — acrylic, collage [ps] on paper
13 x 15 in / 33 x 38.1 cm

(overleaf)
Sequence of Thoughts   2007 — acrylic on paper
30 x 45 in / 76.2 x 114.3 cm

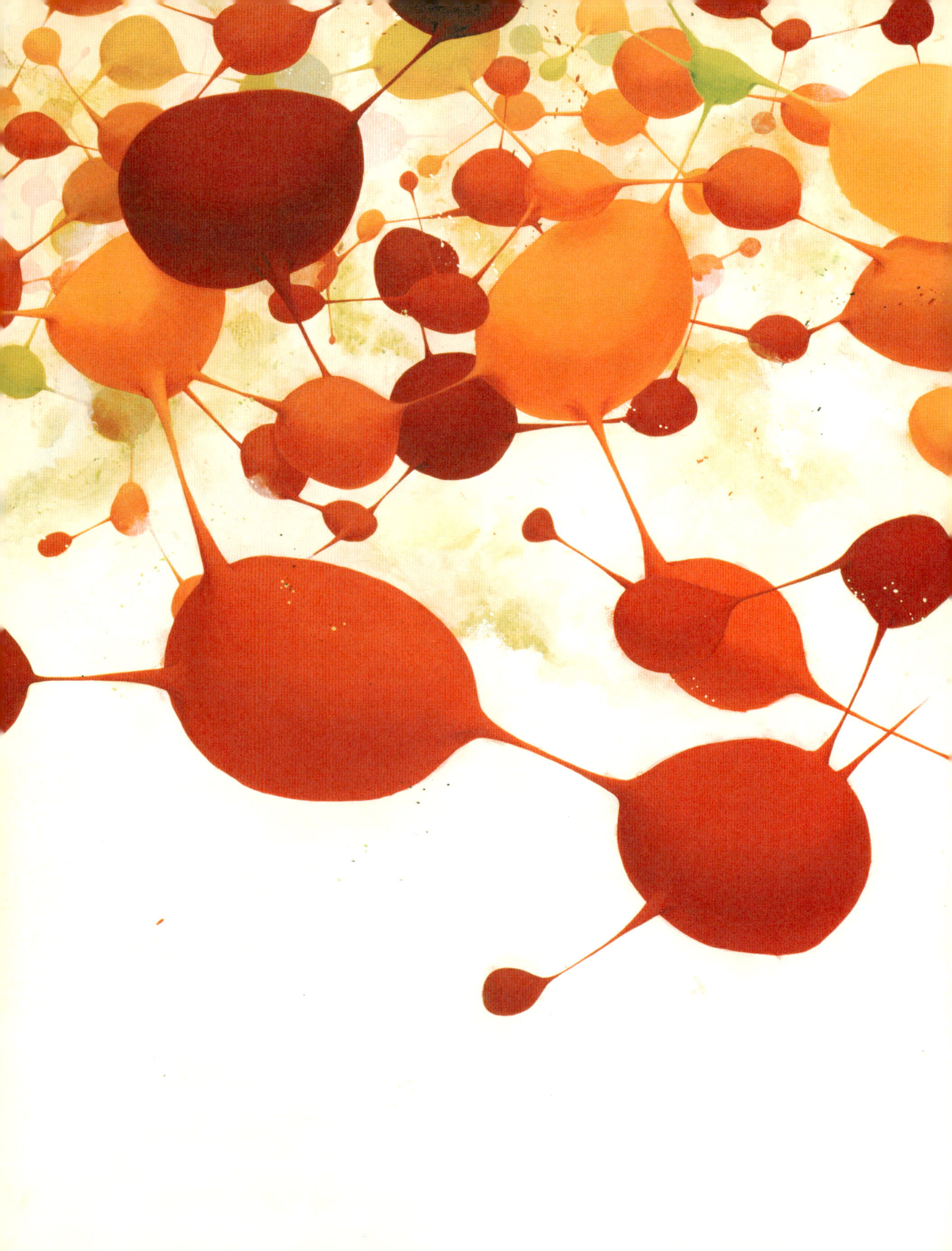

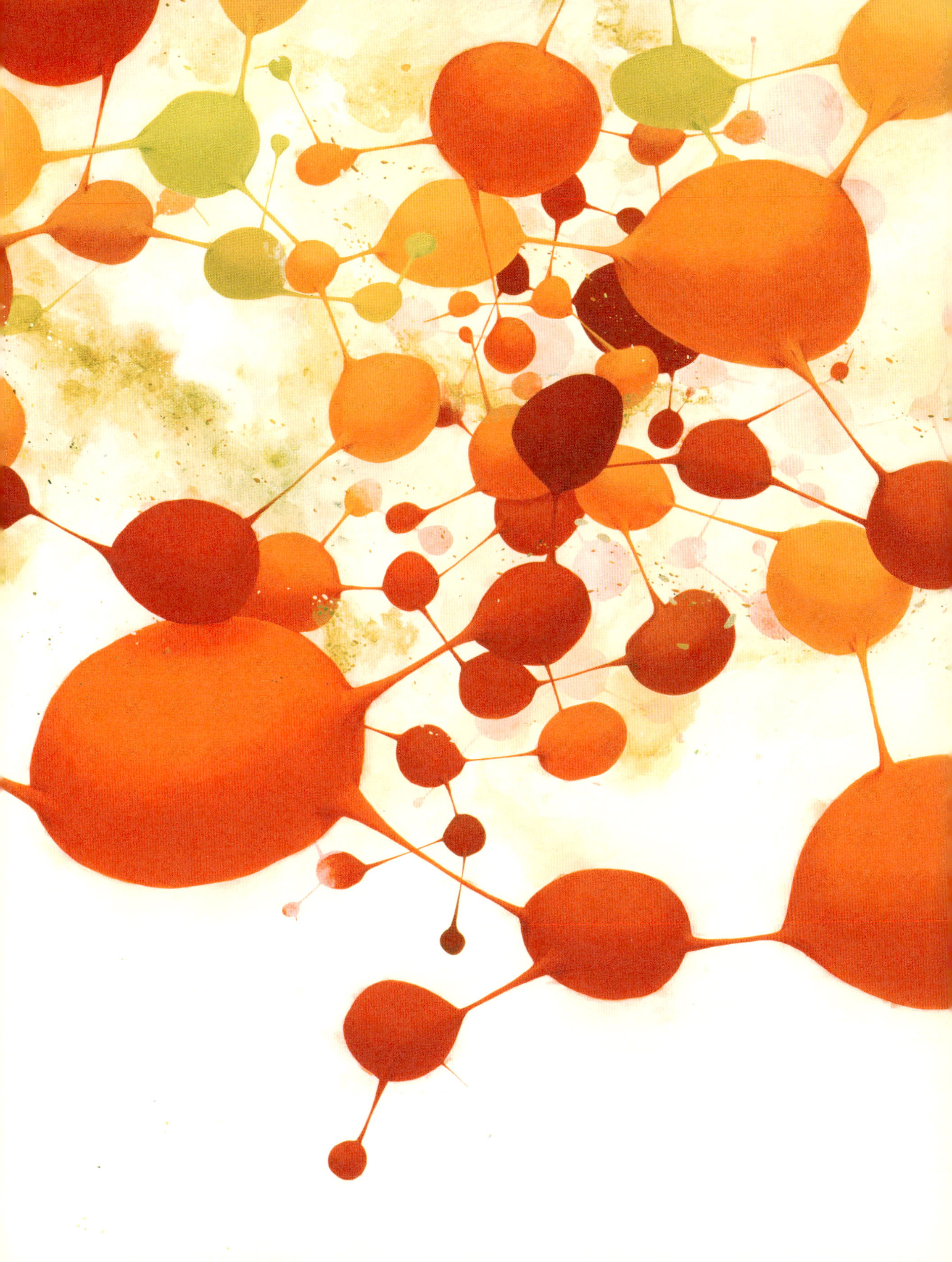

Breaking Blood   2007 — acrylic, collage [ps] on paper
16 x 12 in / 40.6 x 30.5 cm

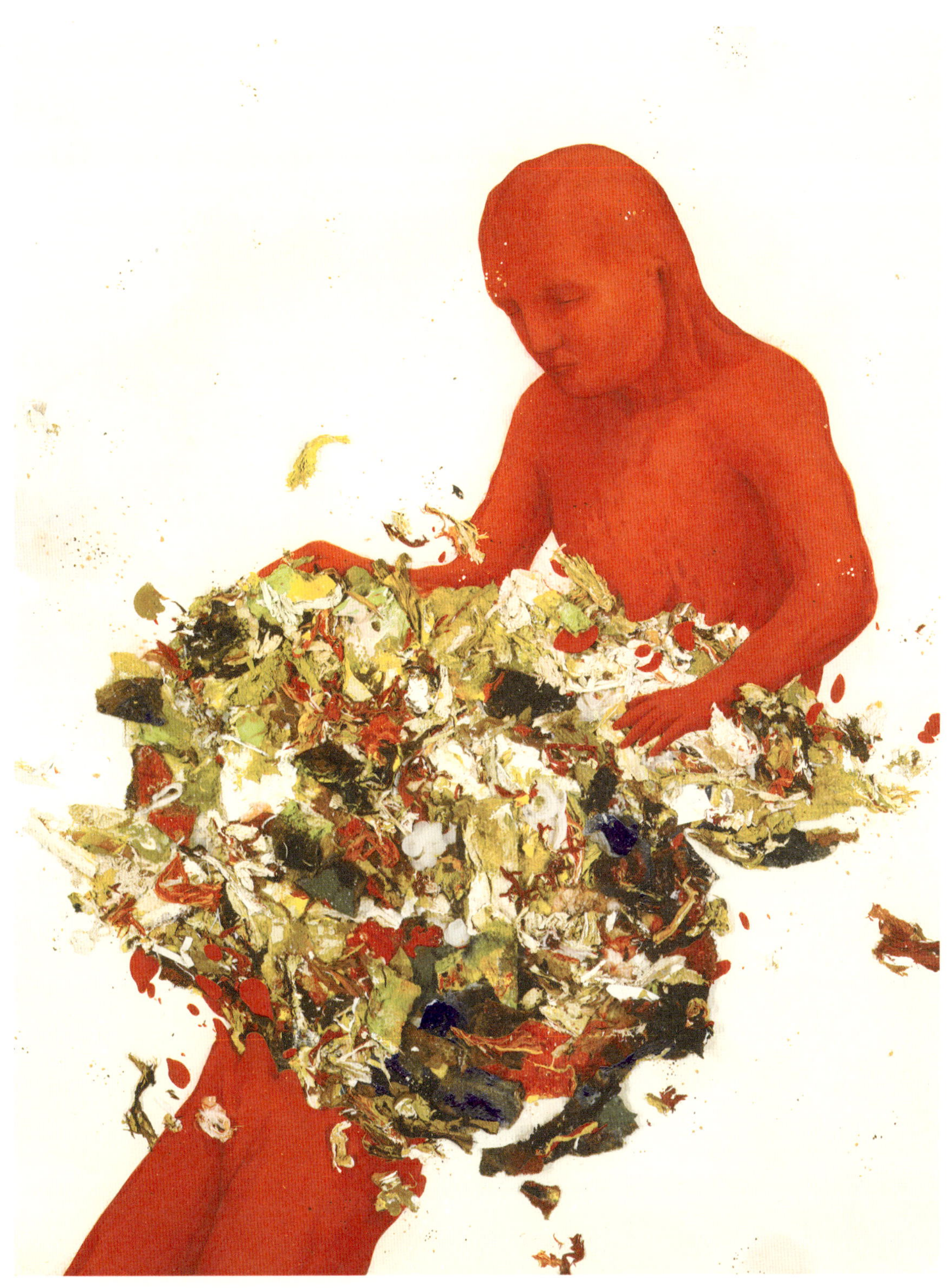

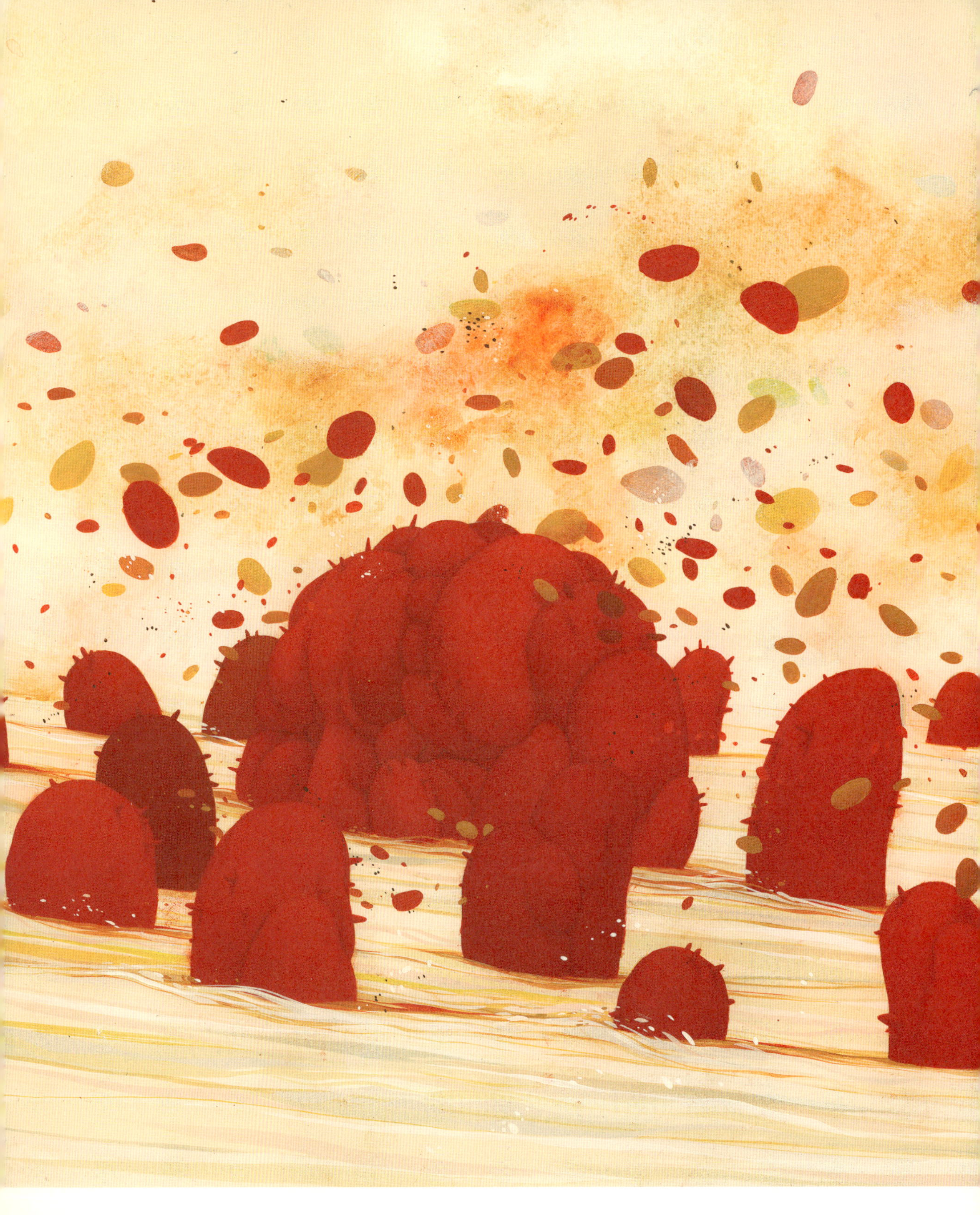

Disguising as Mounded Redness
2007 — acrylic on paper
18 x 26 in / 45.7 x 66 cm

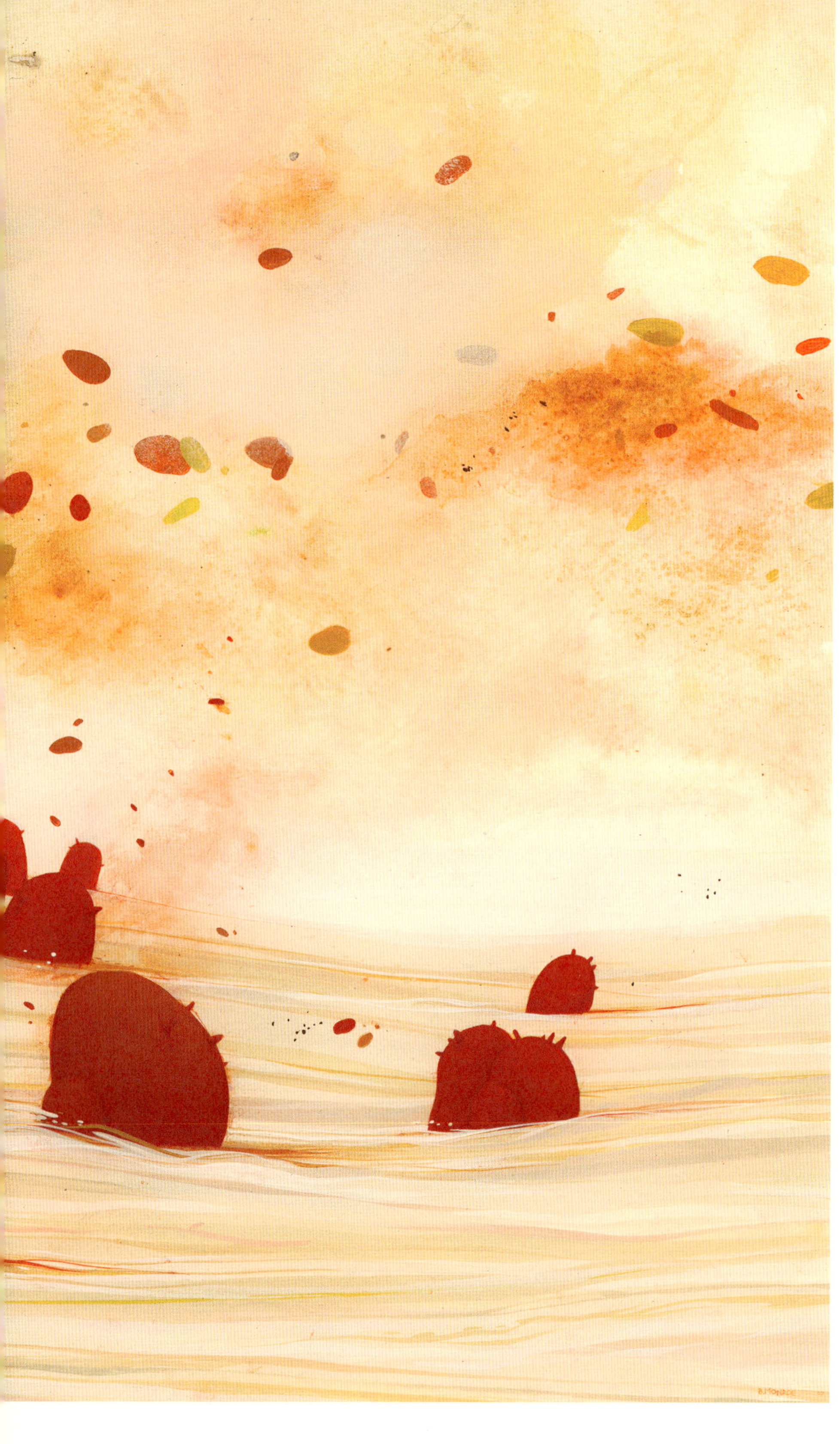

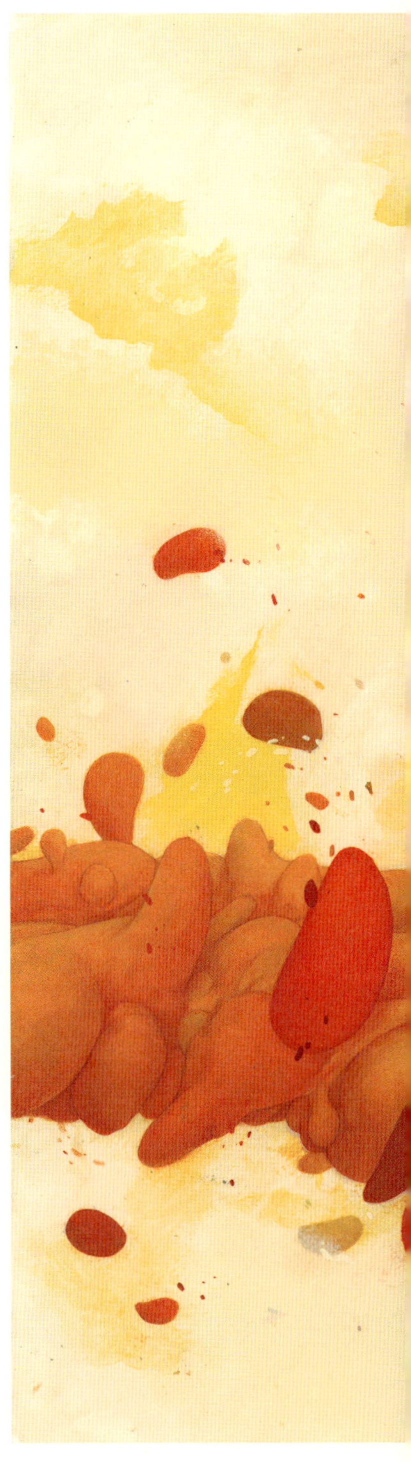

Increase of
Circulation

2007 — acrylic on paper
18 x 26 in / 45.7 x 66 cm

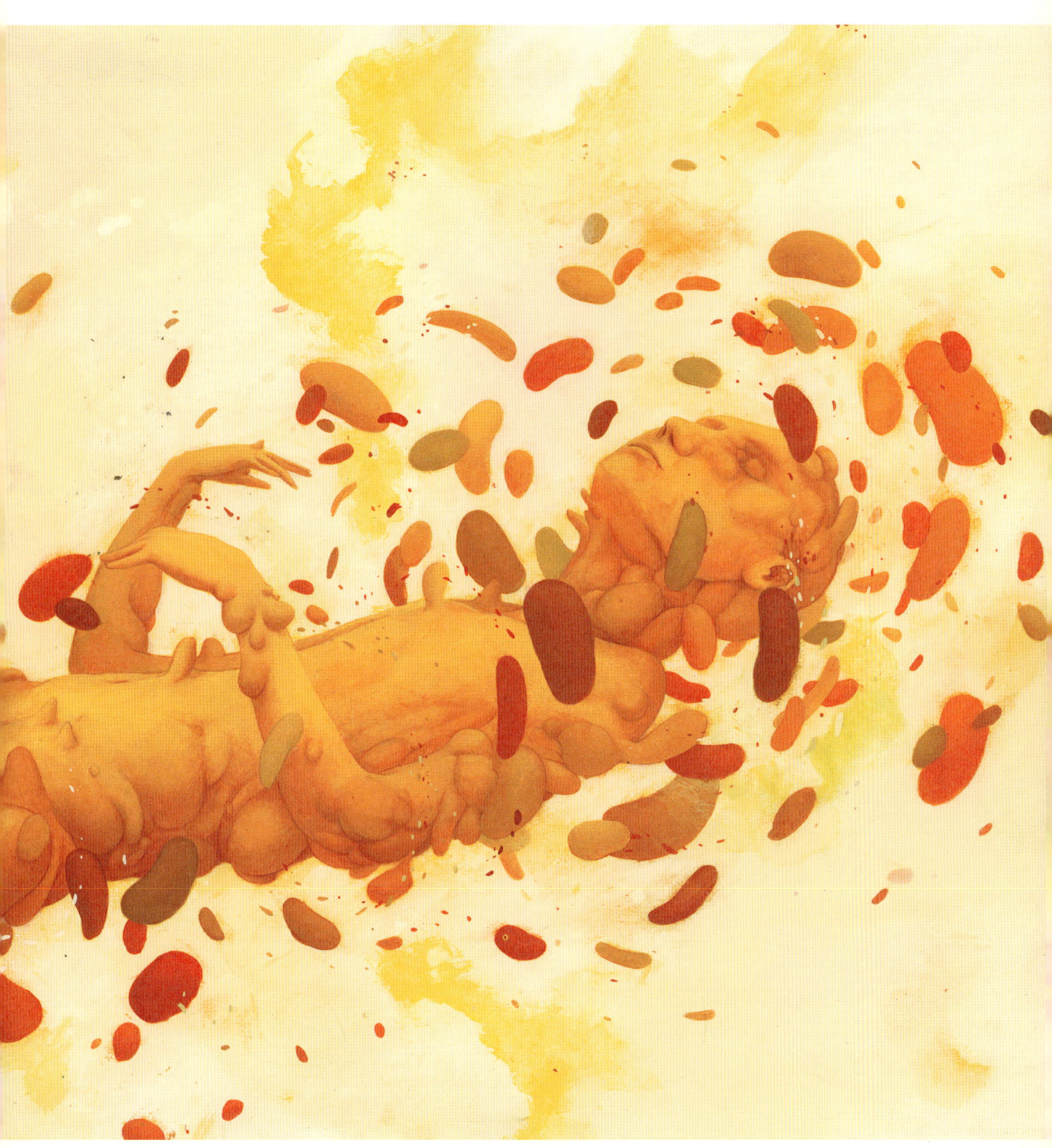

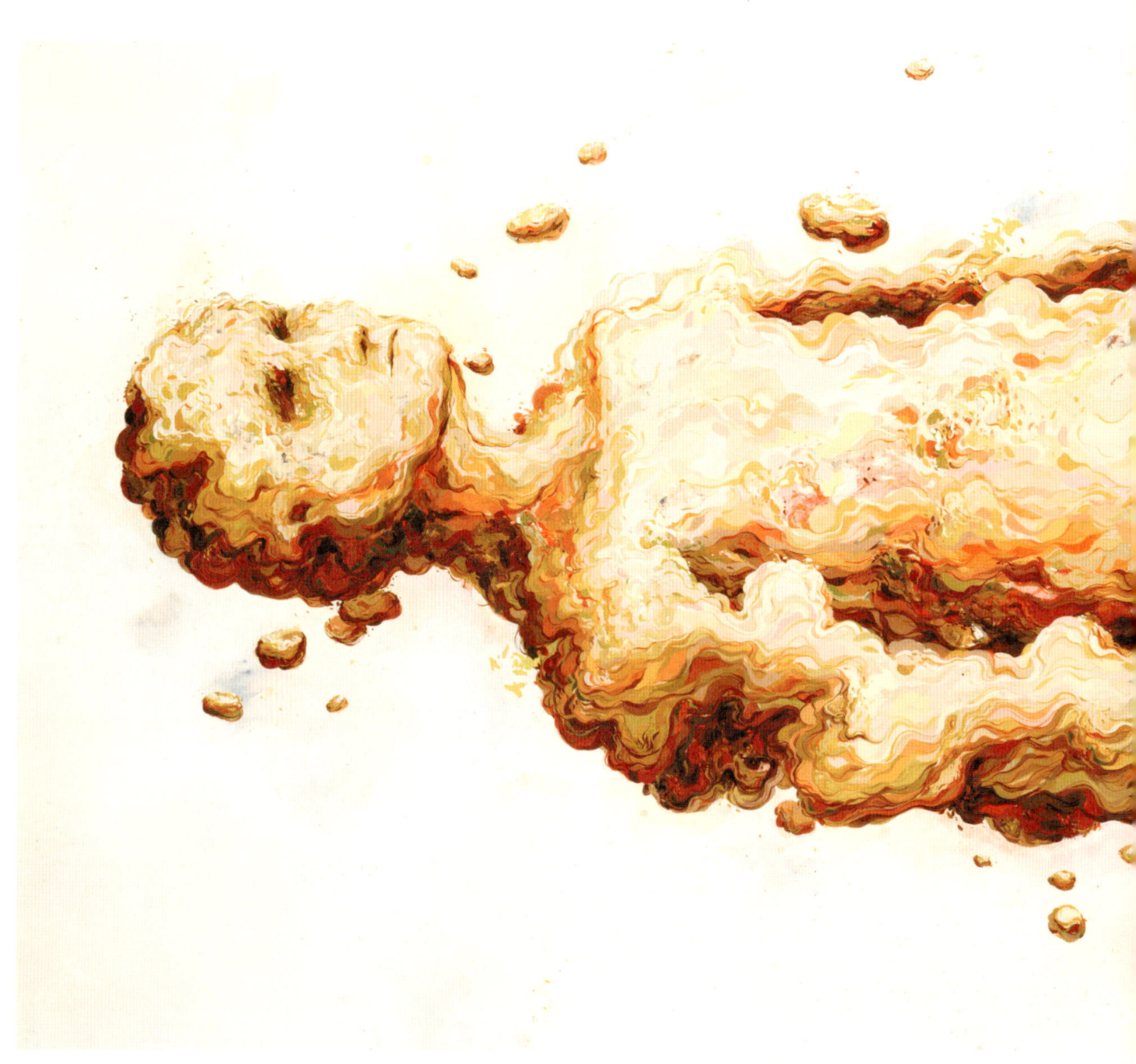

Almost Complete 2007 — acrylic, collage on paper
Manifest 52 x 117.5 in / 132.1 x 298.5 cm

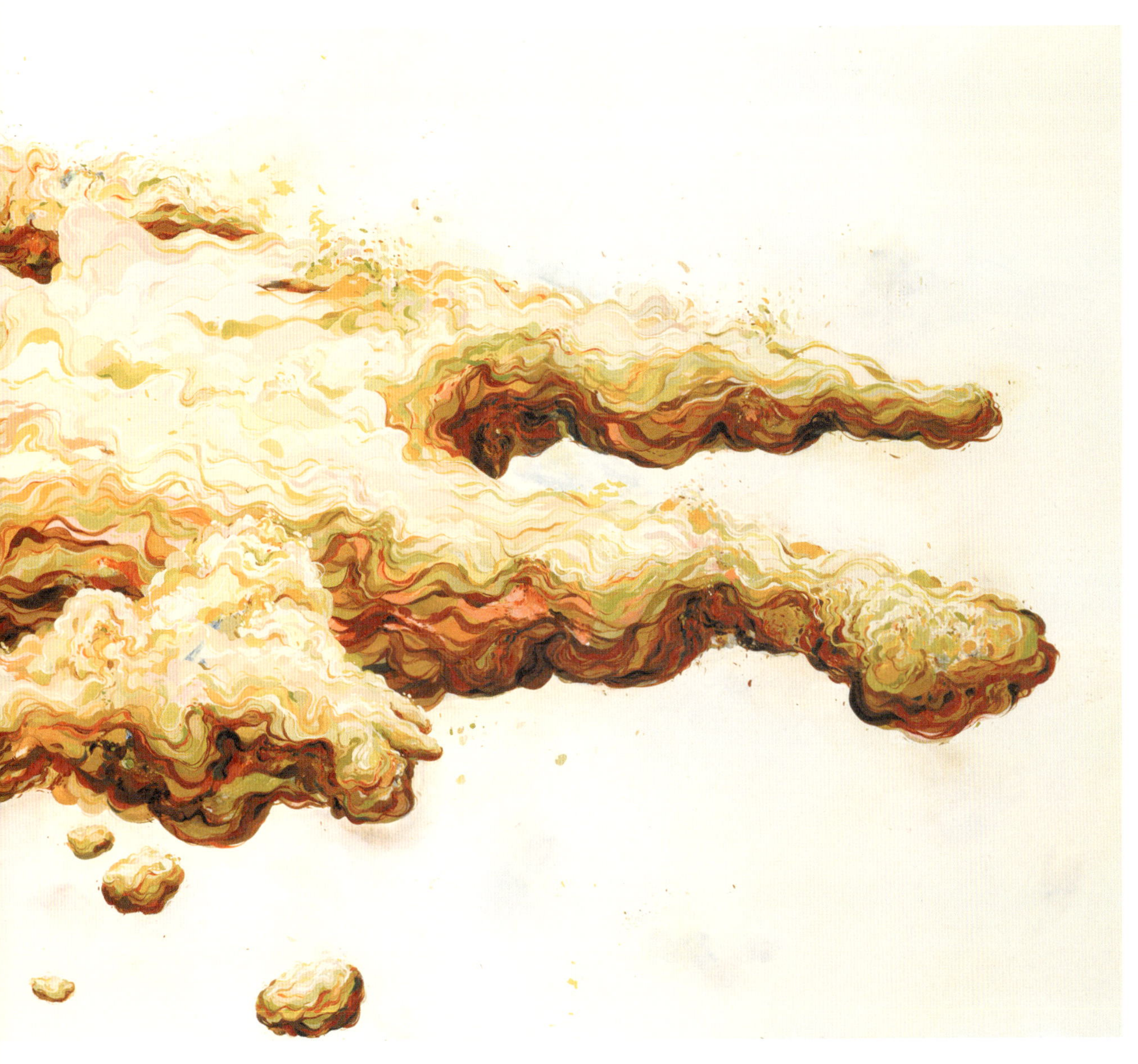

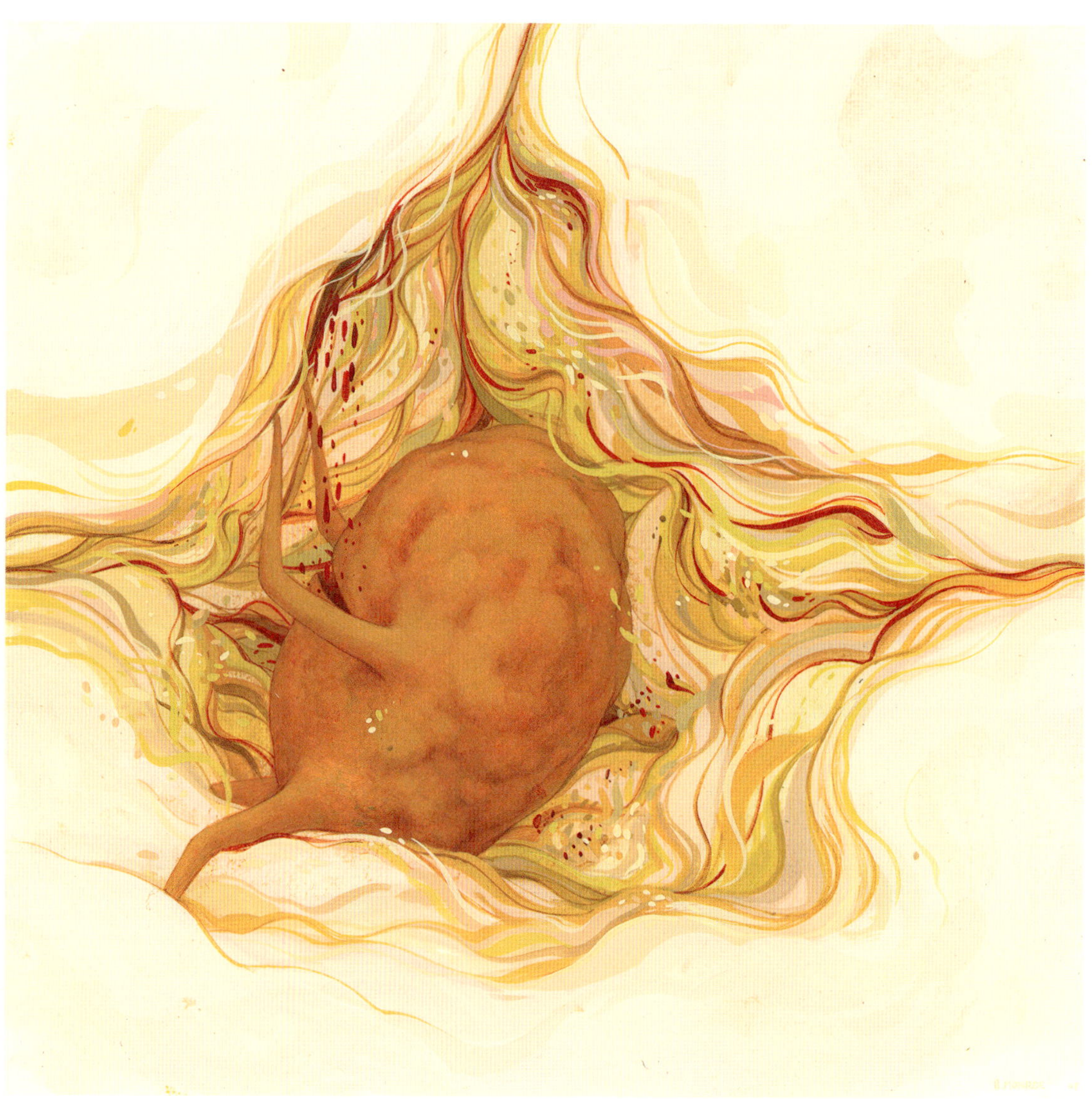

Fulfillment

2007 — acrylic on paper
9 x 9 in / 22.9 x 22.9 cm

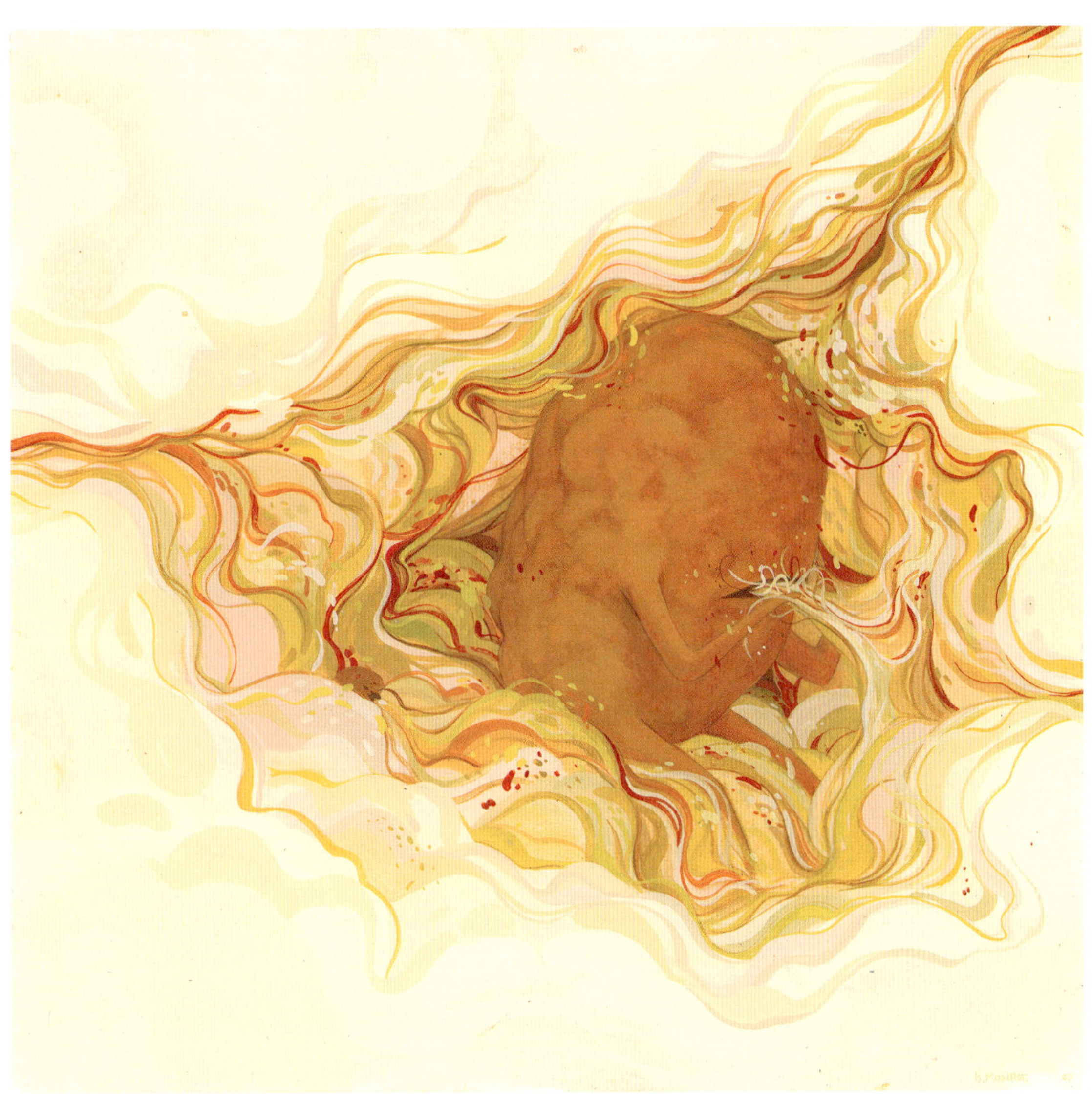

Letting Go	2007 — acrylic on paper
9 x 9 in / 22.9 x 22.9 cm

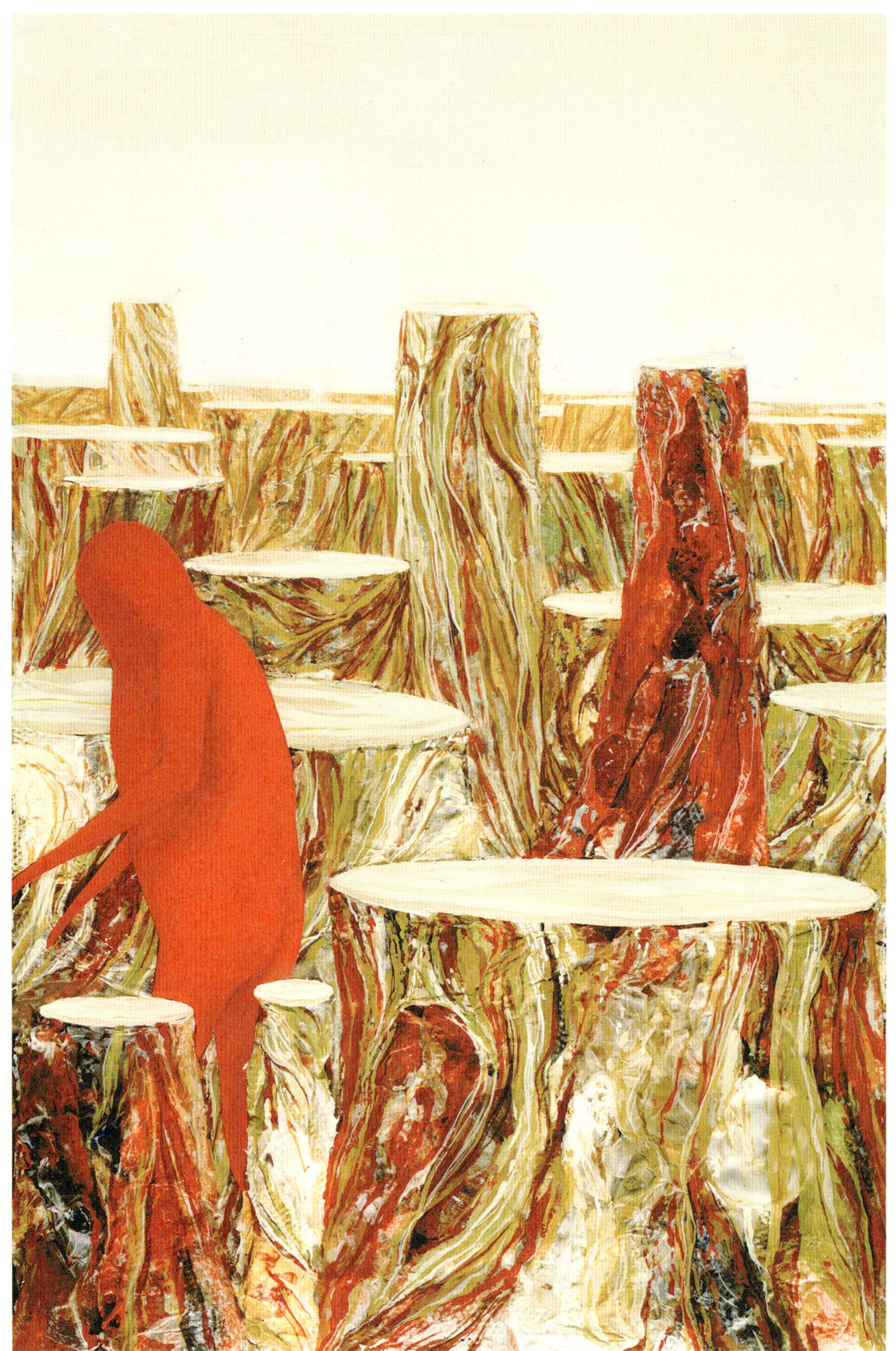

Stepping Through   2007 — acrylic, collage [ps] on paper
the Cracks   14.25 x 9.25 in / 36.2 x 23.5 cm

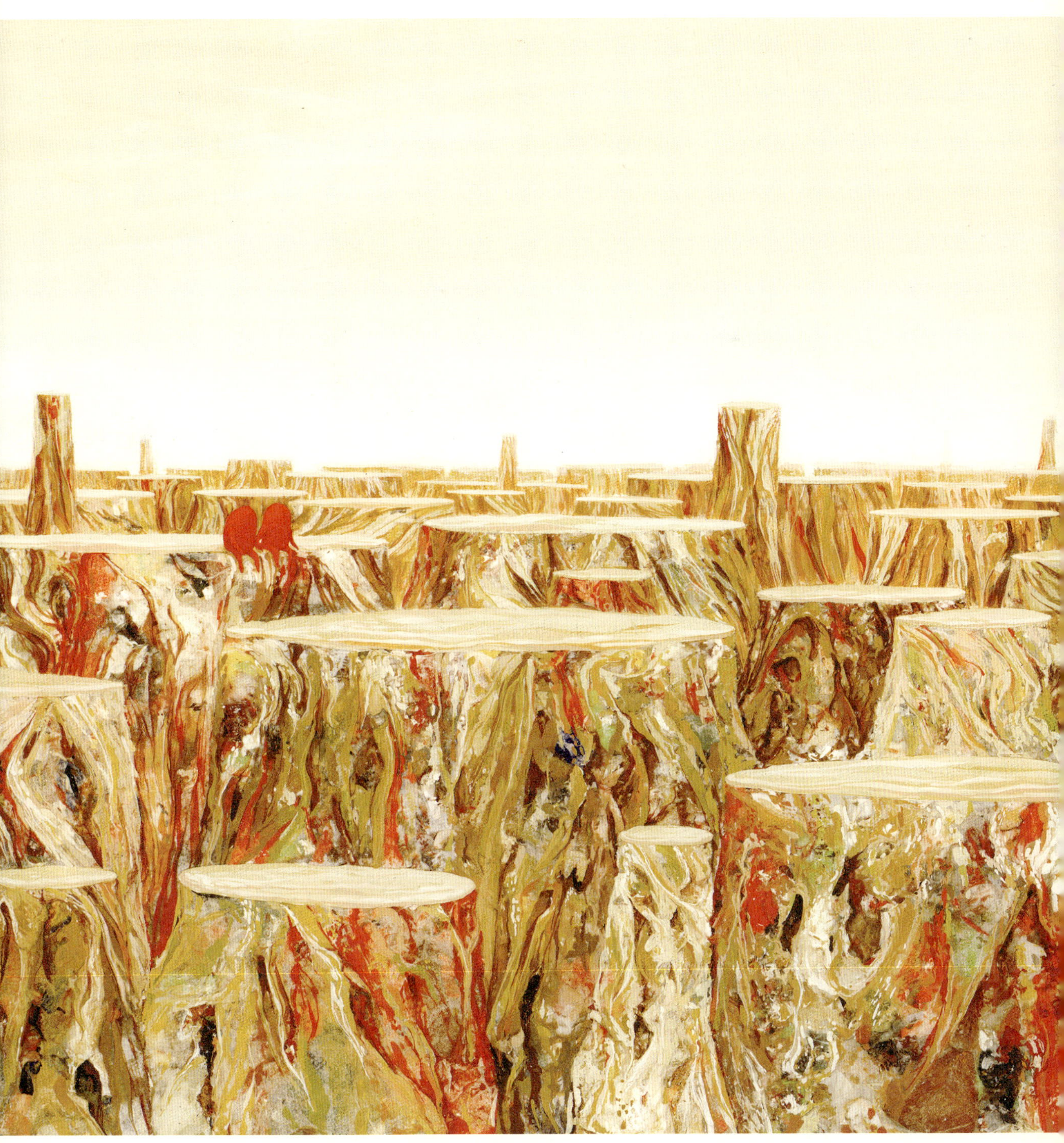

Years 2007 — acrylic, collage [ps] on paper
17 x 17 in / 43.2 x 43.2 cm

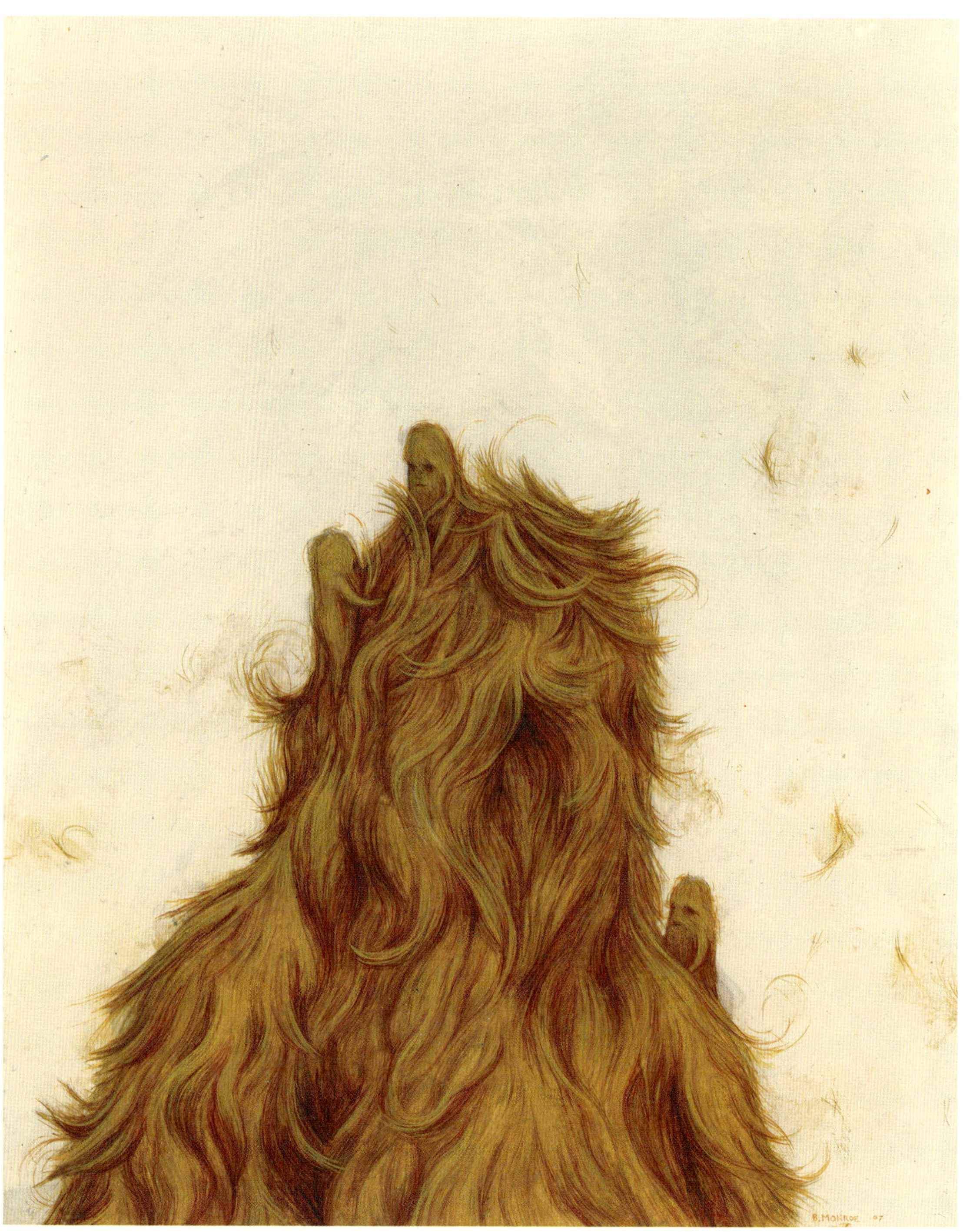

The Hairball from
my Throat (...)

2007 — acrylic on paper
10 x 8 in / 25.4 x 20.3 cm

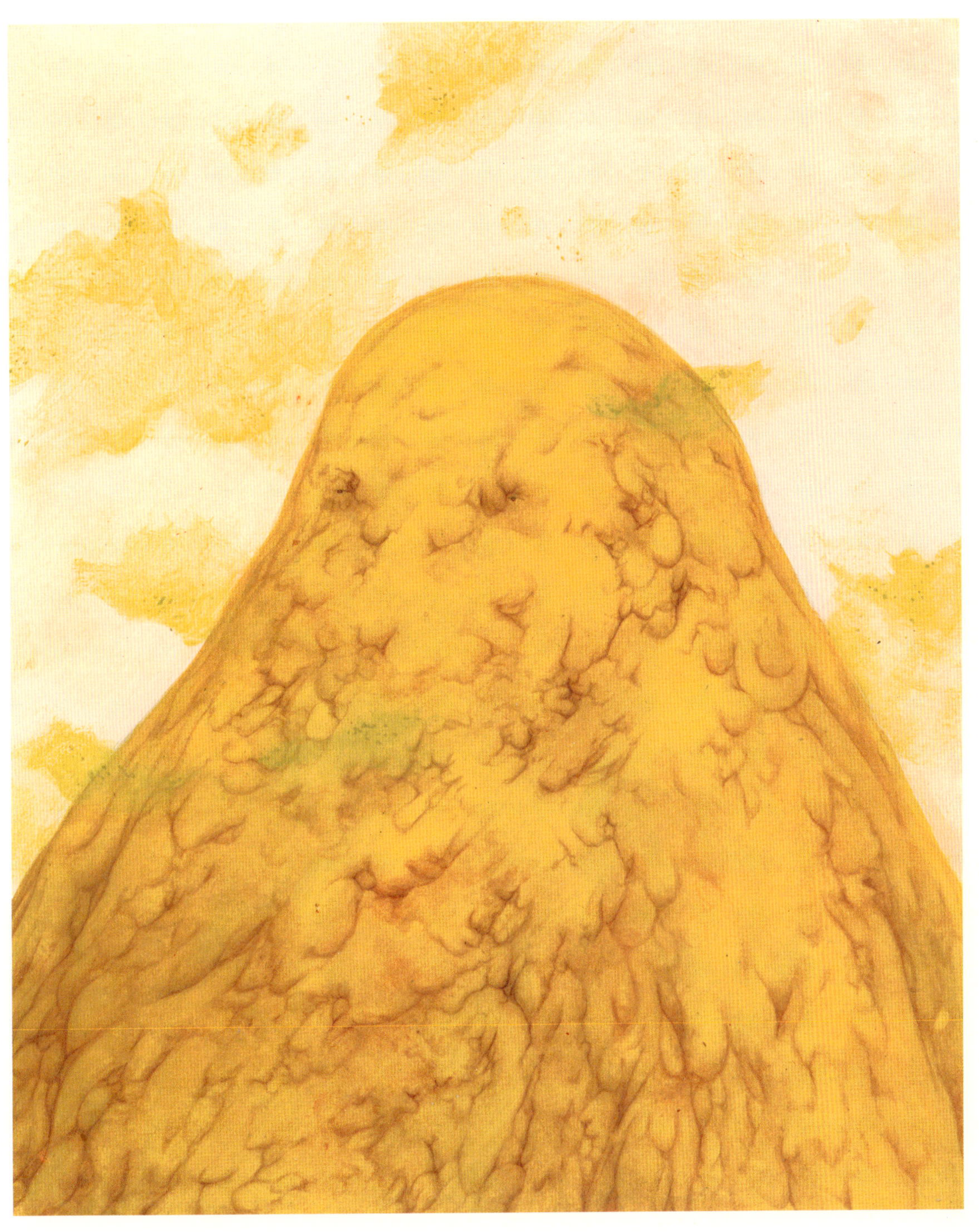

Mr. Suppuration 2007 — acrylic on paper
10 x 8 in / 25.4 x 20.3 cm

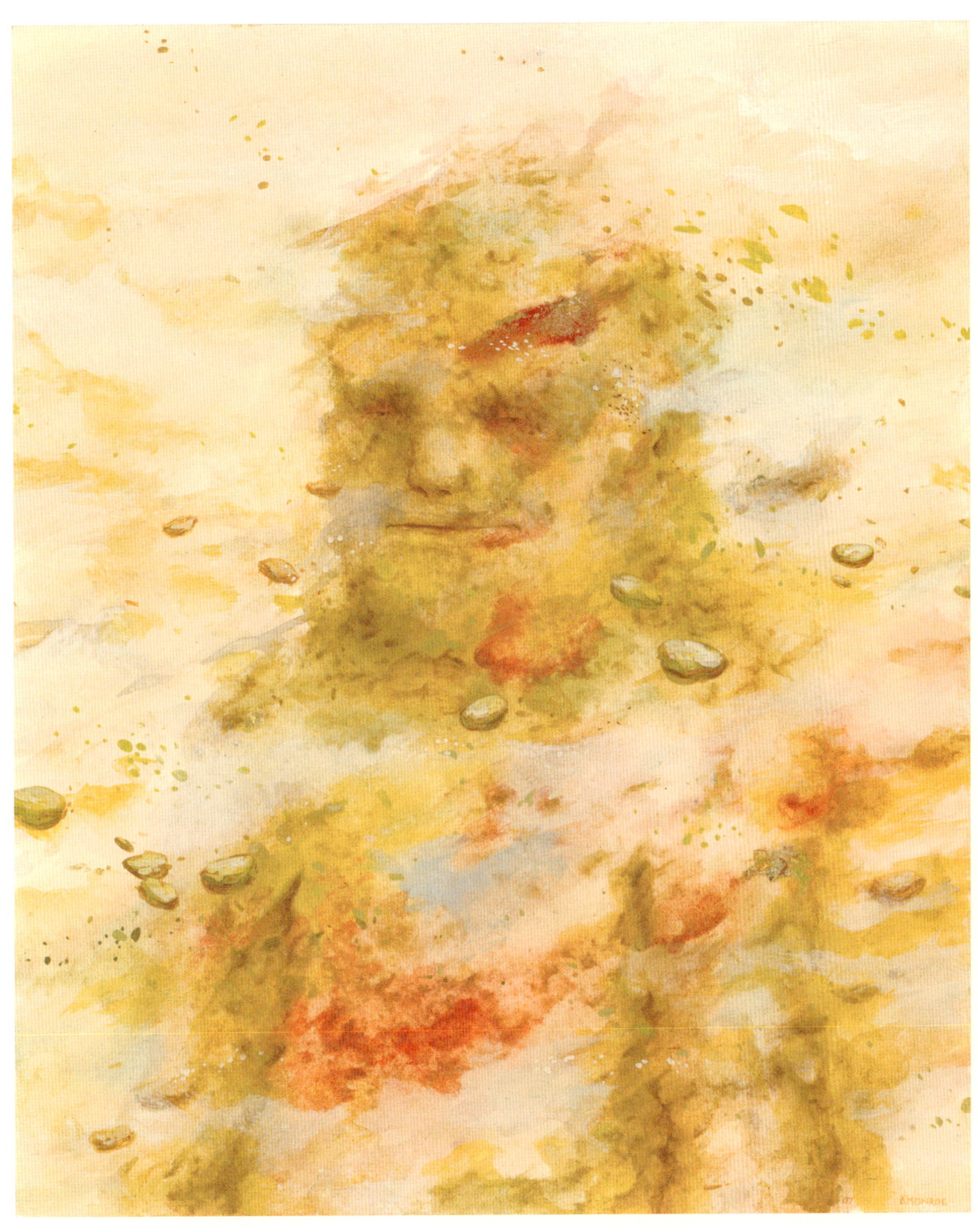

Gastrointestinal
Gas w/ Particles

2007 — acrylic on paper
10 x 8 in / 25.4 x 20.3 cm

(overleaf)
Ritual

2007 — acrylic, collage on paper
26 x 40 in / 66 x 101.6 cm

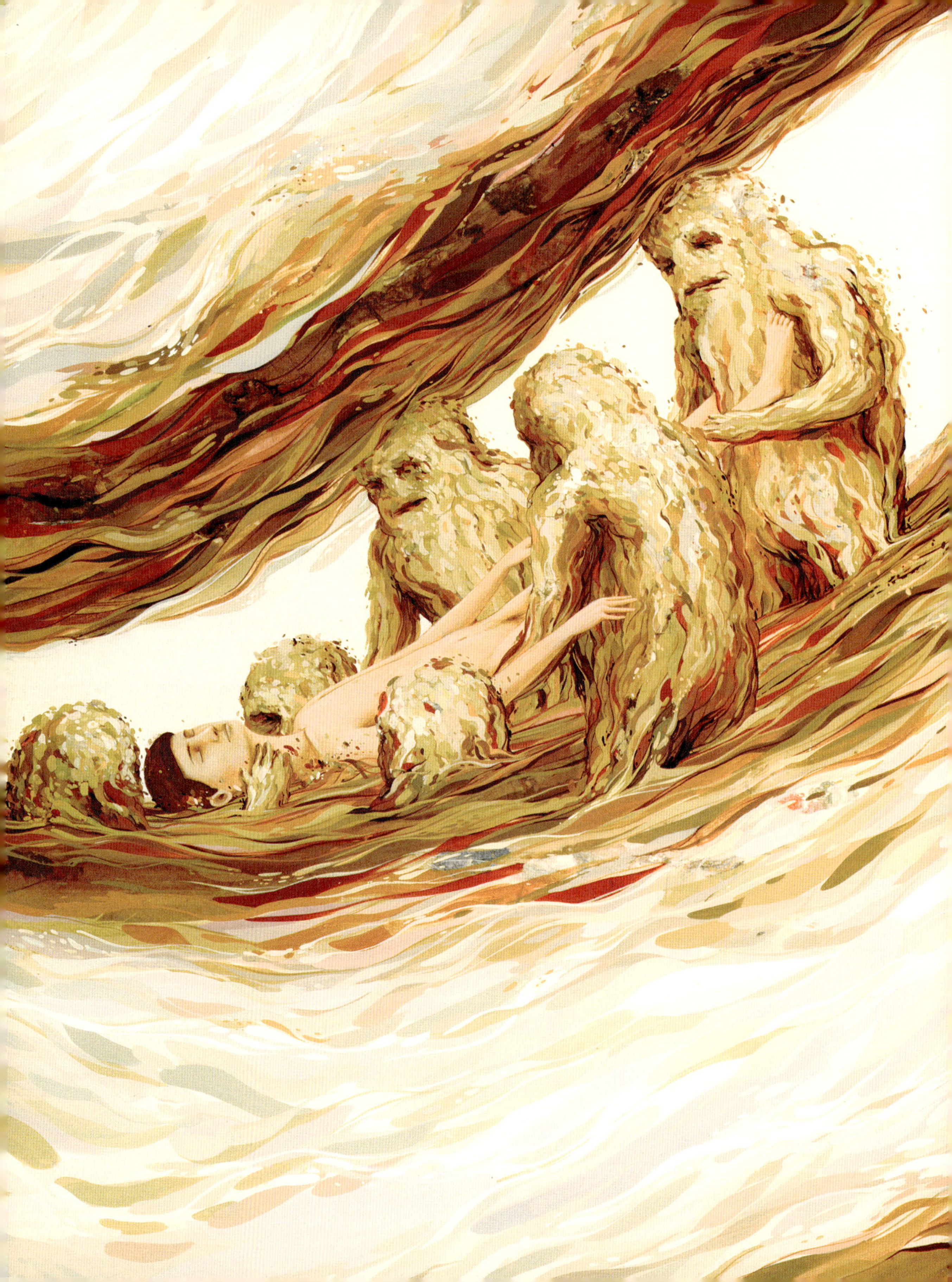

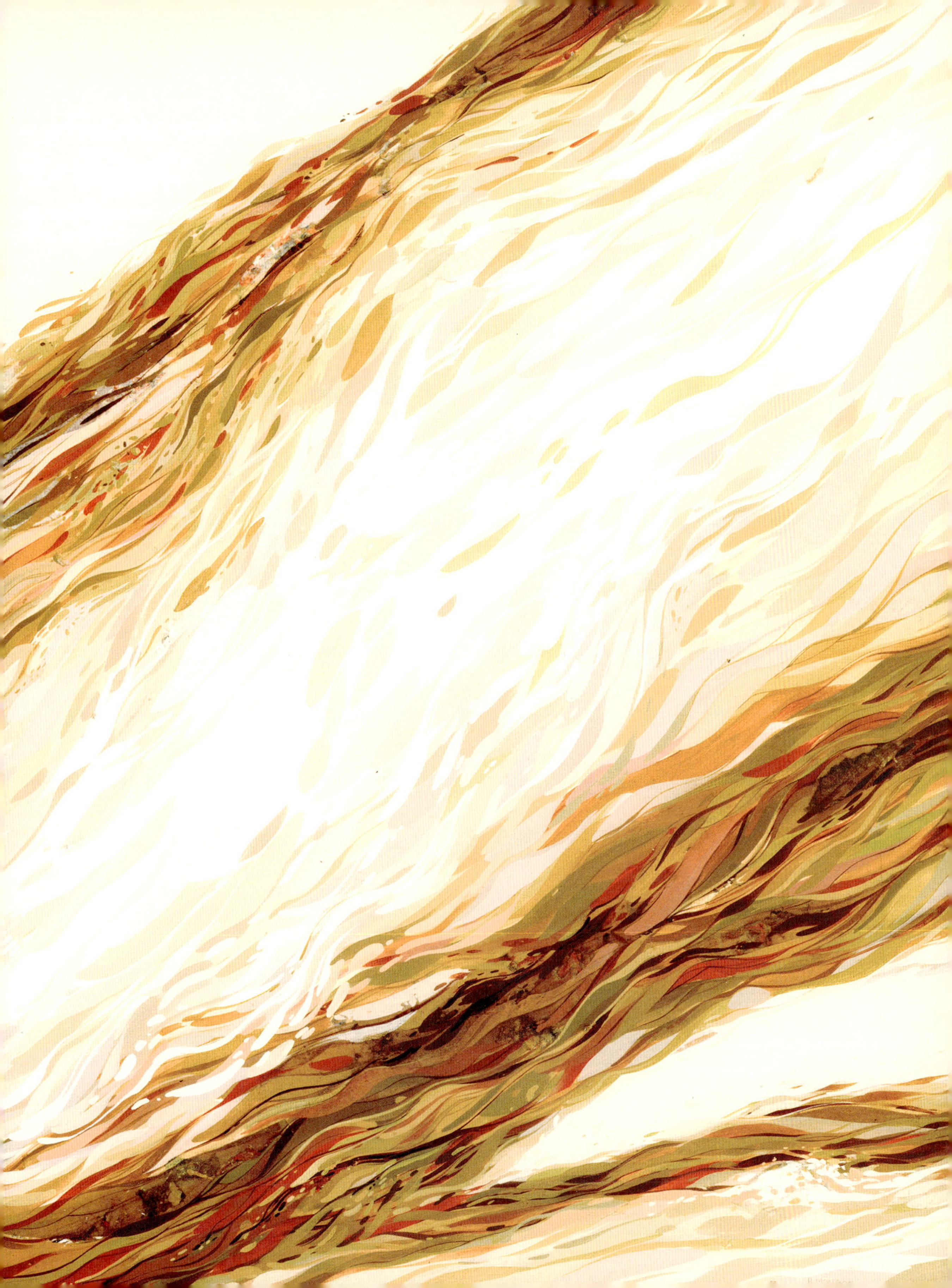

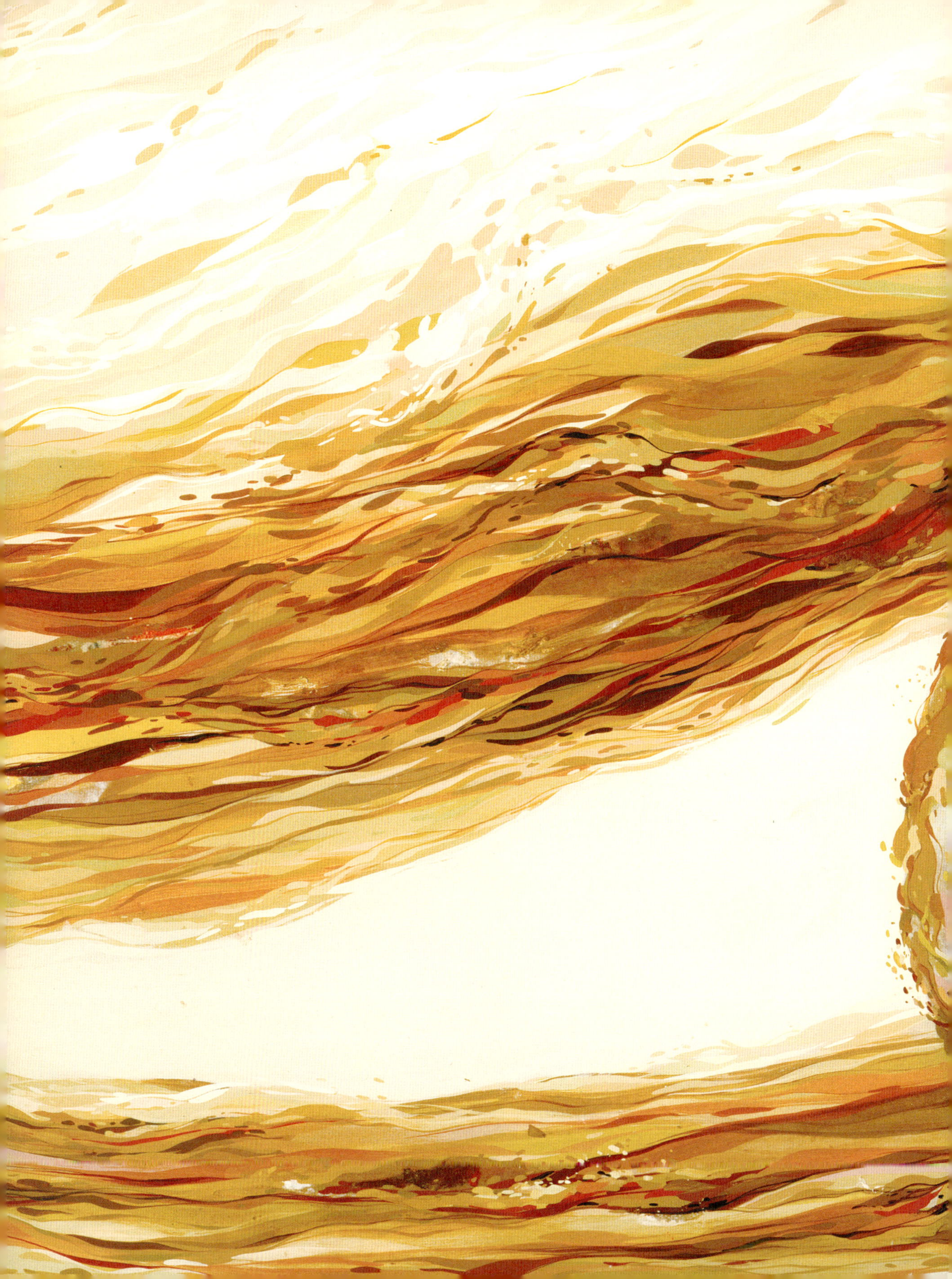

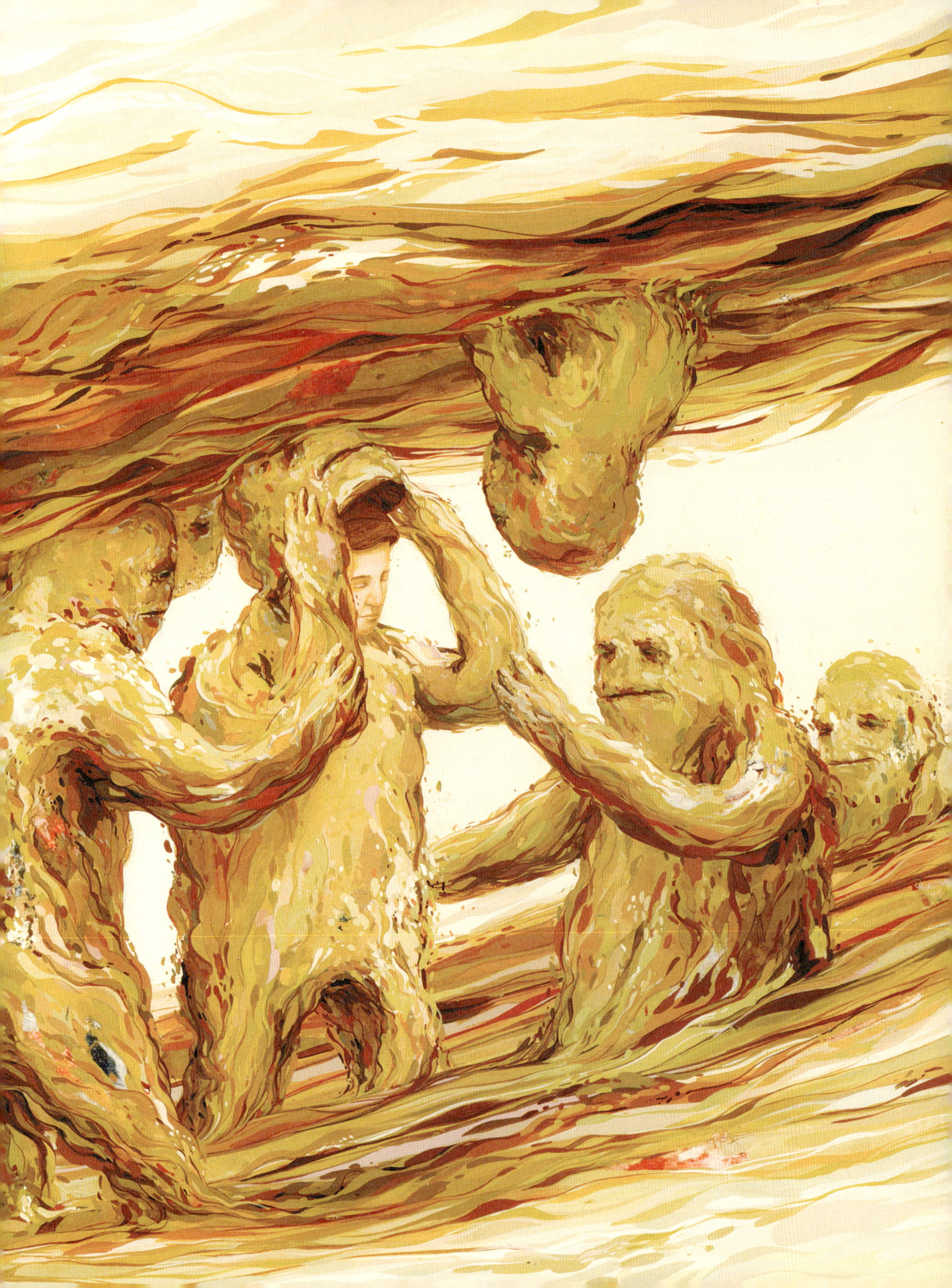

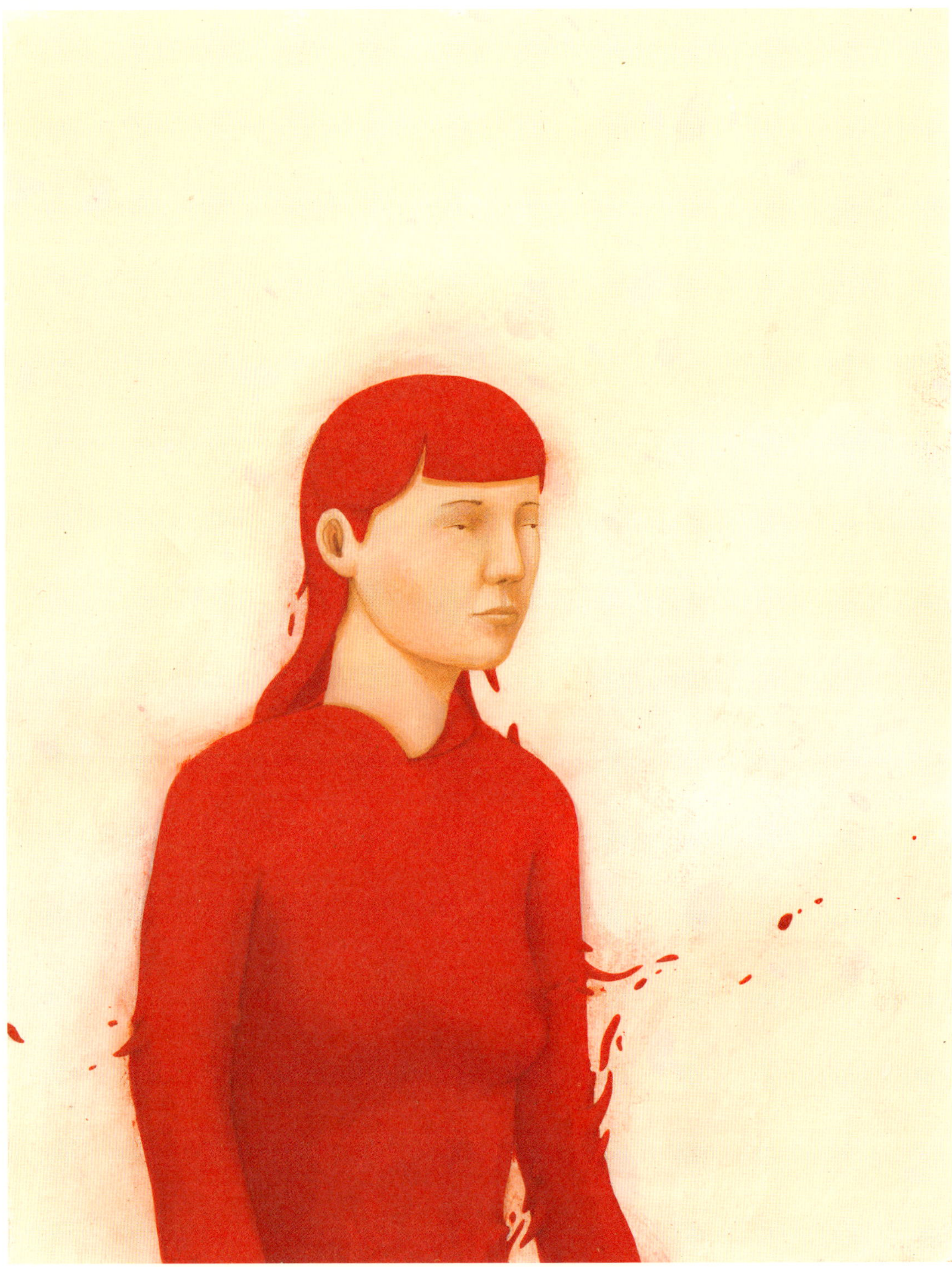

(overleaf)

Assimilation   2007 — acrylic, collage on paper
26 x 40 in / 66 x 101.6 cm

(pg.106-108)

**Meeting Each Other In
Another Place** *(triptych)*

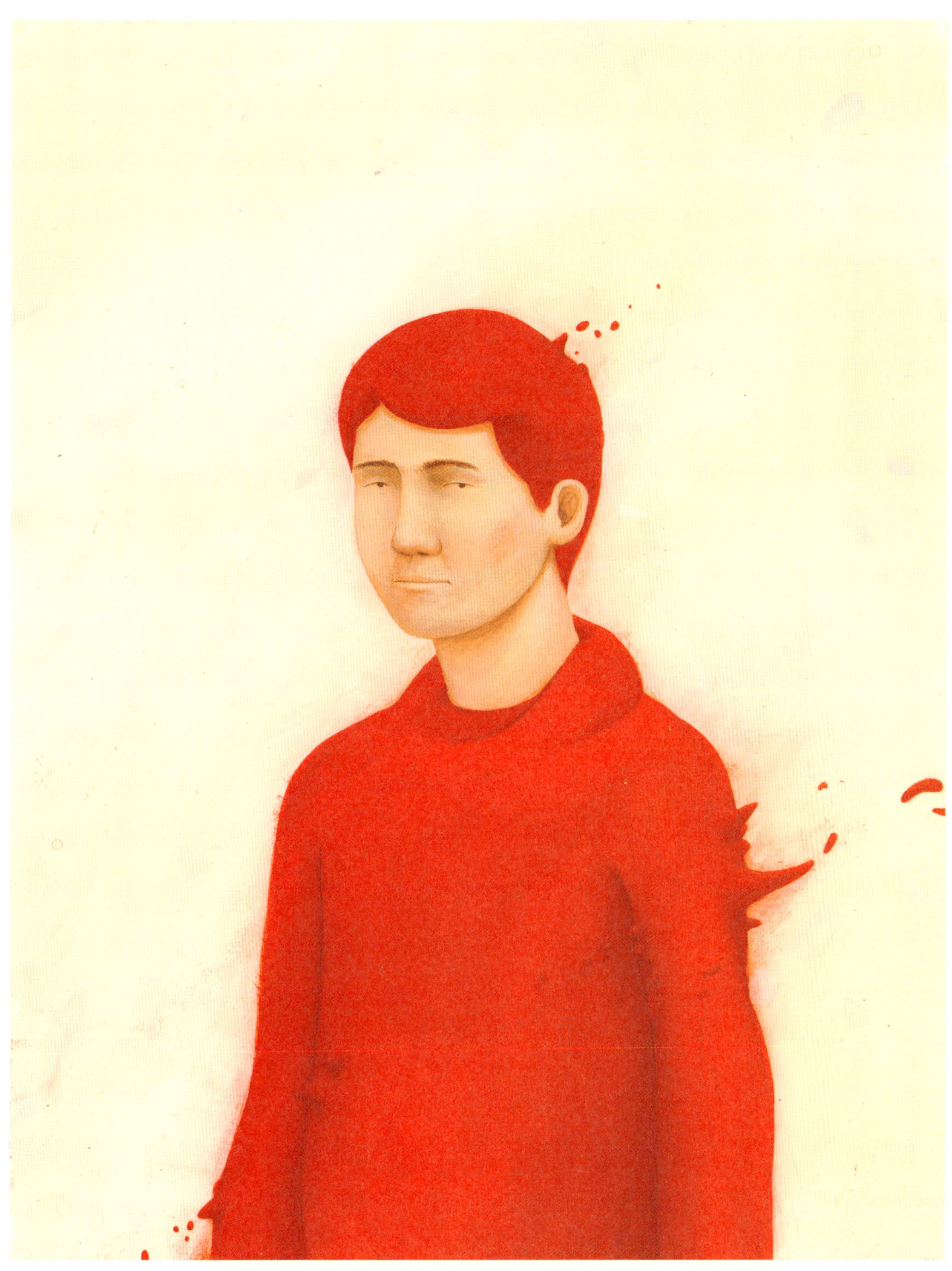

(opposite)
Mind Reading   2007 — acrylic on paper
                    12 x 9 in / 30.5 x 22.9 cm

(above)
Becoming of Me   2007 — acrylic on paper
                    12 x 9 in / 30.5 x 22.9 cm

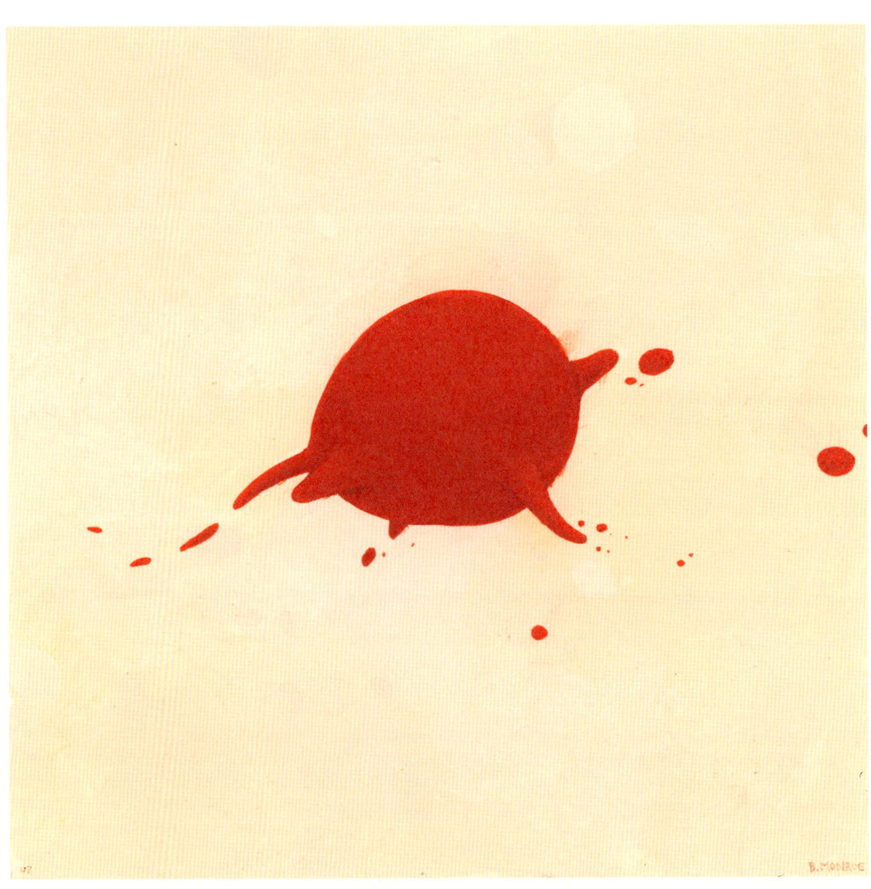

Medium   2007 — acrylic on paper
                       6 x 6 in / 15.2 x 15.2 cm

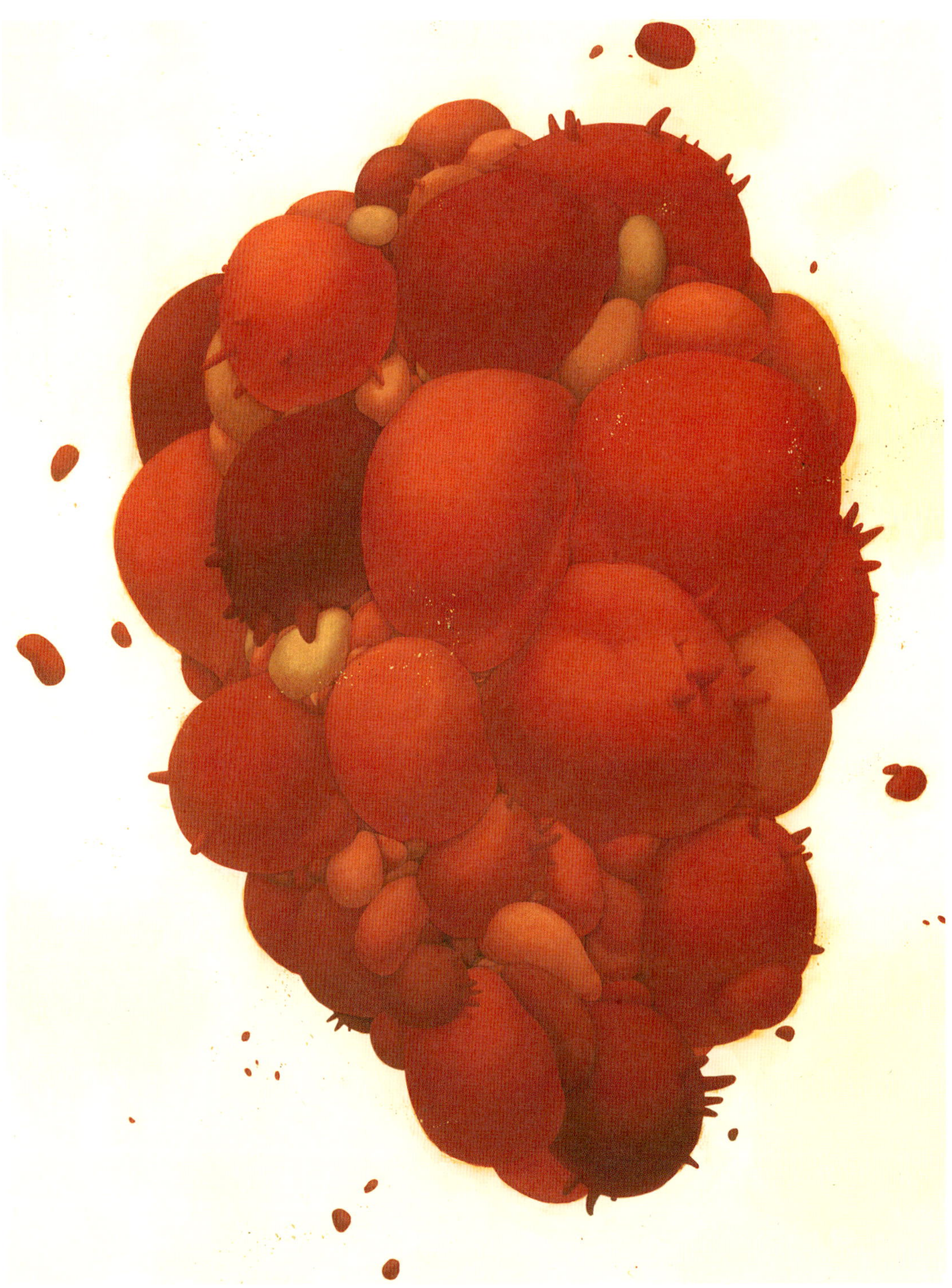

Life as They Know It   2007 — acrylic on paper
60 x 45 in / 152.4 x 114.3 cm

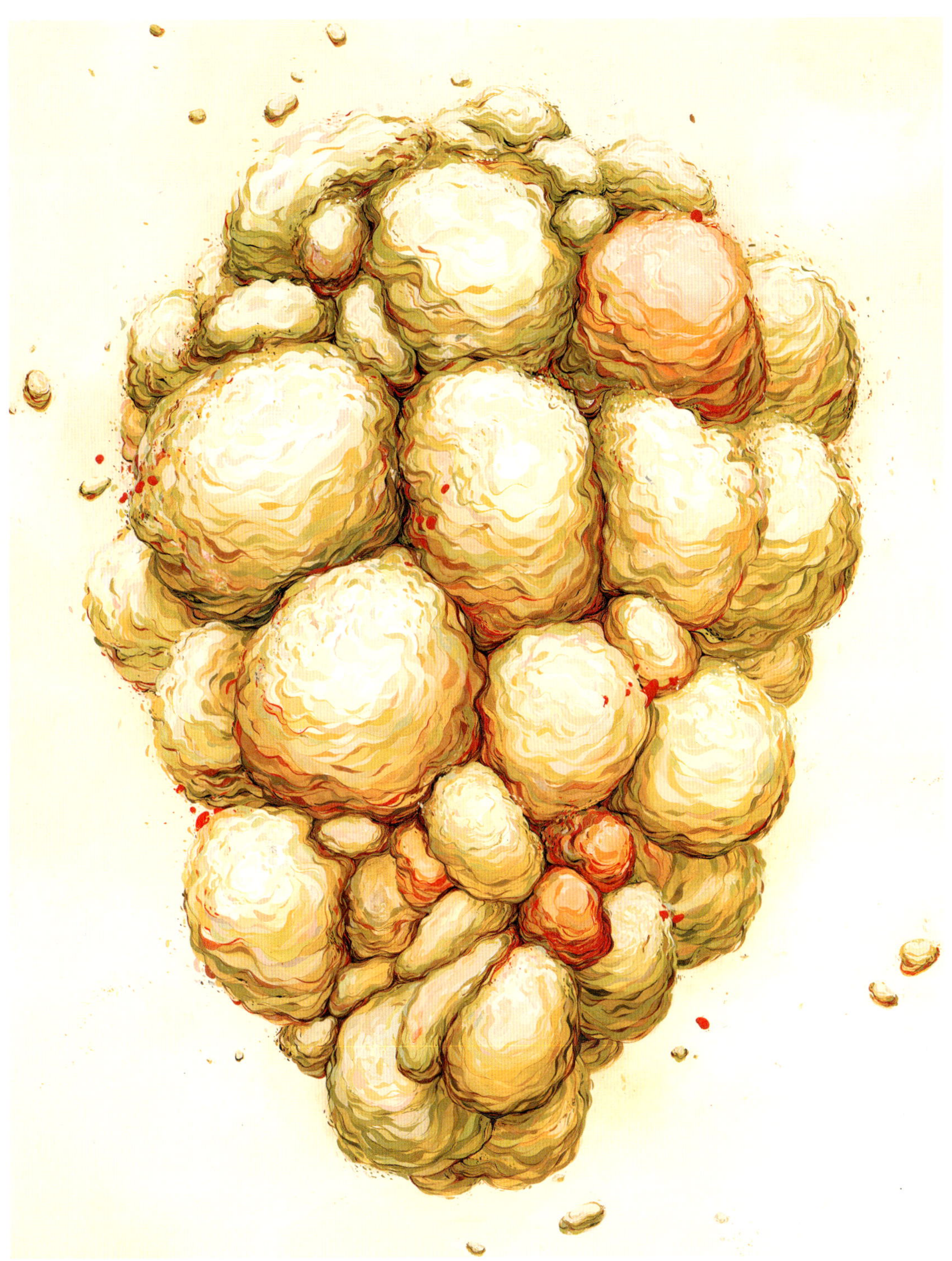

Life as It Knows It   2007 — acrylic, collage on paper
60 x 45 in / 152.4 x 114.3 cm

Sculptures

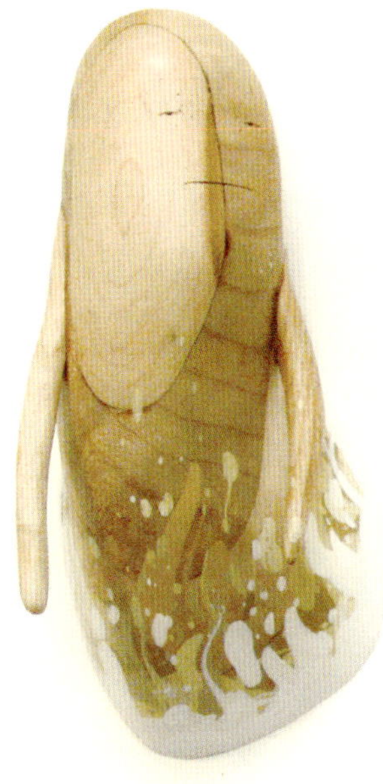

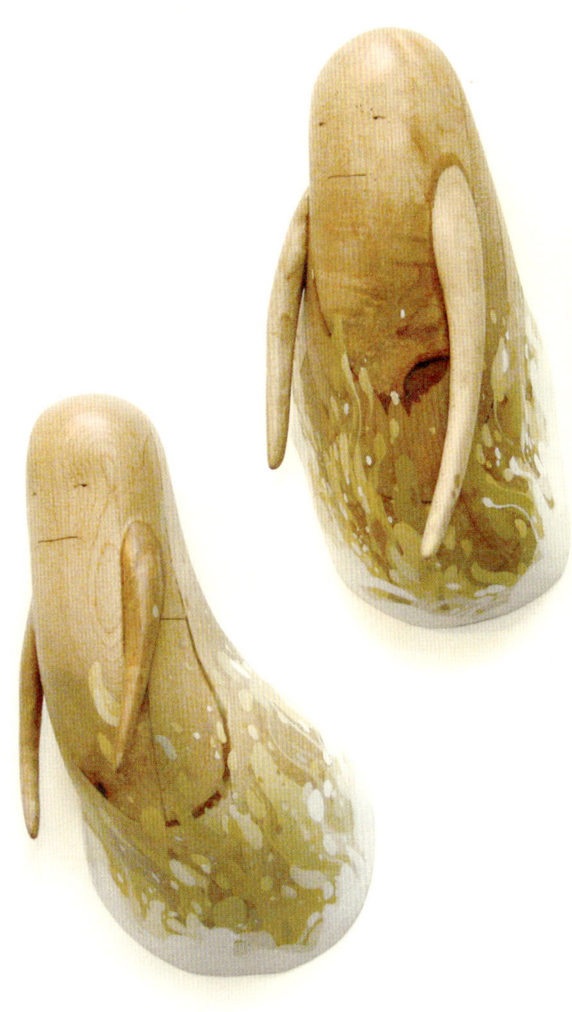

Ghosts   2006 — acrylic on maple
8 x 4.5 x 4 in / 20.3 x 11.4 x 10.2 cm

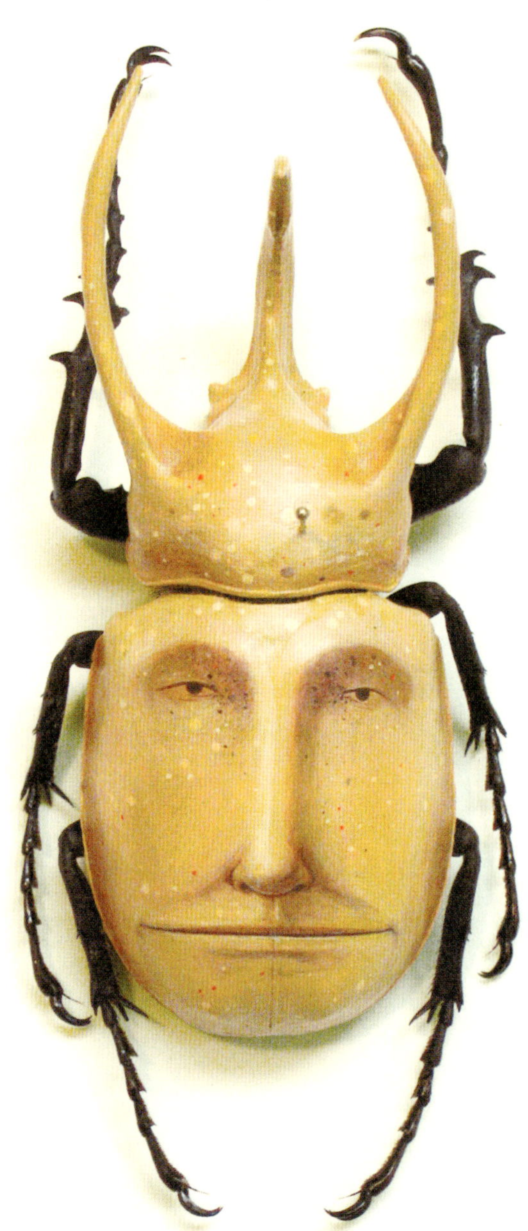

Beetle   2005 — acrylic on beetle
                4.5 x 2.25 x 1.75 in / 11.4 x 5.7 x 4.4 cm

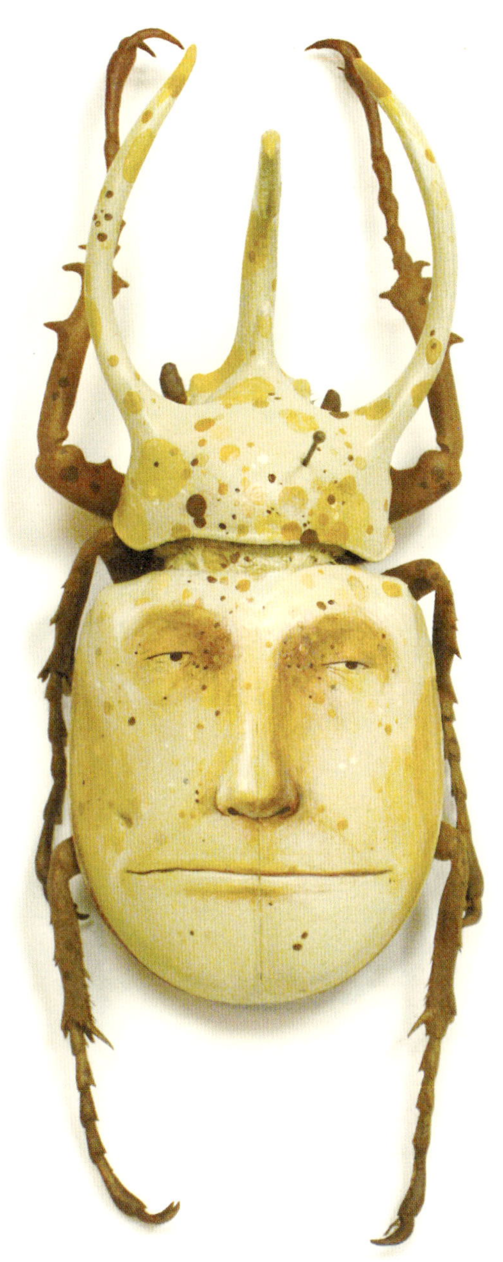

Beetle

2005 — acrylic on beetle
4.5 x 2.25 x 1.75 in / 11.4 x 5.7 x 4.4 cm

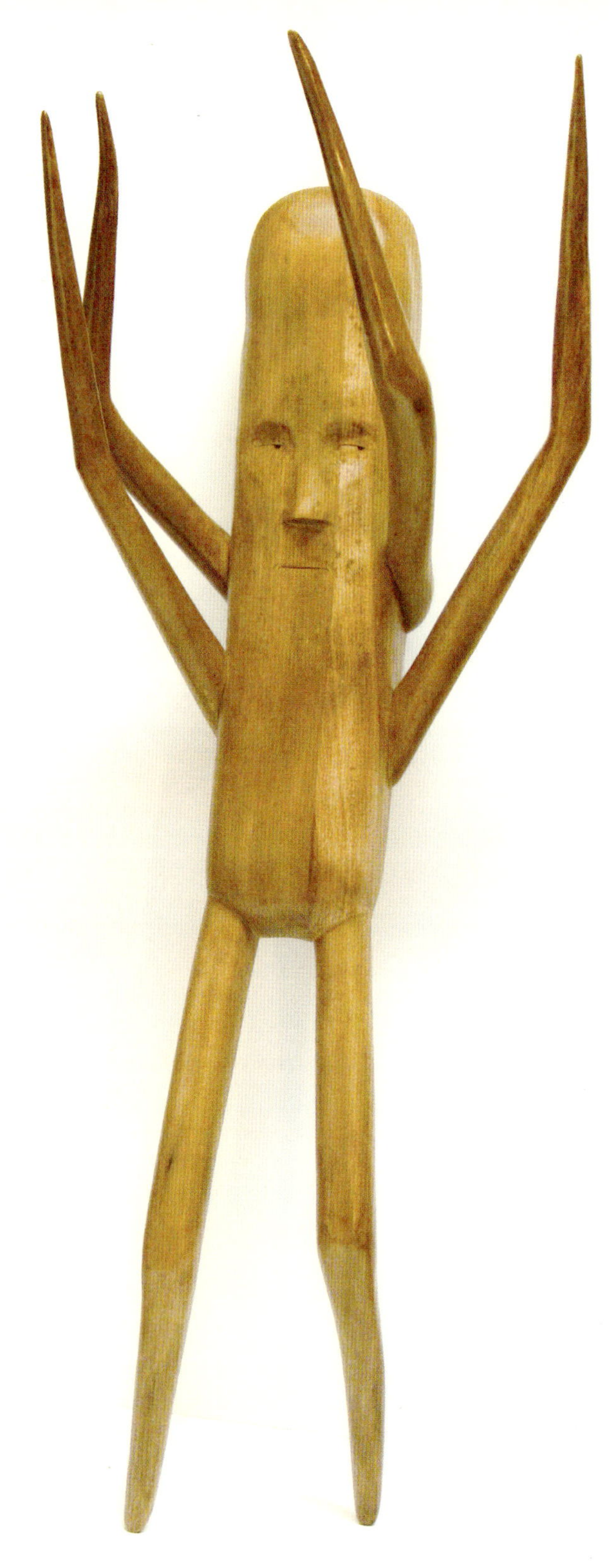

Trying So Hard
to Be

2006 — acrylic on poplar
39 x 18 x 17 in / 99.1 x 45.7 x 43.2 cm

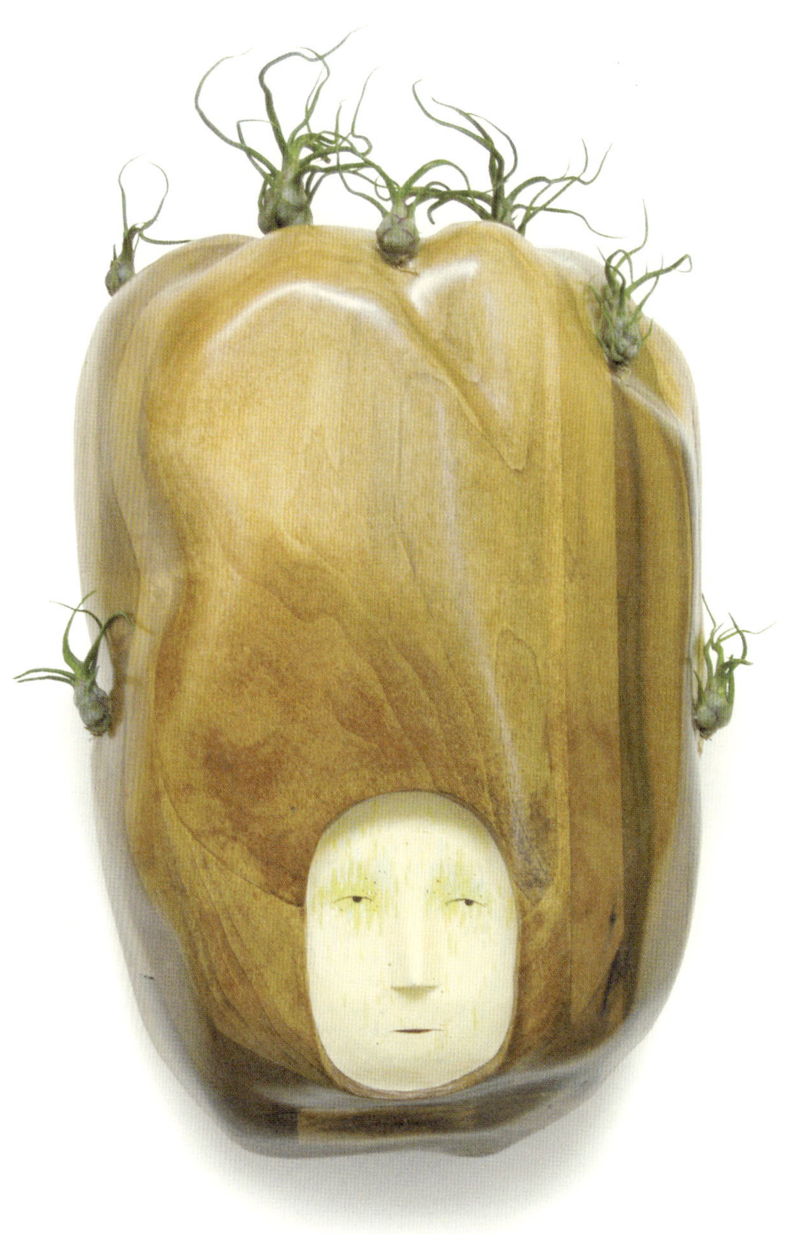

Onion Headed   2005 — acrylic, air plants on poplar
17 x 9.5 x 7.5 in / 43.2 x 24.1 x 19.1 cm

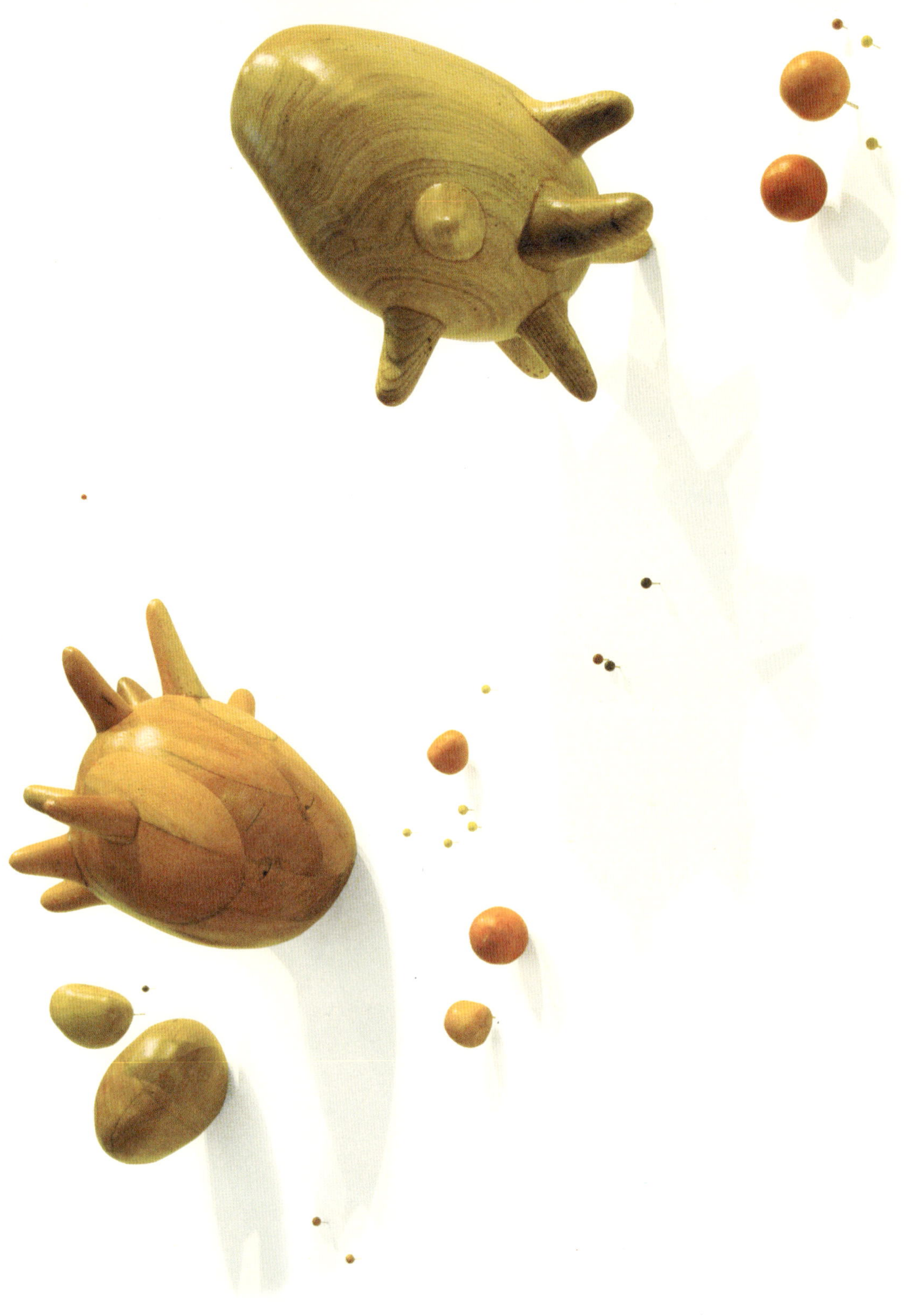

Mycobacterium   2006 — acrylic on various woods
dimensions variable

Claude   2005 — acrylic, grass on various hardwoods
                  12 x 9 x 9.5 in / 30.5 x 22.9 x 24.1 cm

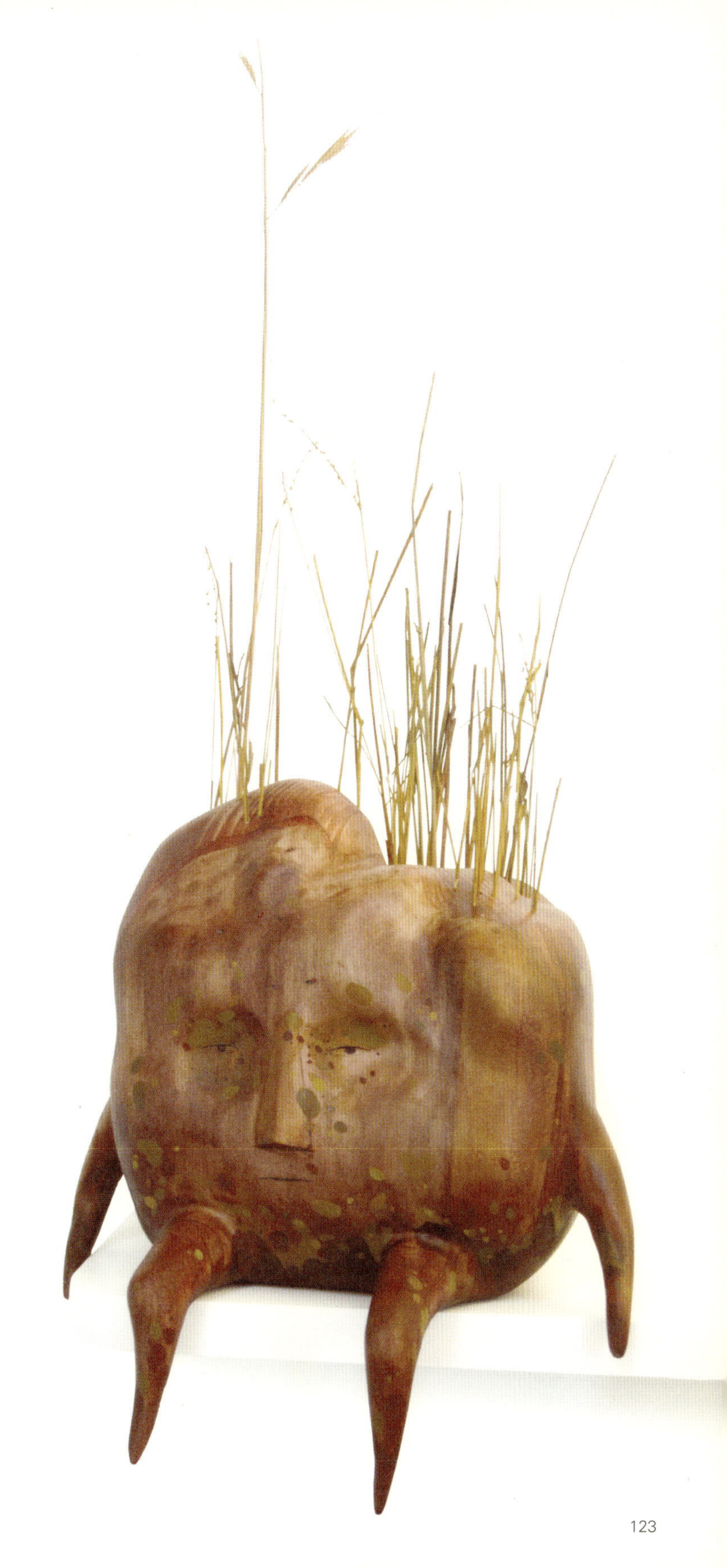

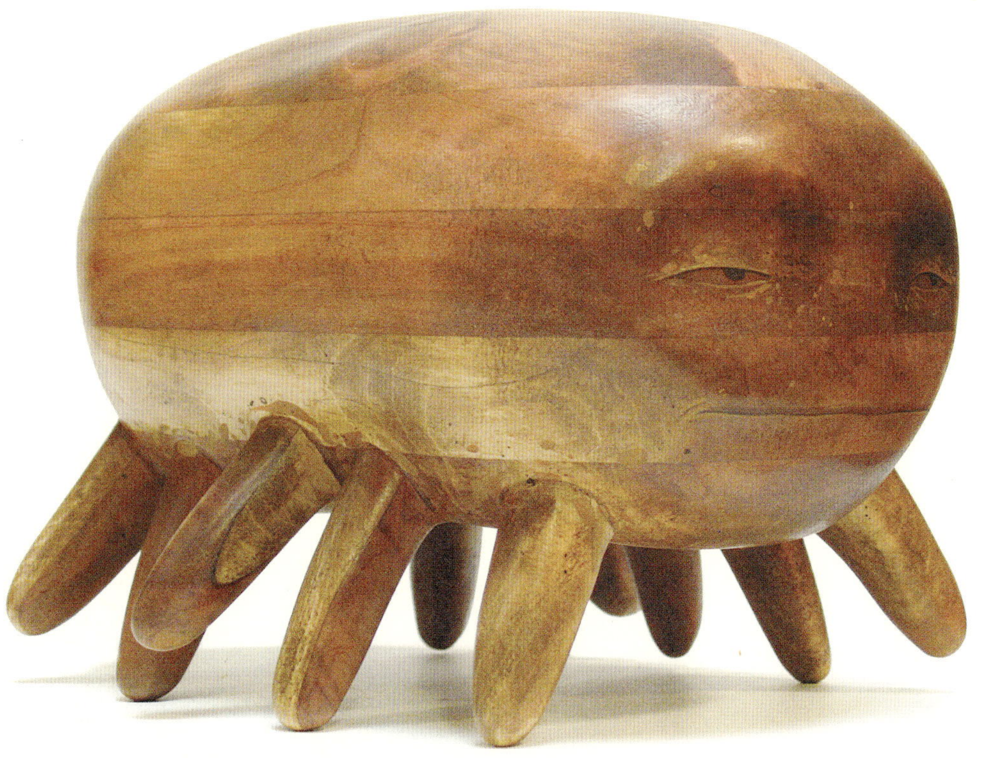

<table>
<tr><td>**Microbe**</td><td>2006 — acrylic on cedar
5 x 5.5 x 7.75 in / 12.7 x 14 x 19.7 cm</td><td>*(opposite)*
Microbe</td><td>2006 — acrylic on cast resin
5 x 5.5 x 7.75 in / 12.7 x 14 x 19.7 cm</td></tr>
</table>

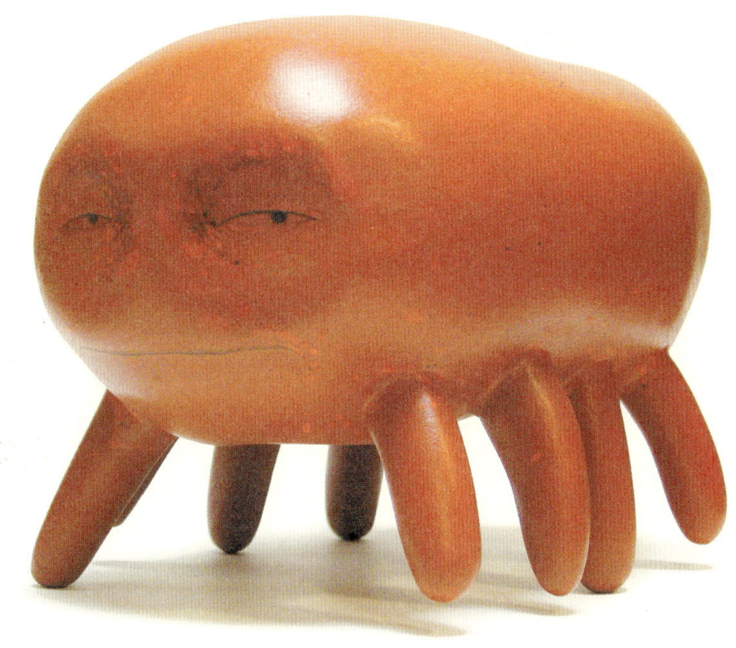

(overleaf)
Microbe Installation   2006 Richard Heller Gallery — mixed media
180 x 60 x 36 in / 457.2 x 152.4 x 91.4 cm

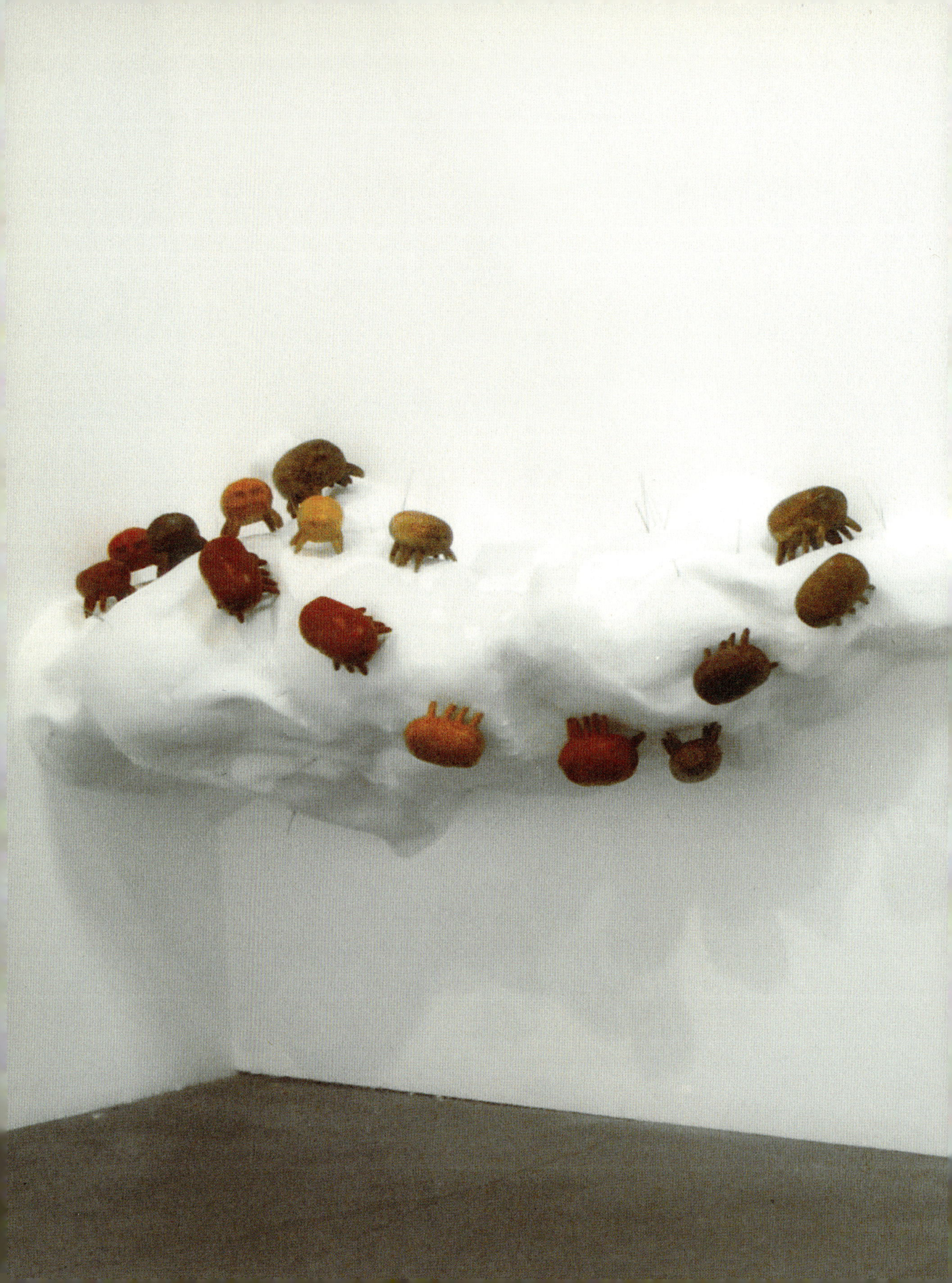

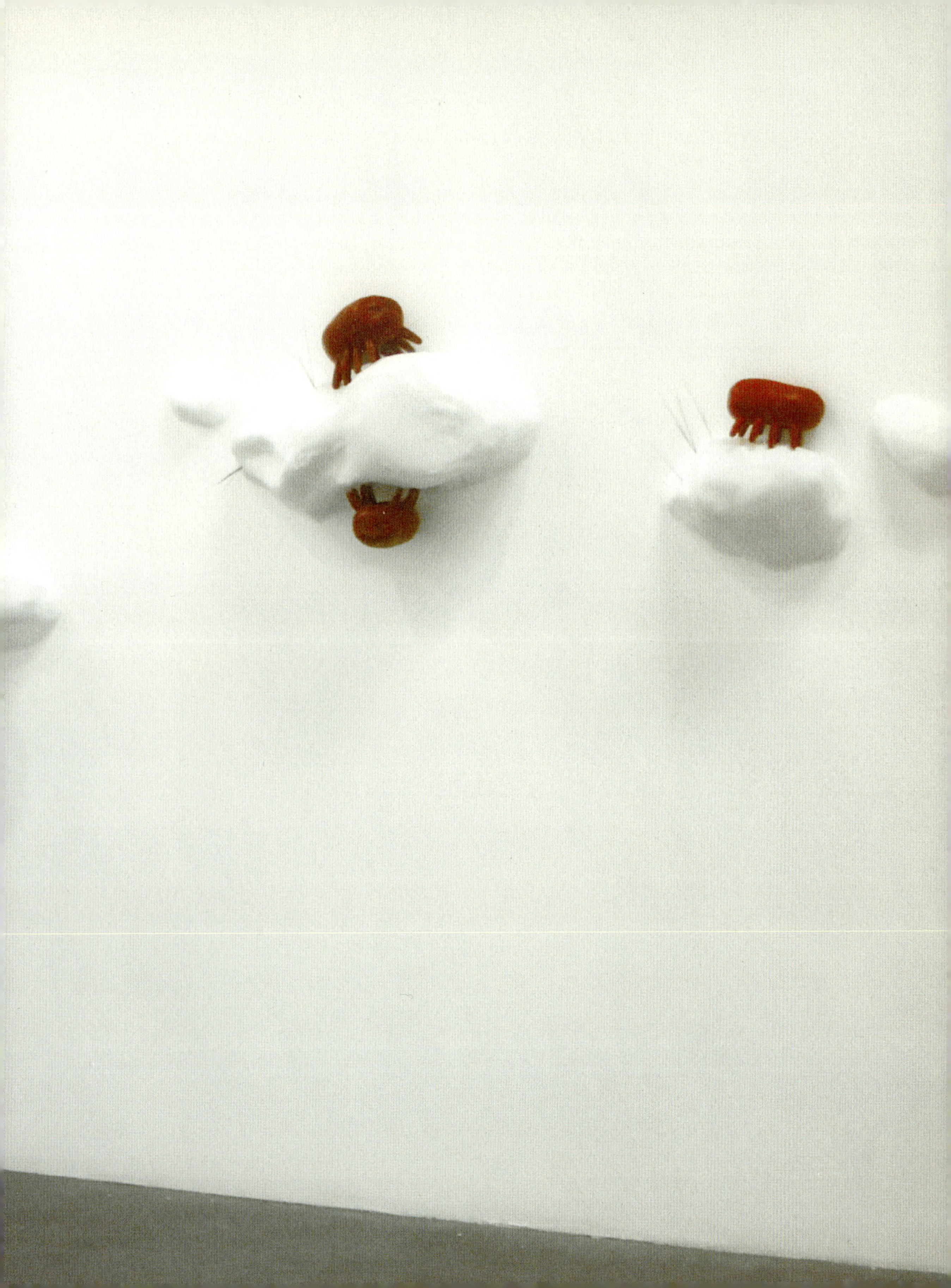

The Spiney	2005 — acrylic on walnut
14 x 7.5 x 8 in / 35.6 x 19.1 x 20.3 cm

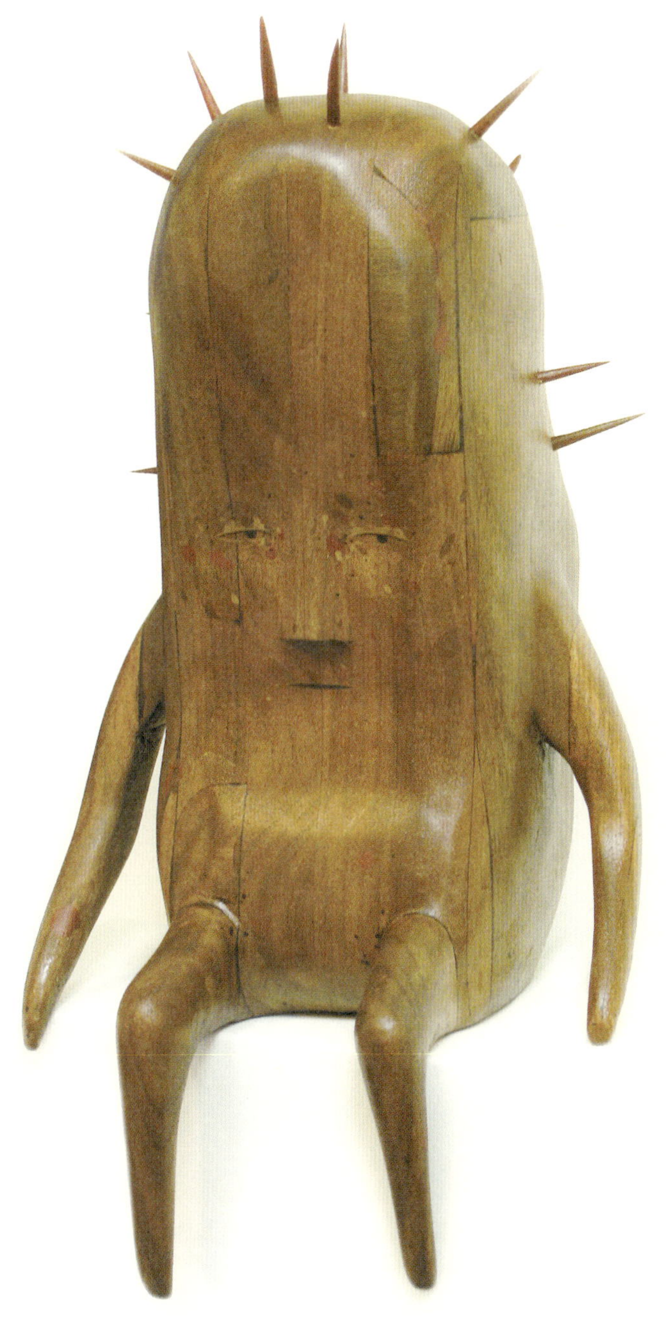

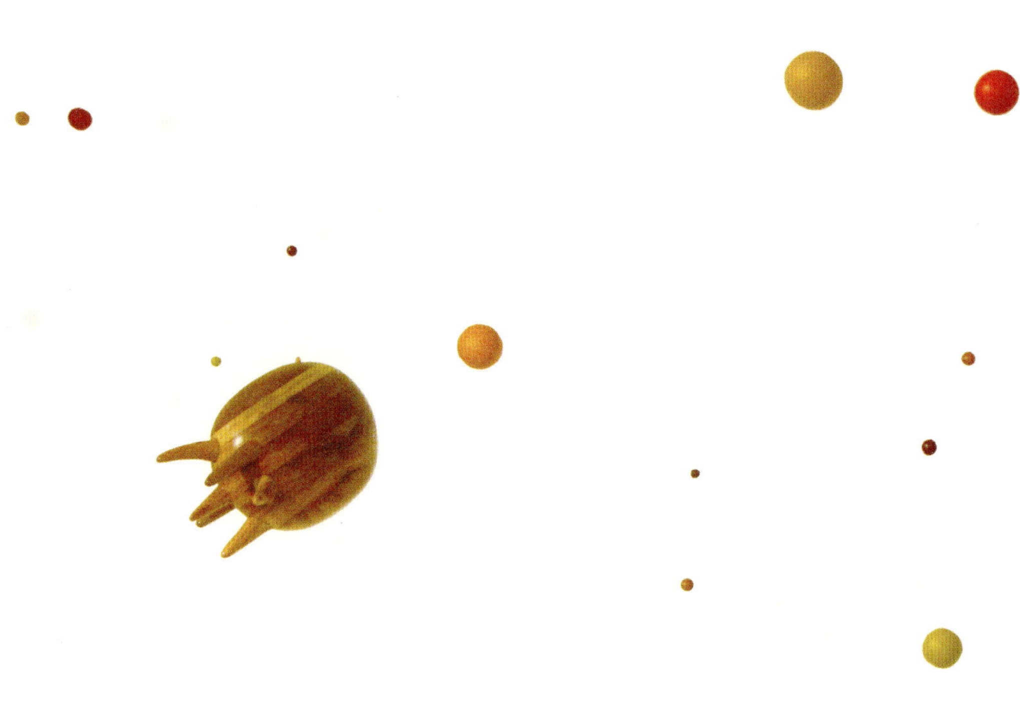

Solid, Liquid, Gas   2007 — acrylic, fishing line on hardwoods
dimensions variable

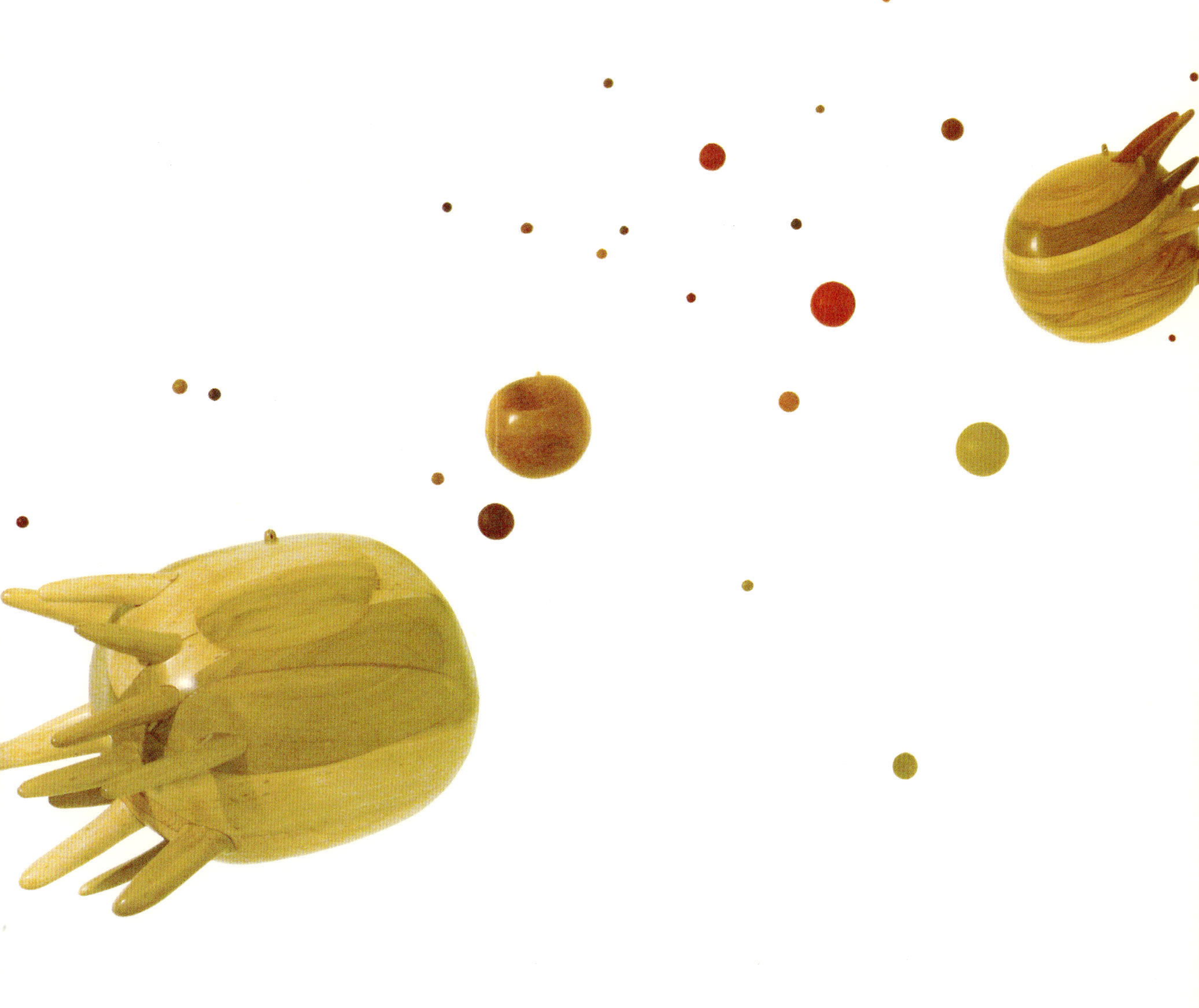

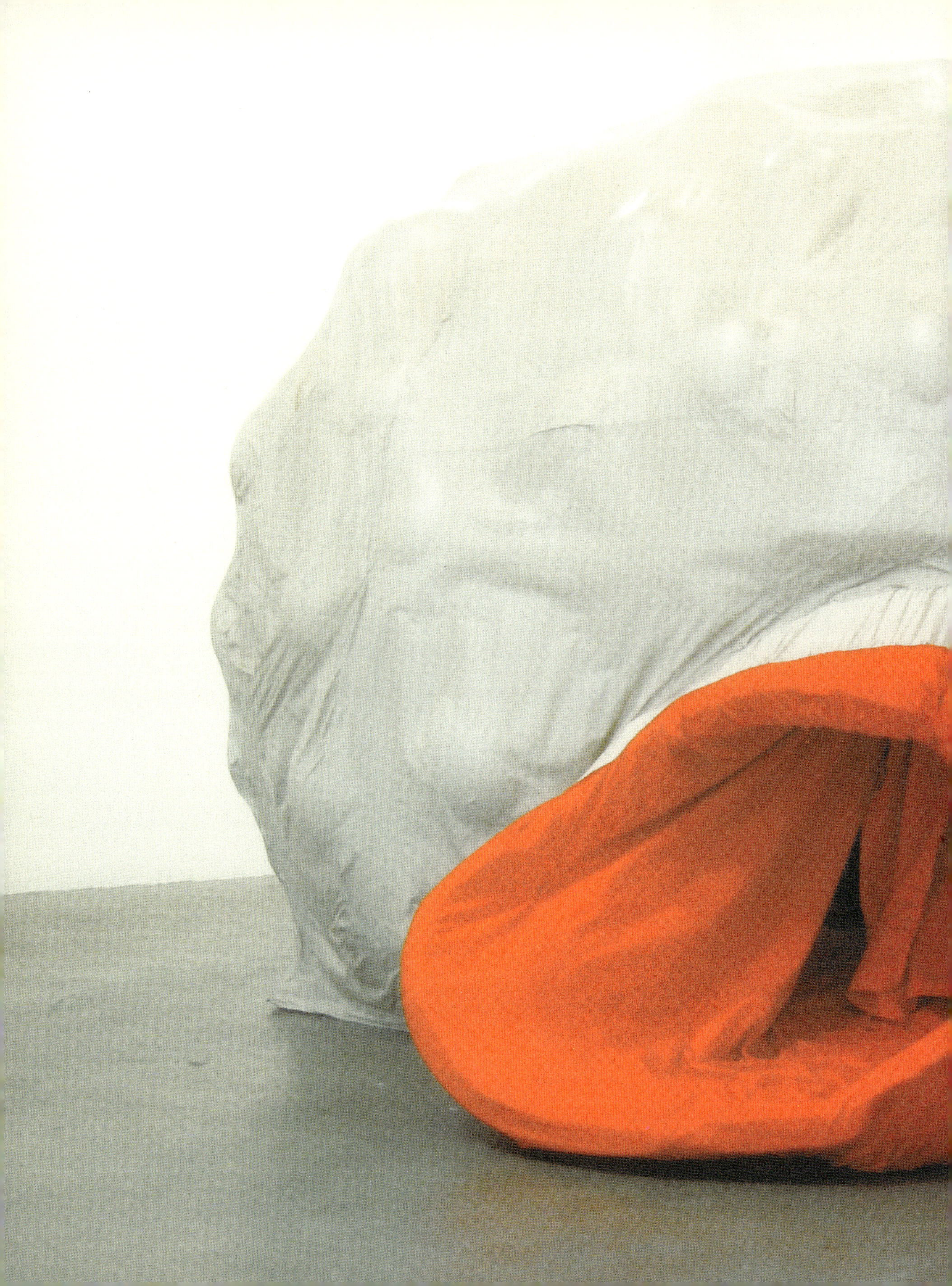

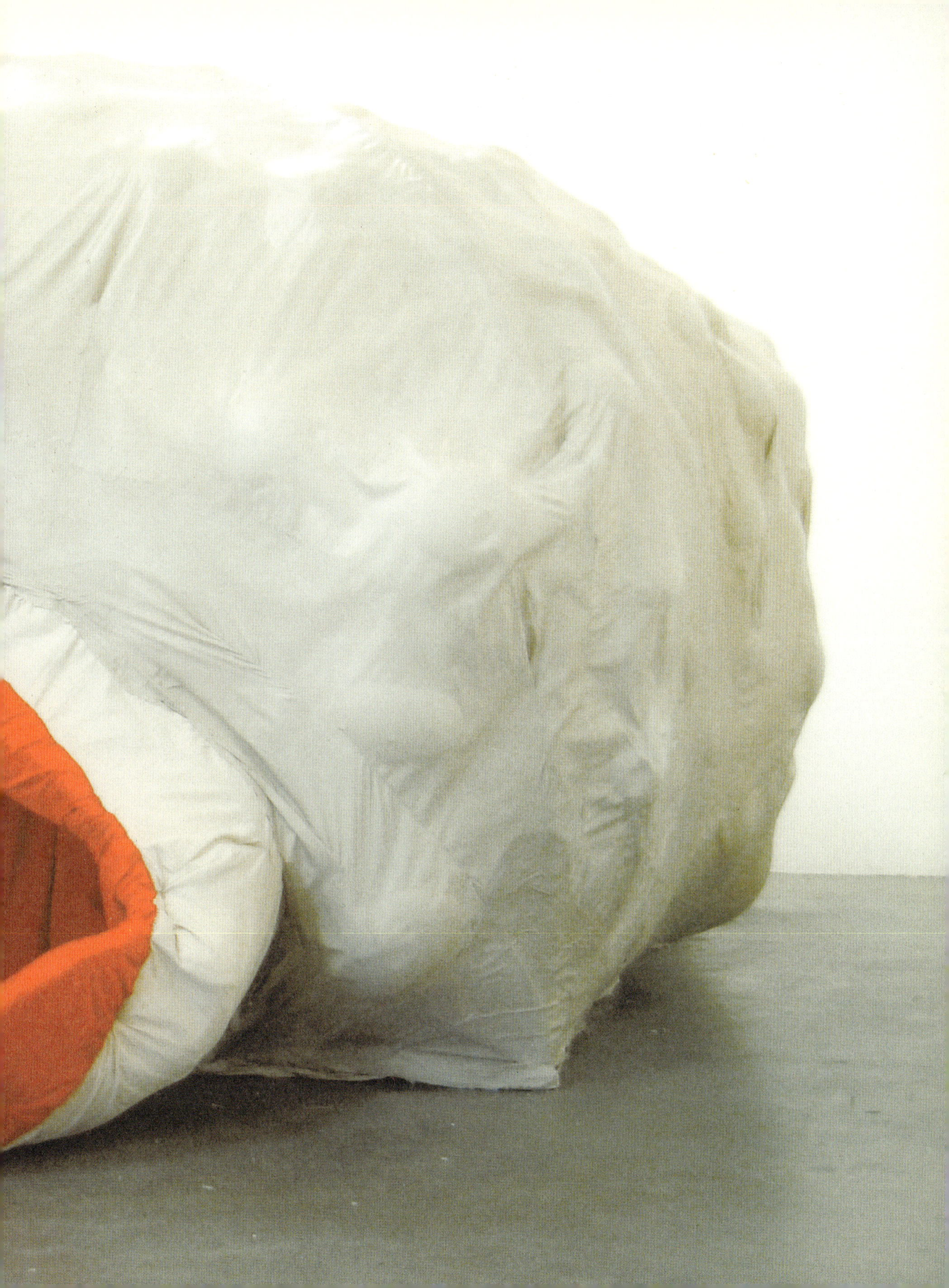

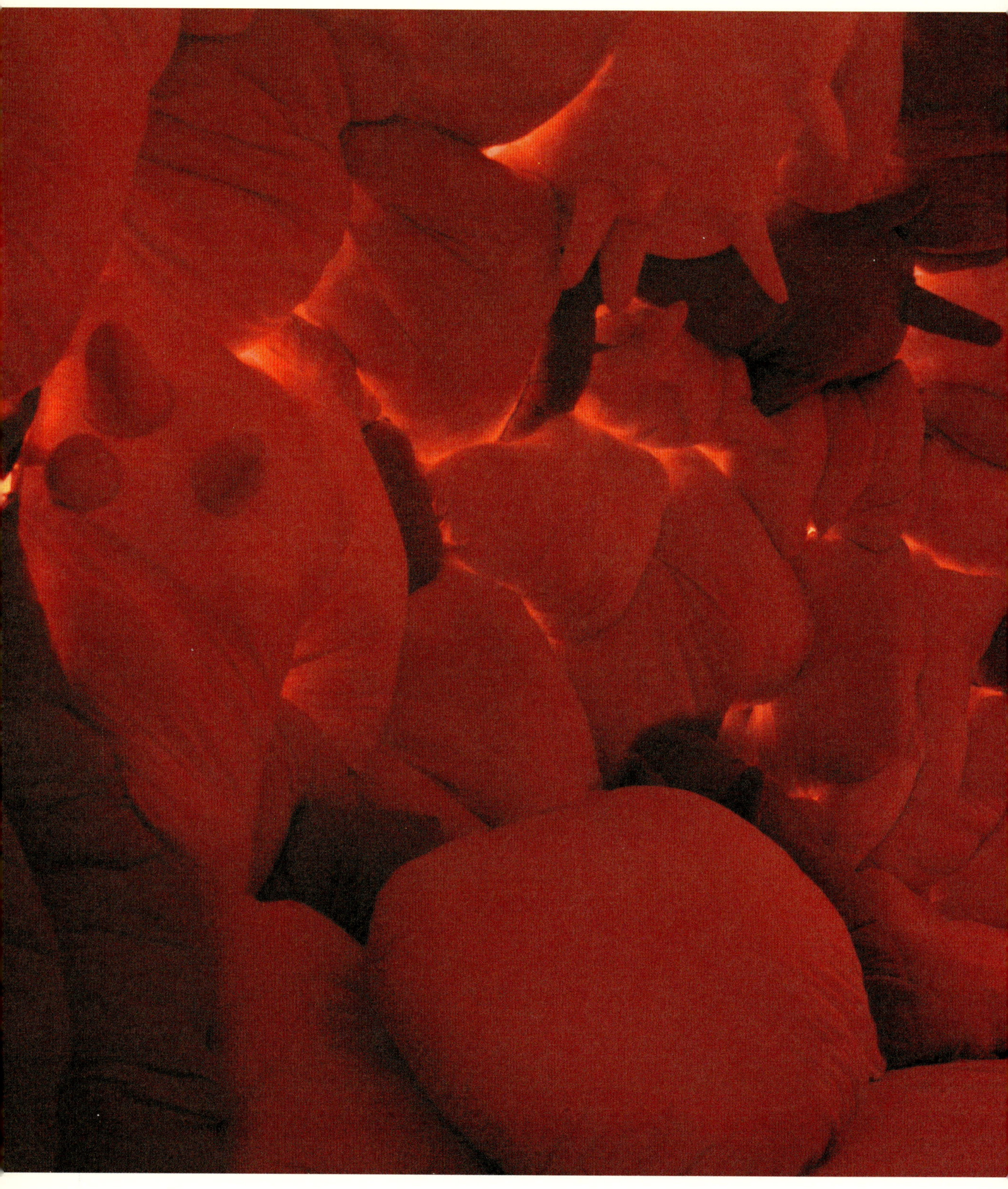

Borborygmi
(interior)

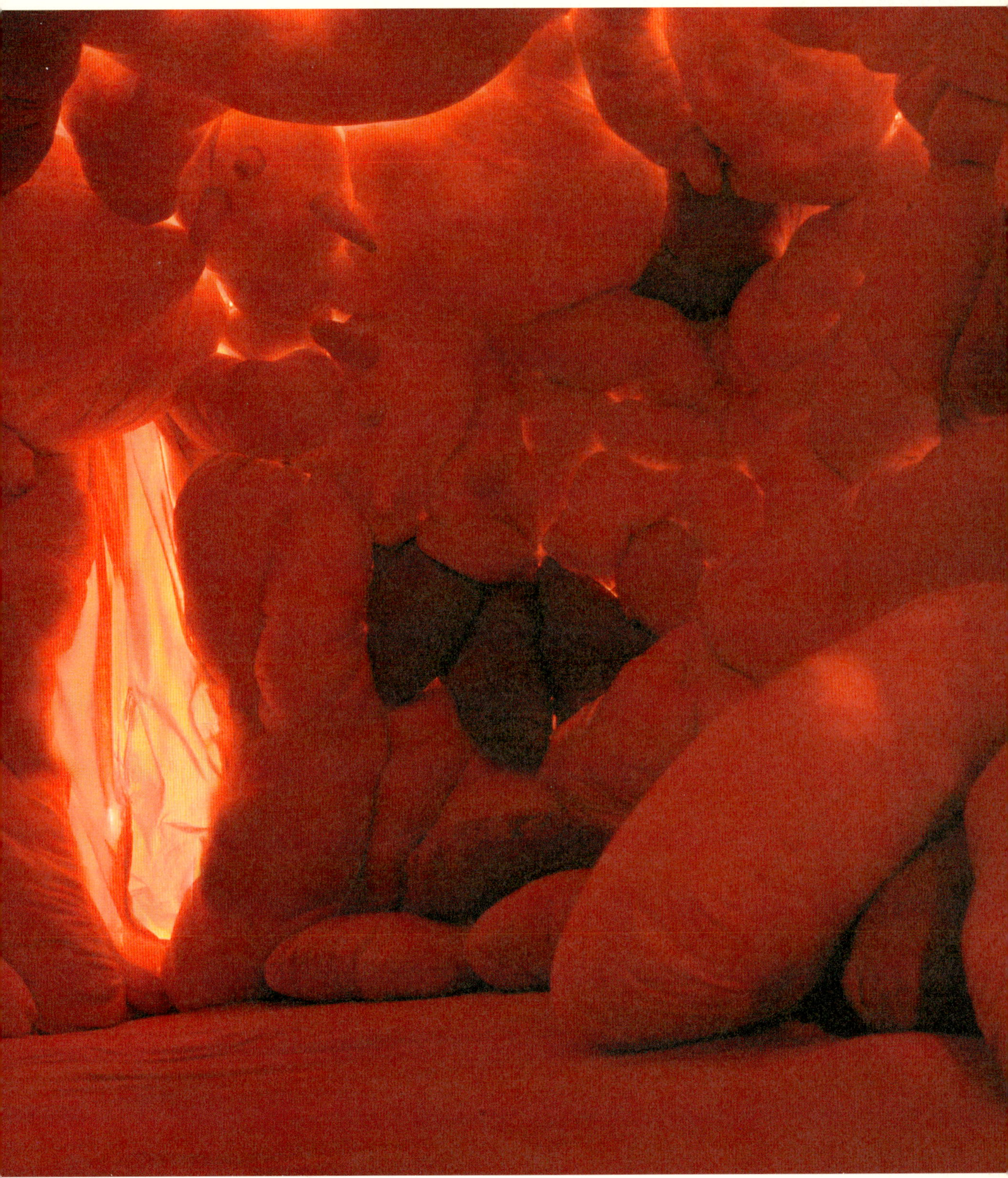

Glossary of Terms
Shana Nys Dambrot

Anthropomorphism (n): the attribution of a human form, human characteristics, or human behavior to nonhuman things, e.g. deities in mythology and animals in children's stories

Archaeology (n): the scientific study of ancient cultures through the examination of their material remains such as buildings, graves, tools, and other artifacts usually dug up from the ground

Artspeak (n): a secret language in which academics congratulate themselves on their superiority, (Usage): the following excerpt from the review I wrote of Brendan's Springtime show at Richard Heller Gallery, Santa Monica, that appeared in the July 2006 issue of *Artweek*:

> "Painter and impresario of the idiomatic post-illustration tribe Brendan Monroe employs a folksy, cartoonish and somewhat maudlin sensibility to express the fact, often forgotten or never realized in the first place, that the planet Earth is a living, breathing being to which human consciousness and existence are inextricably connected. His lexicon is rife with patterns abstracted from the natural world, especially dirt, grass, plants, and rocks, which he either lends anthropomorphized attributes or sets up as representatives of the raw materials of creation. Yet his work is not political; rather it is intimate and personal, metaphorical and romantically symbolist, and manifests a seamless dovetailing of concept and form. Monroe's aggressive tactile compositions are literally built up off the large, heavy paper he favors; visceral architectures of acrylic paint, collages of translucent or colored papers, and a sensual, metonymical topographic impasto. In representing unformed materials of earth and pigment as symbols of creative instinct, and then including literal, dimensional surface, he makes of his work a coherent dualism — it is that which it also represents. In the realm of art the work is paint and paper, in the world of idea it represents a primal, primordial act of self-expression."

Become (v): enter or assume a certain state or condition; undergo a change or development; come into existence

Beyond (prep): on or to the farther side of; outside the understanding, limits, or reach of; above; (n): the life after the present one

Body (n): the main part of the physical structure of a human being or animal, not including the head, arms, legs, or wings; a collection or amount of something, considered as a whole; an individual mass of something, especially water or land

Chaos (n): a state of extreme confusion and disorder; the formless and disordered state of matter before the creation of the cosmos; (physics) a dynamical system that is extremely sensitive to its initial conditions; (Greek mythology)

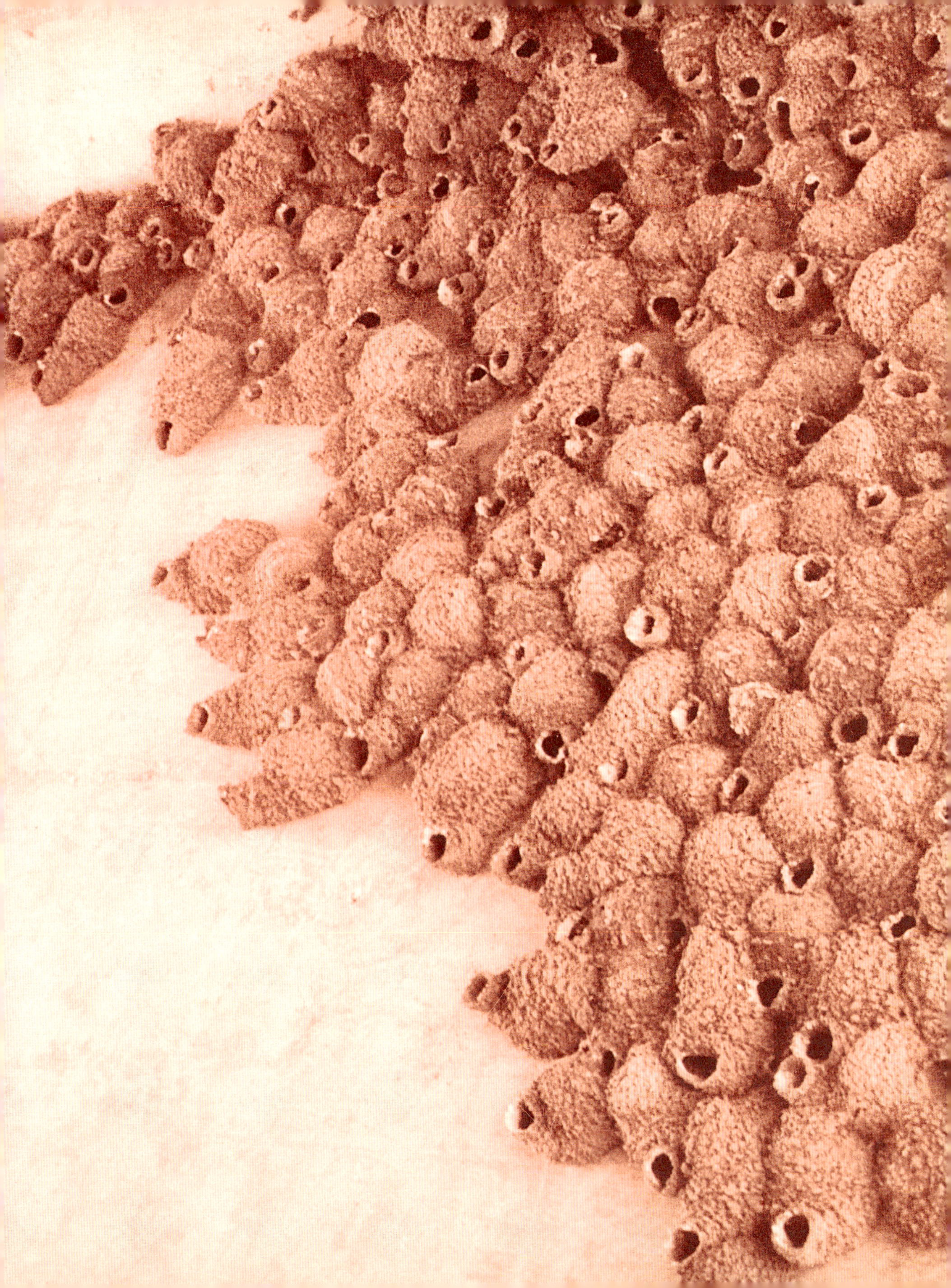

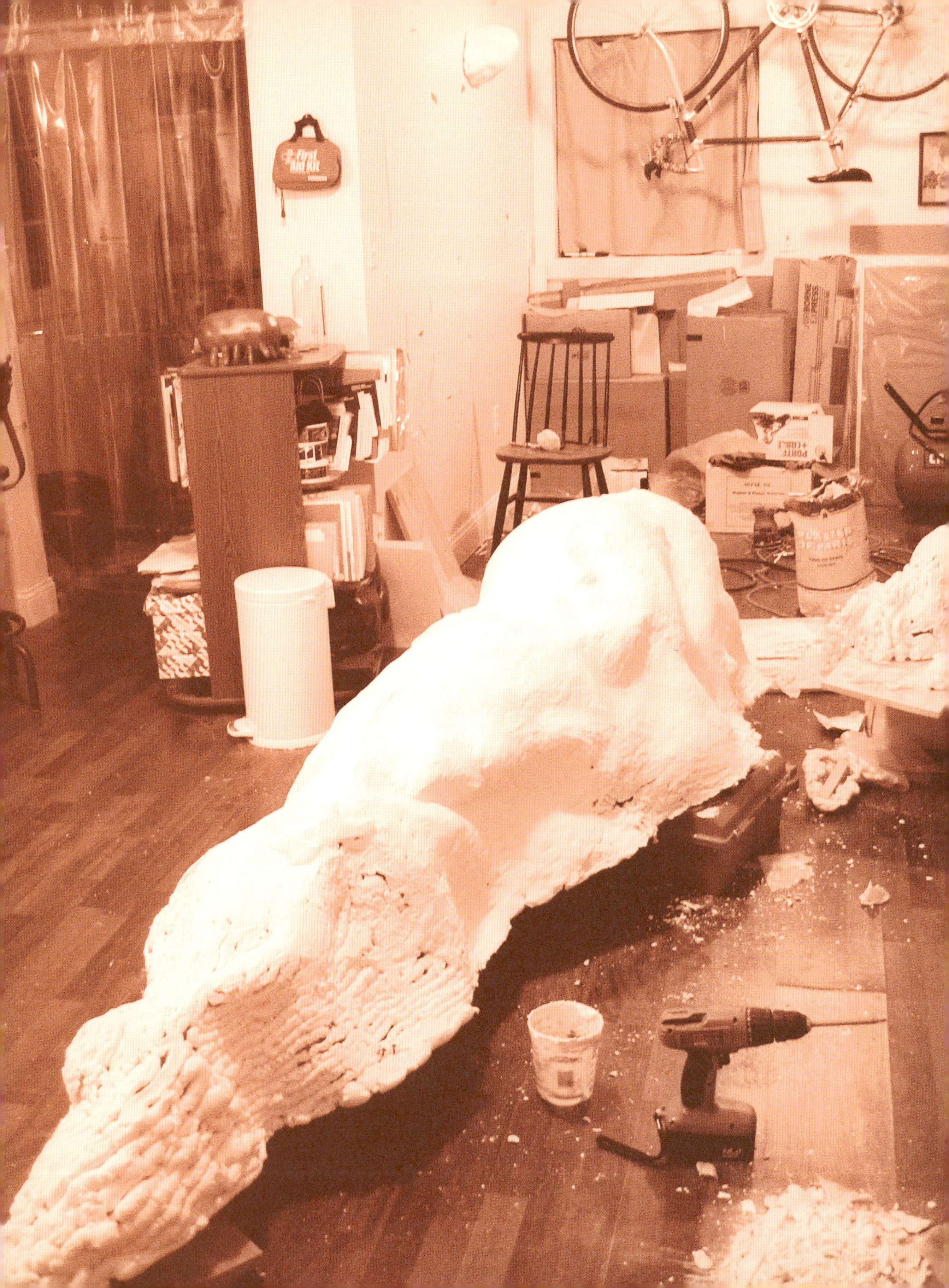

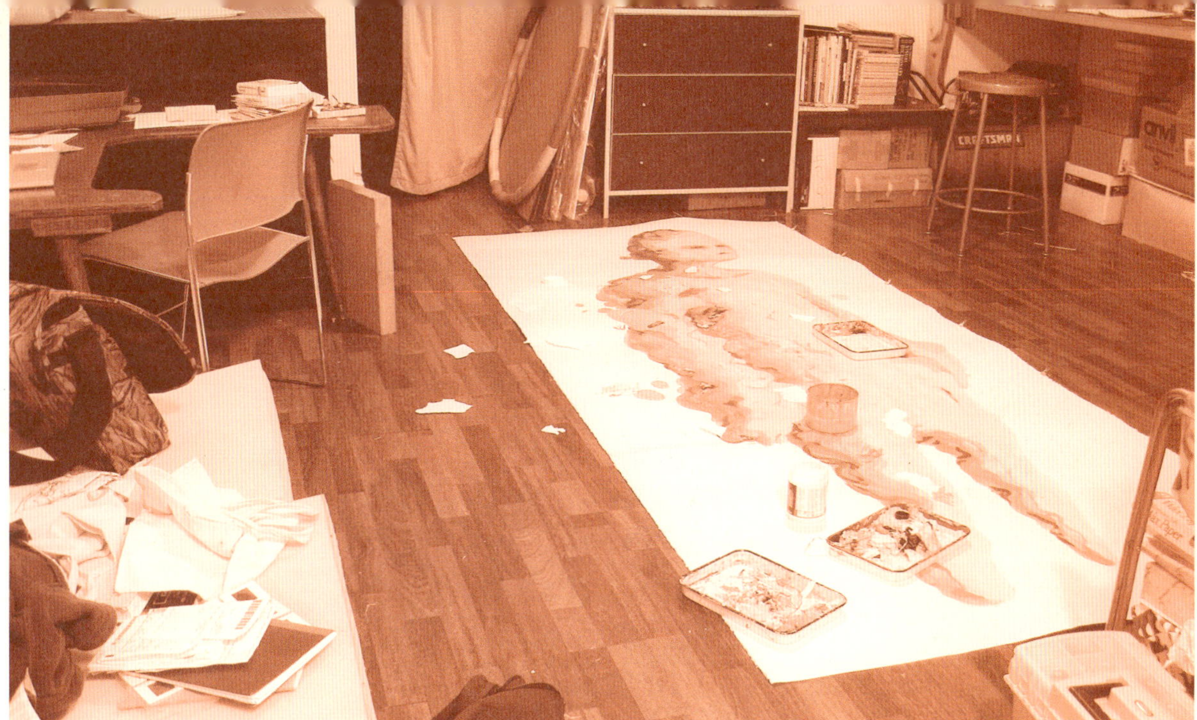

the most ancient of gods; the personification of the infinity of space preceding creation of the universe

Composition (n): the act of combining parts or elements to form a whole; manner of being composed; the resulting state or product; an aggregate material formed of two or more substances; the formation of compounds; a settlement by mutual agreement

Creation (n): the bringing of something into existence; the world and everything in it; a product of human imagination

Disinter (v): to unearth; exhume; bring from obscurity into view

Dream (n): a state of inattention owing to preoccupation with thoughts or fantasies; an involuntary vision occurring to a person awake; something of unreal beauty or charm

Drift (v): to build up and form heaps as a result of the action of the wind or water currents, or cause something such as snow, sand, or leaves to do this; to change or develop gradually, or move slowly from one point or position to another; to be carried along by the flow of water or air

Earth (n): the solid dry land surface of Earth, as opposed to the sea or sky; the soft workable material in which plants grow; all the human inhabitants of Earth; the pursuits of everyday human life, especially as opposed to matters of the spirit; in ancient and medieval philosophy, one of the four elements, earth, air, fire, and water, from which it was believed everything was made

Empathy (n): the transfer of somebody's own feelings and emotions to an object such as a painting

Evolution (n): the theoretical process by which all species develop from earlier forms of life; the gradual development of something into a more complex or better form; a pattern formed by a series of movements

Fable (n): a short story with a moral, especially one in which the characters are animals; a story about supernatural, mythological, or legendary characters and events

Fantasy (n): the combining of distinct parts or elements to form a whole; the manner in which such parts are combined or related; general makeup: the changing composition of the electorate; the result or product of composing; a mixture or compound; arrangement of artistic parts so as to form a unified whole.

Flesh (n): the physical body along with its needs and limitations, as opposed to the soul, mind, or spirit (see below, Hamlet)

Gather (v): to bring people or things together to form a group, or come together to form a group; to pick or harvest a crop; to compile something such as information or ideas from various sources; to accumulate a gradually increasing mass or quantity of something, or be accumulated gradually; to summon up energies, courage, or strength from within; to conclude something from intuition or observation; to draw somebody or something close; to pick or scoop somebody or something up

Germ (n): a microorganism, esp. when disease-producing;

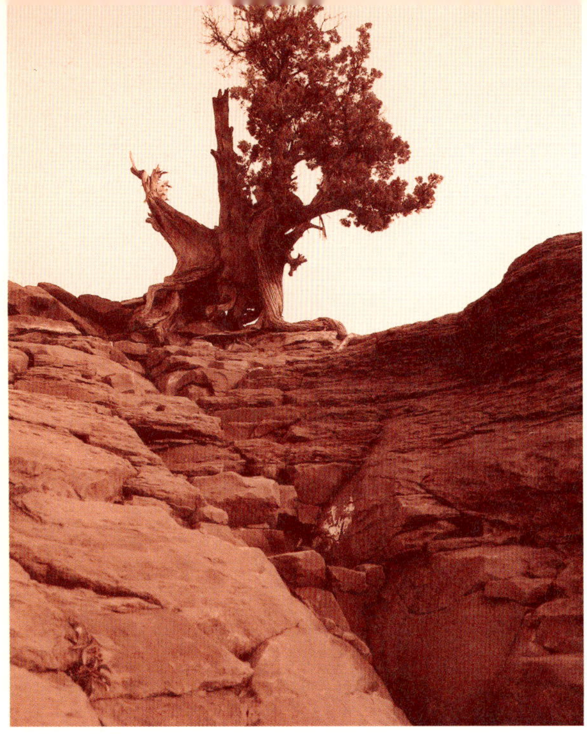

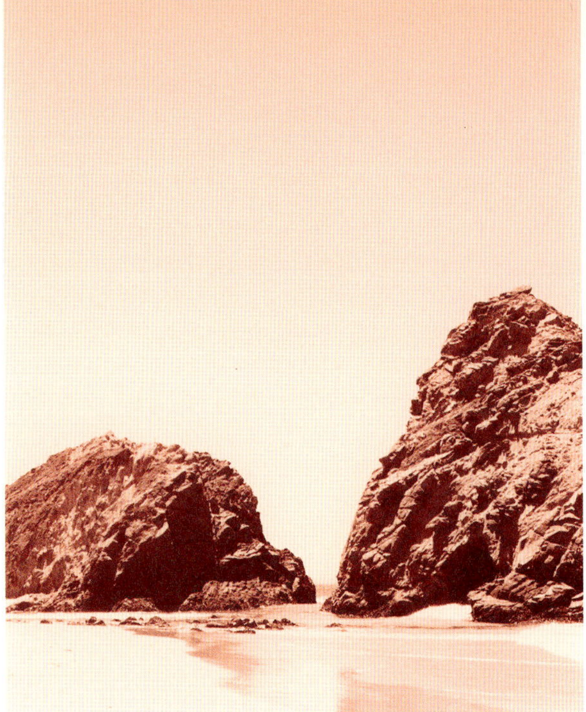

microbe; a bud, offshoot, or seed; the rudiment of a living organism; an embryo in its early stages; the initial stage in development or evolution, as a germ cell or ancestral form; a source of development; origin; seed

Grow (v): to produce something or allow it to be produced as part of a natural process

Hamlet (pn): tragic Shakespearean character who said, "O that this too too solid flesh would melt, thaw and resolve itself into a dew…"

Heal (v): to make healthy, whole, or sound; restore to health; free from ailment; to repair or reconcile; settle; to free from evil; cleanse; purify; to effect a cure (of a wound, broken bone, etc.) to become whole or sound; mend

Holistic (n): characterized by the view that a whole system of beliefs must be analyzed rather than simply its individual components; taking into account all of somebody's physical, mental, and social conditions in the treatment of illness

Incubate (v): to form or develop something such as a plan or an idea slowly and quietly over a period of time, or be formed or developed in this way

Inspiration (n): an inspiring or animating action or influence; something inspired, as an idea; a result of inspired activity; a thing or person that inspires; a divine influence directly and immediately exerted upon the mind or soul; the drawing of air into the lungs; inhalation

Integration (n): an act or instance of incorporating or combining into a whole; behavior that is in harmony with the environment; the organization of the constituent elements of the personality into a coordinated, harmonious whole

Jabberwocky (n): writing or speech with nonsensical words [coined by Lewis Carroll in "Jabberwocky," poem in *Through the Looking Glass* (1871)]

> `Twas brillig, and the slithy toves
>> Did gyre and gimble in the wabe:
>> All mimsy were the borogoves,
>> And the mome raths outgrabe.
>
> "Beware the Jabberwock, my son!
>> The jaws that bite, the claws that catch!
>> Beware the Jubjub bird, and shun
>> The frumious Bandersnatch!"
>
> He took his vorpal sword in hand:
>> Long time the manxome foe he sought—
>> So rested he by the Tumtum tree,
>> And stood awhile in thought.
>
> And, as in uffish thought he stood,
>> The Jabberwock, with eyes of flame,
>> Came whiffling through the tulgey wood,
>> And burbled as it came!

Join (v): to bring or put together or in contact; connect; to come into contact or union with; to bring together in a particular relation or for a specific purpose; unite; to meet or engage in (battle or conflict); to be contiguous or close; adjoin

Jung, Carl: 1875-1961, Swiss psychiatrist and psychologist. worked then broke with Freud. here's some things he said:

Tree in Sedona, AZ
2006

Beach in Big Sur, CA
2006

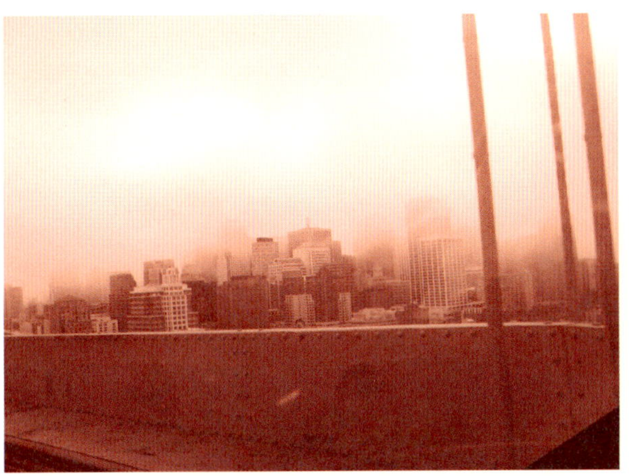

i   A man who has not passed through the inferno of his passions has never overcome them.

ii   As far as we can discern, the sole purpose of human existence is to kindle a light in the darkness of mere being.

iii   Everything that irritates us about others can lead us to an understanding of ourselves.

iv   In all chaos there is a cosmos, in all disorder a secret order.

v   In my case Pilgrim's Progress consisted in my having to climb down a thousand ladders until I could reach out my hand to the little clod of earth that I am.

vi   Man's task is to become conscious of the contents that press upward from the unconscious.

Kinetics (pn): the branch of mechanics that studies the actions of forces in producing or changing the motion of masses.

kinnikinnick=kinnikinnic (n): a mixture of bark, dried leaves, and sometimes tobacco, formerly smoked by Indians and pioneers in the Ohio valley; any of various plants used in this mixture; literally "that which is mixed"

Kiva (n): a large chamber in a Pueblo Indian village, often wholly or partly underground, used for religious ceremonies and other purposes

Lao-tzu: Chinese philosopher reputed founder of Taoism [Taoist propriety and ethics emphasize the Three Jewels of the Tao; namely, compassion, moderation, and humility. Taoist thought focuses on wu wei ("non-action"), spontaneity, humanism, and emptiness. An emphasis is placed on the link between people and nature. Taoism teaches that this link lessened the need for rules and order, and leads one to a better understanding of the world]

Life (n): the general condition that distinguishes organisms from inorganic objects and dead organisms, being manifested by growth through metabolism, a means of reproduction, and internal regulation in response to the environment; the animate existence or period of animate existence of an individual; a corresponding state, existence, or principle of existence conceived of as belonging to the soul; the general or universal condition of human existence; the course of existence or sum of experiences and actions that constitute a person's existence; animation; liveliness; spirit; resilience; elasticity; the force that makes or keeps something alive; the vivifying or quickening principle; pungency or strong, sharp flavor, as of substances when fresh or in good condition; nature or any of the forms of nature as the model or subject of a work of art

Lost (adj): I am not lost; I am here. The path is lost

Malevich, Kasmir (Russian Painter, 1878-1935) From his Suprematist Manifesto circa 1915

Nothing in the objective world is as "secure and unshakeable" as it appears to our conscious minds. We should accept nothing as predeter-

San Francisco, CA
2006

Atlantic Ocean
2006

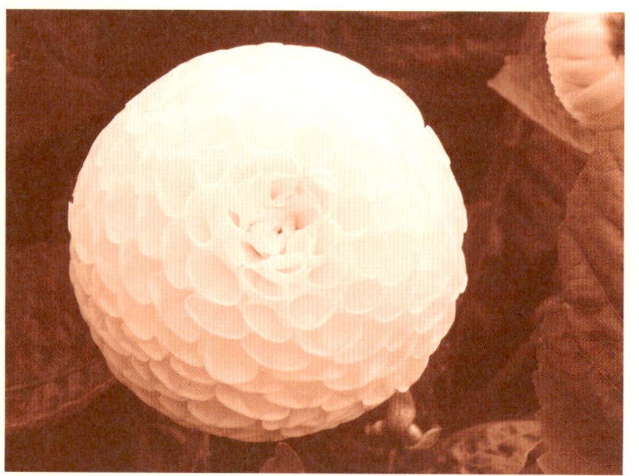

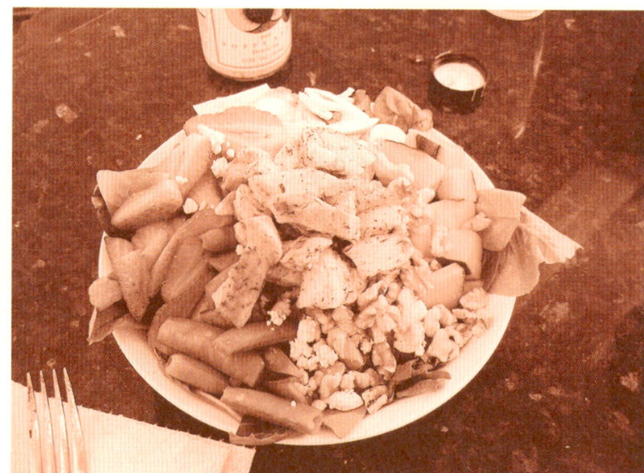

mined as constituted for eternity. Every "firmly established," familiar thing can be shifted about and brought under a new and, primarily, unfamiliar order. Why then should it not be possible to bring about an artistic order? ... Our life is a theater piece, in which nonobjective feeling is portrayed by objective imagery.

Matter (n): the material substance of the universe that has mass, occupies space, and is convertible to energy; something that is extended in space and persists through time, and is contrasted with mind; the substance of which any physical object consists or is composed; physical or corporeal substance in general, whether solid, liquid, or gaseous, esp. as distinguished from incorporeal substance, as spirit or mind, or from qualities, actions, and the like; a substance discharged by a living body, especially pus; that which relates to form as potentiality does to actuality

Multivocal (adj): having many or different meanings of equal probability or validity

Nature (n): the physical world including all natural phenomena and living things; the forces and processes collectively that control the phenomena of the physical world independently of human volition or intervention…

Nymph (n): in mythology, a minor goddess or spirit of nature inhabiting areas of natural beauty such as woods, mountains, and rivers and traditionally regarded as a beautiful young woman; the larva of some insects such as mayflies, dragonflies, and grasshoppers that resembles the adult and develops into the adult insect directly, without passing through an intermediate pupa stage

Oracle (n): somebody or something considered to be a source of knowledge, wisdom, or prophecy; the most sacred area in either of the Temples mentioned in the Bible, often referred to as the Holy of Holies

Organic (adj): forming a basic and inherent part of something and largely responsible for its identity or makeup; being made of parts that exist together in a seemingly natural relationship

Perihelion (n): the point in the orbit of a celestial body that is nearest to the Sun (the point farthest from the sun is called aphelion)

Primordial (adj): existing at the beginning of time or of the development of something; essential or basic to something; relating to cells, tissues, organs, or organisms at the earliest stage of development

Quiver (v): to shake rapidly with small movements; (n): a long narrow case for holding arrows; those arrows

Quixotic (adj): ending to take a romanticized view of life; motivated by an idealism that overlooks practical considerations; tending to act on impulses; referring to Don Quixote, hero of a novel by Miguel de Cervantes

Regenerate (v): to form again, or become formed again; to return from a state of decline to a revitalized state, or cause something to do this; to replace lost tissue or a lost limb or

Flower in Bloom / Chicken Salad
2006

Evah Fan in "Borborygmi" stuffing
2006

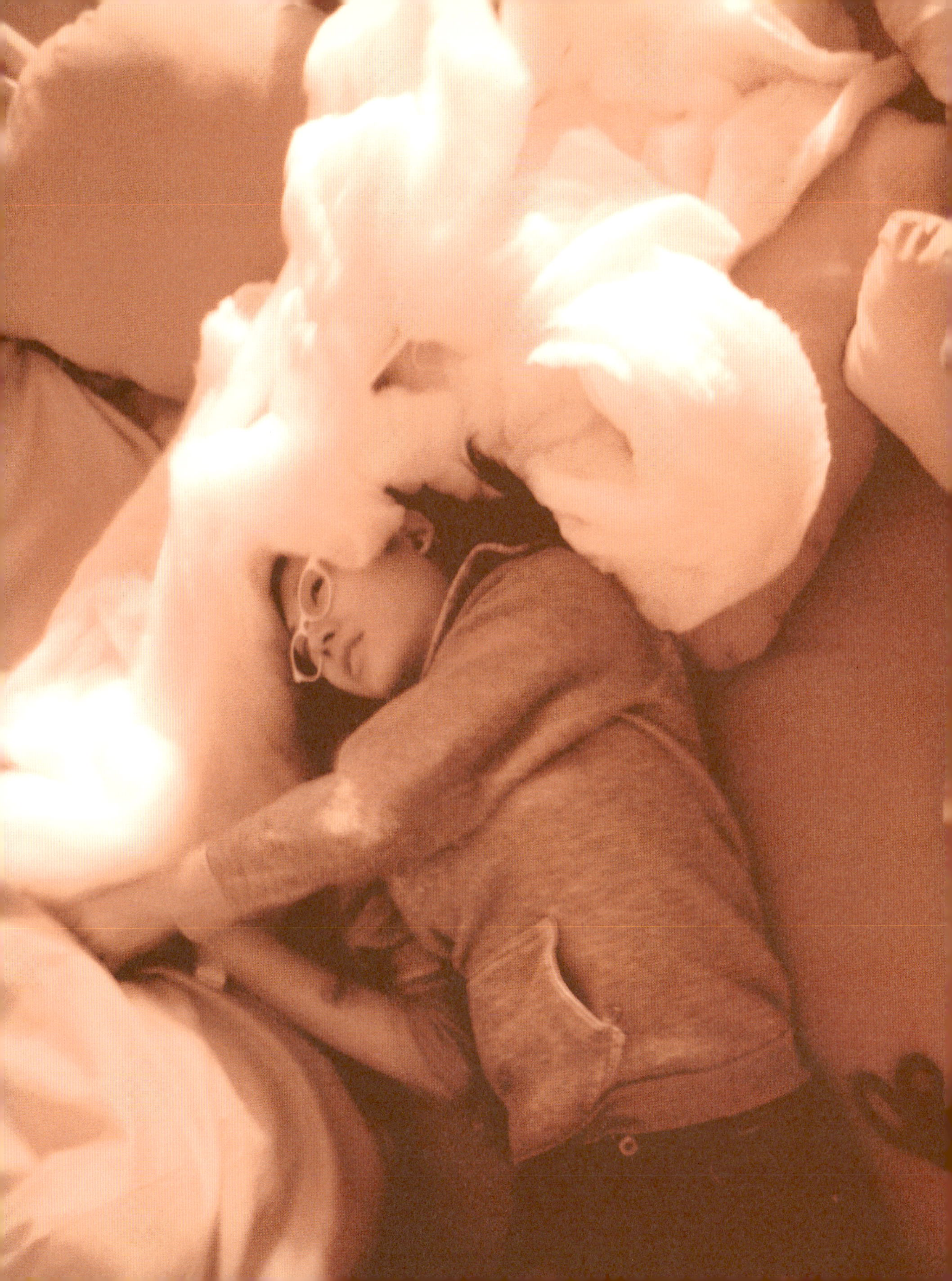

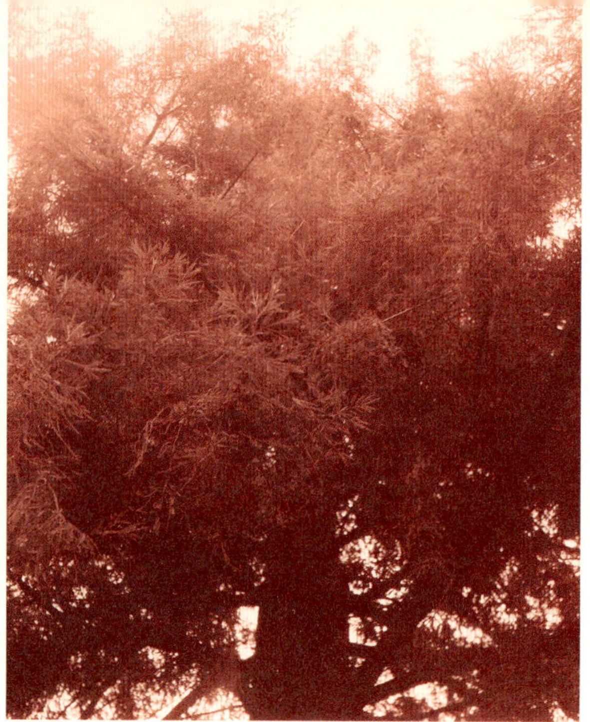

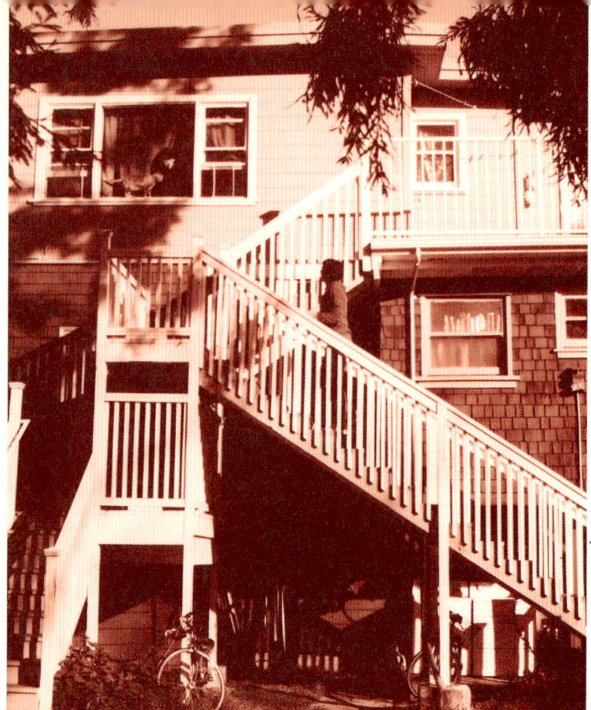

organ with a new growth, or grow again after loss; to restore and renew somebody morally or spiritually; (adj): spiritually reborn, renewed, or restored to health

Sonnet No. 18:

> Shall I compare thee to a Summer's day? / Thou art more lovely and more temper- ate / Rough winds do shake the darling buds of May / And Summer's lease hath all too short a date / Sometime too hot the eye of heaven shines / And oft' is his gold complex- ion dimm'd / And every fair from fair some- time declines / By chance or nature's changing course untrimm'd / But thy eternal Summer shall not fade / Nor lose possession of that fair thou owest / Nor shall Death brag thou wan- derest in his shade / When in eternal lines to time thou growest / So long as men can breathe, or eyes can see / So long lives this, and this gives life to thee.

Symbol (n): something that stands for or represents some- thing else, especially an object representing an abstraction; an object or act that represents an impulse or wish in the un- conscious mind that has been repressed

Transcend (v): to go beyond a limit or range, e.g. of thought or belief; to exist above and apart from the material world

Transcendent (adj): in Kant's philosophical system, exceed- ing the limits of experience and therefore unknowable ex- cept hypothetically; superior in quality or achievement; above or outside all known categories; existing outside the material universe and so not limited by it

Transcendental (adj): independent of human experience of phenomena but within the range of knowledge

Uproot (v): to pull a plant and its roots from the soil; to dis- place somebody or something from a home or habitual envi- ronment; to remove or destroy something completely

Urania (pn): ancient Greek Muse of Astronomy, planetary namesake, ancient friend of seafarers and other navigators and travelers

Visceral (adj): proceeding from instinct rather than from rea- soned thinking; characterized by or showing basic emotions; relating to or affecting one or more internal organs of the body

Weather (n): the state of the atmosphere with regard to tem- perature, cloudiness, rainfall, wind, and other meteorological conditions; (adj.): toward the wind; (v): to change color or be- come worn because of prolonged exposure to the weather, or make something do this; to endure the damaging effects of; to come safely through a crisis or difficult time

X (n): the archetypal variable in mathematical equations; the traditional method of marking locations on maps; a crude substitute for a person's signature; shorthand for Christ

Yearning (n): a strong desire, often tinged with sadness; a feeling of affection, tenderness, or compassion

Youth (n): the period of human life between childhood and

Tree outside Berkeley studio, CA
2007

Evah & Brendan's Berkeley apartment, CA
2007

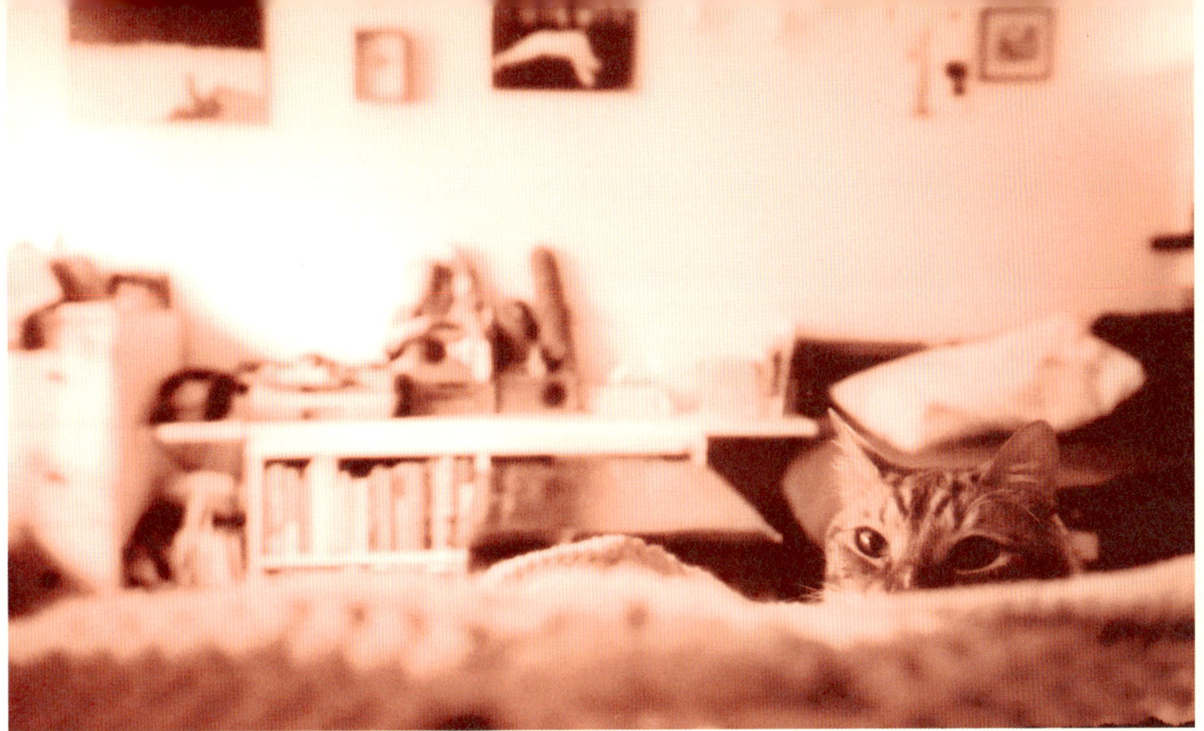

maturity; the first stage in landscape formation in which fast-flowing streams travel down steep mountain valleys

Zoarium (n): a collection of distinct organisms that together form a compound organism

Zoomorphism (n): the use of animal figures in art and design, or of animal symbols in literature; the attribution of animal forms or characteristics to gods

Jalapeño
Jordan Stark, 2007

Interview with
Dr. Simon F. Park

SP How do you arrive at a finished painting? Do you have a preformed image in your mind and work closely to this or do your works evolve on the canvas?

BM That can go a few ways. Sometimes I have a pretty good idea of what I want to achieve and I can just paint it till it's done, starting from my pencil sketch. Most of the time it's not that simple though. I often find that as I go along working on a piece things will look bad if they go how I thought might have been good, so things are moved around, painted over, and added to. If I'm lucky, the painting will just sort of be finished. After a long enough time of working on something so closely, taking a step away can give me the better complete visual of it as having been finished, then I stop.

SP Where do your ideas for a painting/artwork come from? Do they arise spontaneously or are they triggered by events or things that you see?

BM There's usually a kind of narrowing down of ideas. The bigger ideas starting with being interested in microorganisms and the world that is ours on a smaller and overlooked level. So from there I try and draw in my sketchbook, but that doesn't always happen. More specific ideas come out of readings, experiences, or even just me simply admiring things as beautiful objects.
For example, a few months back I did this painting "Eat-

ing Shit" *[pg 75]*, where the little yellow blob guy is eating a burger that looks to be made of something trashy. That one came out of some decisions I made at the time, that resulted in a nervous worry about my life, future, career, and if I made the right choice. . .

SP "Redness" *[pg 60]* could be interpreted as a surreal representation of a clot of human red blood cells. When such clots form in the human body they can cause illness and often death as they lead to strokes and heart attacks. Where did the inspiration for this work come from?

BM I like the idea of these red cell-like shapes living, merging, and mutating. They could be in the process of multiplying to form something larger or they could be wrapping themselves around a core meaning to keep it protected. Actually, I think I was most inspired to make this because of the color. I tend to have a love for warm colors and particularly pure red. My favorite thing about making this piece was the idea of bringing life into that color with basic but sort of sensuous forms.

SP "Ballet of Arterial Lights" also appears to have a medical theme. It could be interpreted as a representation of the particles in blood that lead to cholesterol deposition and thus the narrowing of arteries that can be a prelude to heart attacks or strokes. Where did the inspiration for this work come from?

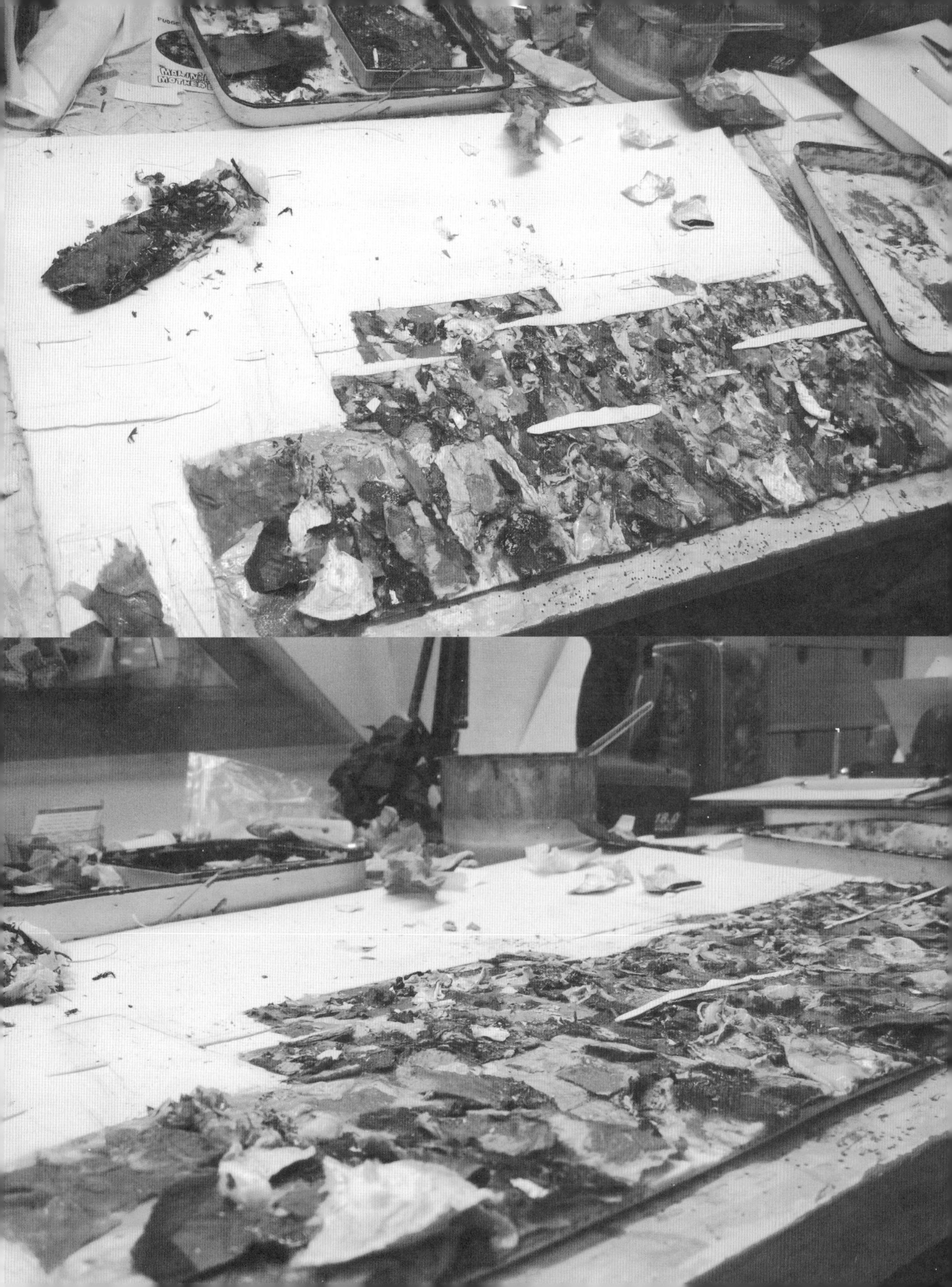

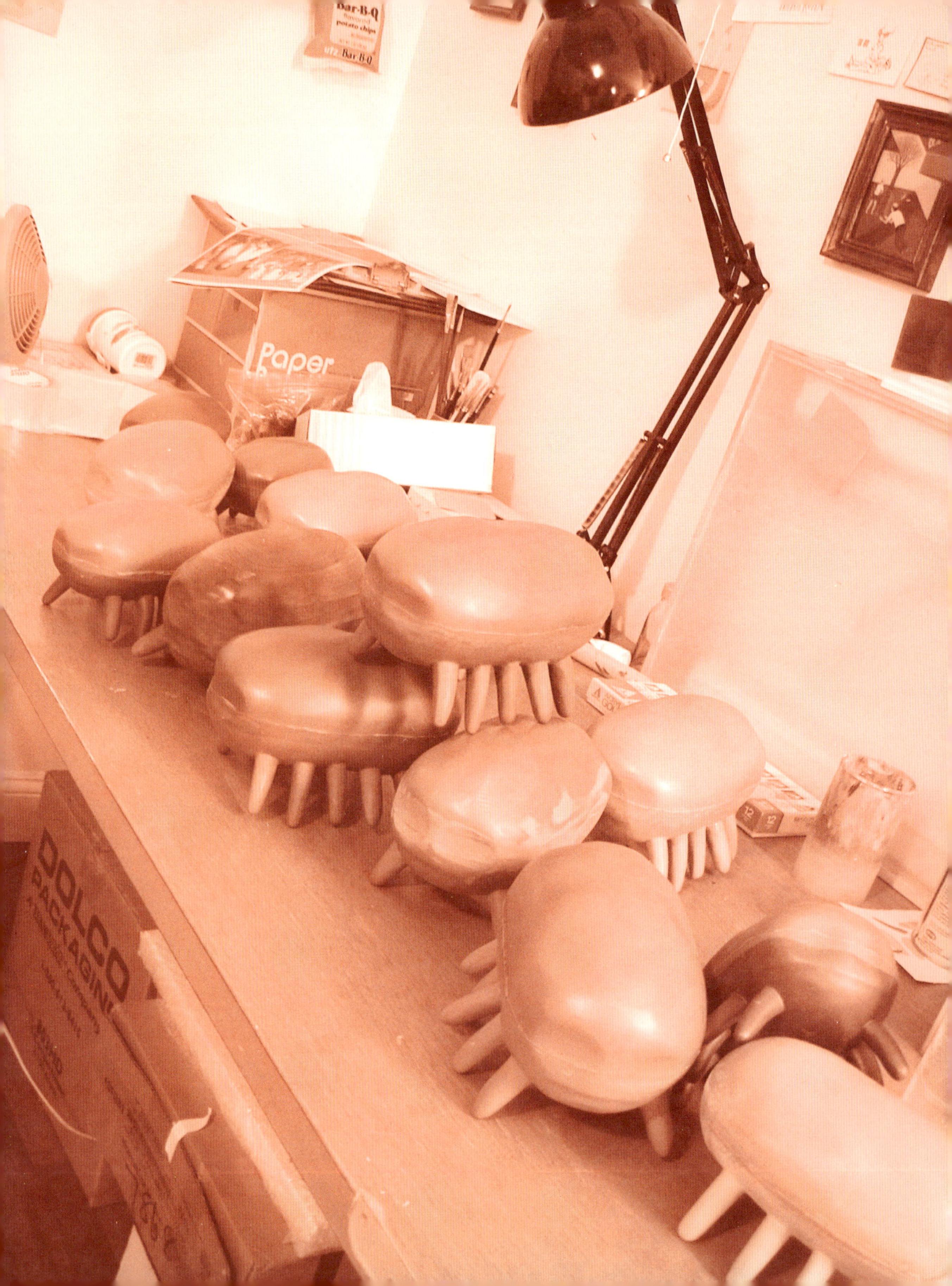

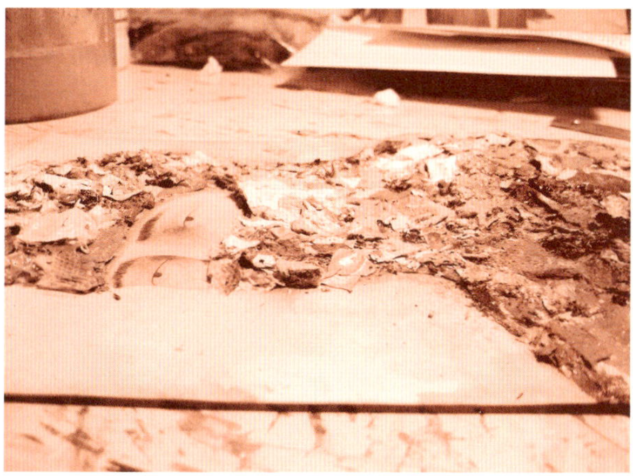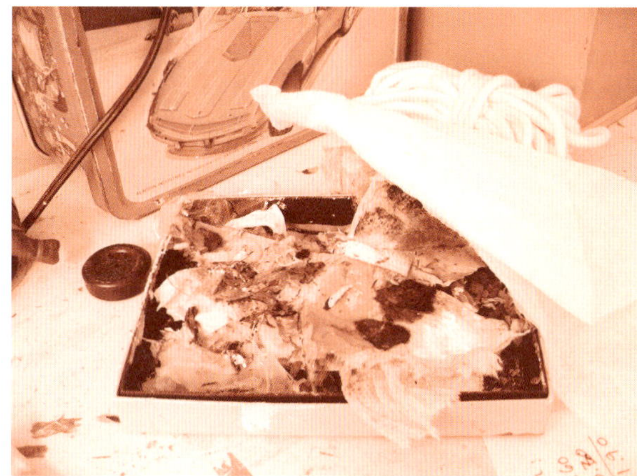

BM This one comes more directly from an idea of flowing fluids and the multitude of possibilities of what could be in that fluid. The title is referring to the smaller and more colorful particles nimbly finding their ways around the dirtied fat cholesterol build up that could be terrible for a blood stream.

SP In the UK there is an insect larvae called a caddisfly, which builds a silk cocoon and then coats it with material from its environment (like gravel) for protection and camouflage. "Suits Me" *[pg 26]* and "Personal Ninja" *[pg 61]* seem to mimic this natural theme. Are the figures hiding from something?

BM I don't think hiding, but protecting themselves could be part of it. The paint scrapings are collected by me as I go along with other work. Paint dries on the palette and I scrape it off with a razor blade then put it in a box. So in these paintings the scrapings or basically trash (compost as Mike described) are meant to be collections created over a long period of time that these people have worked hard to create. Some others like this are "Can't Hold it Up" *[pg 19]* and "Can't Keep it Down" *[pg 18]*.
When I was in school I worked at an aquarium store and they sold decorator crabs, they also have those collecting behaviors like the caddisfly. Sea life in general has a ton of other really interesting creatures.

SP I remember watching the original version of "Fantastic Voyage" in which a team of miniaturized people are injected into a human body to treat a life threatening illness. In this science fiction film one of the characters swims free in the blood stream of the patient and is attacked by the body's immune system, the components of which build up to form a coating on the miniature body. "Suits Me" seems reminiscent of this process as the individual seems to be covered by an accretion of material. Is this person in the painting under attack?

BM I don't think I've ever seen that film, but now I really want to. I have seen "Innerspace," sounds like a similar idea of small people going inside bodies.
The person in "Suits Me" isn't under attack. Actually I mean for him to be OK with everything going on, to be pleasantly satisfied. I think in the majority of my work I'd like the characters to have this sort of "this is normal and usual" attitude. In this one there are those little red mite-like things burrowing and working through his scrapings suit. They are more meant to have a friendly symbiotic relationship.
The painting "Greater Mitosis" *[pg 50 / 51]* I think is actually a little closer to the "Fantastic Voyage" person being attacked, but I hope my image is less clear to whether the external cellular things are helping or harming.

SP A lot of your works contain imagery that seems to be inspired by microbiology. Where does your insight into the mi-

Personal Ninja [pg. 61] / Scrap box
2006

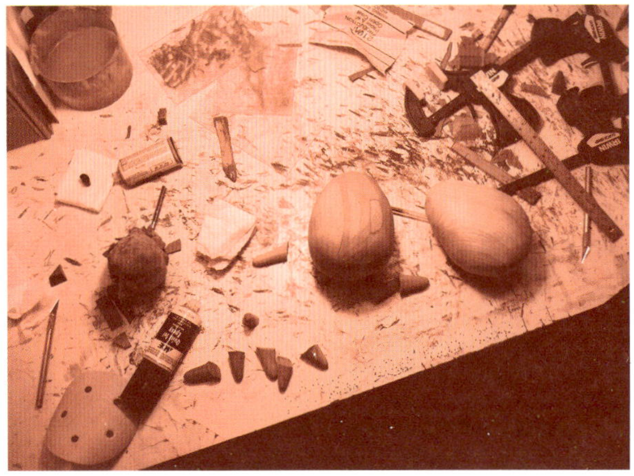 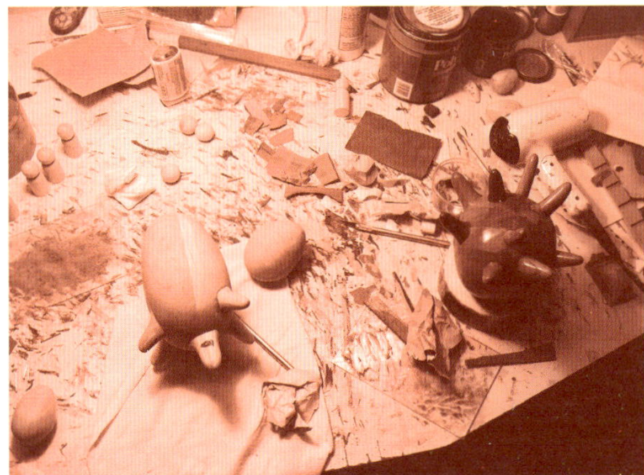

crobiological world come from and why are you inspired to reference it?

BM I've always been interested in sciences. It's one of those things that came easy to me and I enjoyed it through school when I was young. I really didn't like English or History type classes, but Math and Science I did. My parents helped that too, they met while my mother was between lab jobs at USC Medical Center and I think my dad at the time was in residency to be a medical doctor. Now my dad is no longer a doctor and my mom is teaching High School Science courses. They also really got me into outdoorsy stuff, camping, nature, gardening. I've only studied Biology and Chemistry in community colleges, so I would only consider myself somewhat knowledgeable of basics in the subjects.
My work has been referencing the microbiological world for about the past two years. Before that there was more outdoors, trees, deserts, swamps and such. Only more recently I have begun to read again more in detail about my references, though that sometimes but doesn't always cross over into my work.

SP The human body sheds around 7 million skin scales per minute. Many of the figures in your work are indistinct and surrounded by particles. Does this reflect the leakage of this microscopic tissue from our bodies, and through this, the merging of the human form with its environment?

BM It is definitely a merging or mingling with the surrounding environment. It's not just figures either, most of my paintings have these particles in some way or another. I like the idea of every little thing being a smaller part of a larger world or even universe. These pieces and parts of figures can travel between images then blend, pass through, and flake off of others. It's all these little things that turn into building blocks for the larger forms.

SP Soil is Nature's most complicated and vital organ, and like the human liver, it is a supplier of nutrients, a recycler of waste material and detoxifier of poisons. Given time, and the opportunity, it will even recycle the human form. The agents of soil's remarkable transformations, and thus its ability to provide sustenance to other life, are the bacteria. Two of your works, "Growth of a Growth" *[pg 40 / 41]* and "Holding Seams" *[pg 20 / 21]* contain figures emerging from or being subsumed by soil. Are these inspired by soil's remarkable microbiological properties?

BM "Holding Seams" is about the life of soil growing and making eventually what could be a human. I guess going the opposite direction of decomposing. I wasn't thinking about soil's microbiological properties though. While "Growth of a Growth" is a little more like being in a limbo place, between above and below. If you look closely you'll see the cells (more particles) just underneath the surface. I made a few paint-

Sculptures in progress
2006

(opposite)
Lily pads at Conservatory of Flowers in San Francisco, CA
2006

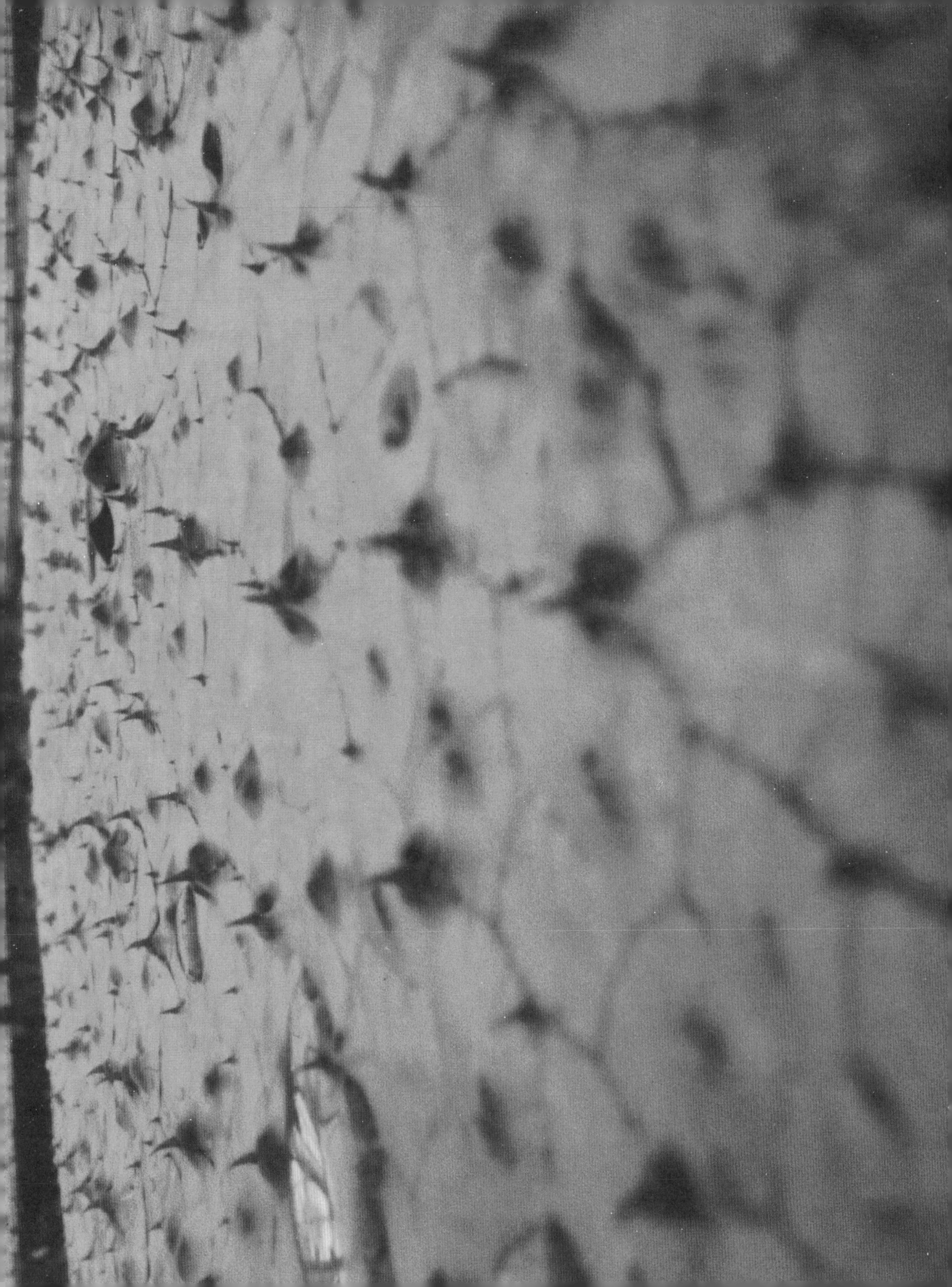

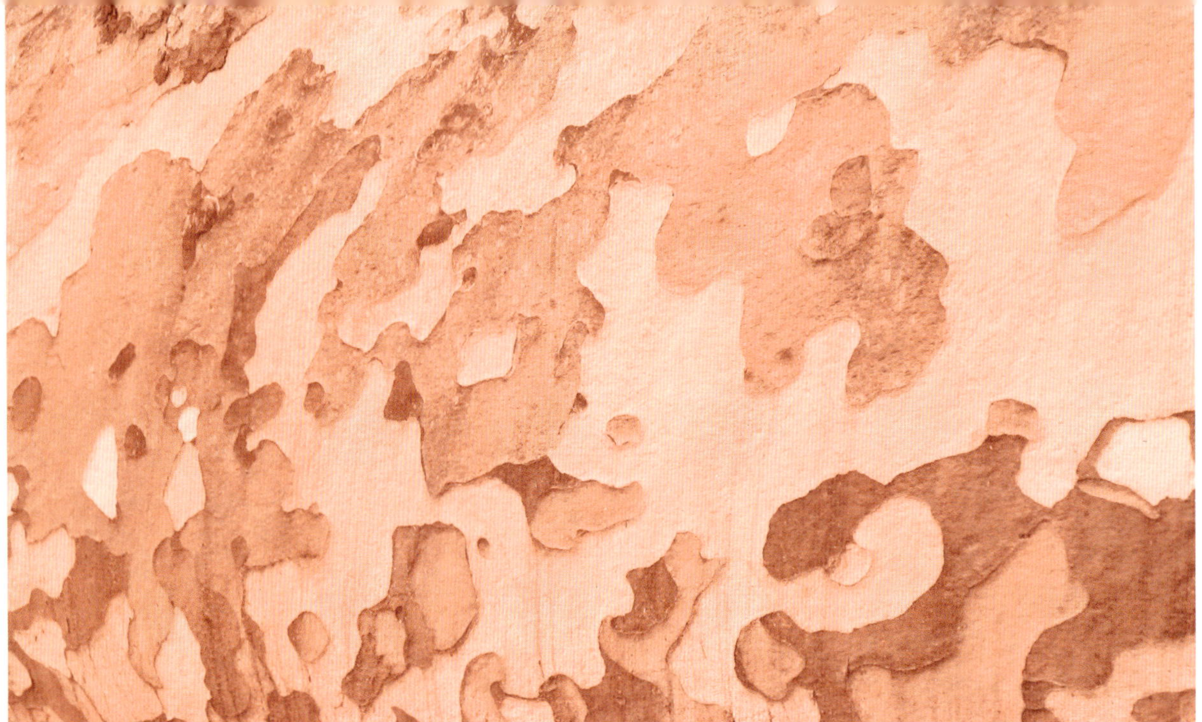

ings at this time that were kind of like a transition from the top levels to the inside micro levels. This series came from earlier work of the smaller life that could exist in grass and dirt, then the ground sort of became a living being and the surface was turned into layers of what could be skin. The grass on top was now like hair and there were all sorts of new things to explore above and below. Then I started thinking more about microbiology, but having to deal with beings rather than soil.

SP There is a recurring male figure in some of your works that appears as a child in "What am I?," and as an adult in "Allergens" *[pg 16]*, "Having No Other Choice" *[pg 22]*, and "Becoming of Me" *[pg 107]* . The figure possesses a melancholic quality. Is this a reflection of aspects of your own outlook on life?

BM I don't think I have a melancholic look on life. Though he (the male figure) is often some part of me. I would like him to have a quiet knowledge and calm position in the images. He's not exactly in a happy mood but I hope not too sad of a mood either. Though maybe that just ends up happening. Sometimes I worry about where things are going, like this career, where life is going to take me, if things will go where I want them to go. . . but in general I tend to keep a good outlook on things and focus on brighter sides.

SP Many of your works contain general references to microbiology in terms of the reoccurring shapes that you use. Why then does the sculpture "Mycobacterium" *[pg 121]* contain an explicit reference to a particular genus of bacteria and one that can cause tuberculosis and leprosy?

BM I came across Mycobacterium in an old textbook I found somewhere. I was thinking that these bacterium, although terrible for us, must be really happy to find the right host and be able to multiply like crazy. So I liked these happy dancing microorganism-like sculptures to have that perspective.

SP Most of us will suffer from a disease caused by a bacterium at one or more points in our lives. Have you ever been on the wrong end of a bacterial infection?

BM I don't think so. Nothing serious at least, for the most part I'm pretty lucky or healthy, I don't get sick too often. I guess I have had infected cuts here and there, but still nothing too bad.

SP "Having No Other Choice" is a very moving painting that seems to explore our humanity, and in particular, our responsibility for the welfare of the other creatures with which we share our planet. Is the painting based on your own experiences with animals?

Sycamore tree in Sedona, AZ
2006

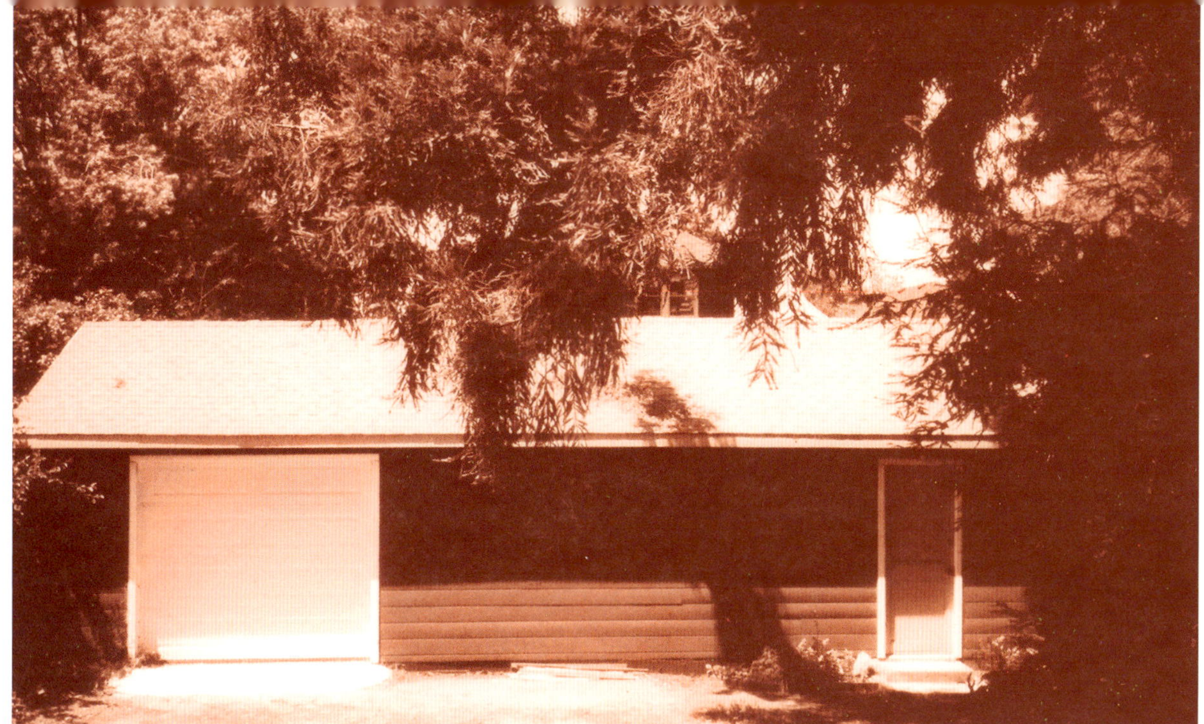

BM Not directly and not even in any indirect specific experience, but it is about those moments that all of us will probably have to go through at some point or another in our lives. Those things that make us ache but we know we have to go through with them.

SP Do "Stranded" *[cover]* and "Frequency Composition" represent a deliberate move towards more abstract paintings that refer less to the real world?

BM They sort of grew on their own. I've been painting this flow of blobby stuff for a while, mostly working it in to situations, but sometimes I feel like it's nice to have it stand on its own as a free flowing organic shape. I don't think my whole body of work is going in an abstract direction, but I do like some images working their way into the language of all the paintings together.

SP Your work is heavily inspired by biology and both your parents have a medical background so why did you choose to express your creativity through art rather than via a science based career?

BM I've always enjoyed both. When I started community college and was supposed to be deciding what to do with my life I found myself pursuing both biology and art, but I never thought anyone would be able to feed themselves by making art. At some point I found that there were people out there that were not famous, and did very well with art. I didn't know that before. And I guess I leaned in the art direction because maybe it was a little more exciting to me at the time. The end result of working for myself as an artist might have sounded more appealing than working in a lab, but at this time I also didn't realize all the possibilities a science related career might go. I think I just had a dreamy idea of being an artist.

Evah & Brendan's Berkeley studio, CA
Jordan Stark, 2007